MY STREET
Memories and Reflections

by Diana Ruth Krohn

Tovim Press
book publishing services that are simply, Tov!

Published in the USA by Tovim Press, LLC.

My Street, Memories and Reflections

Cover design by Chasya Katriela Eshkol

ISBN: 978-0-9994786-5-3

Published by Tovim Press, LLC.

TovimPress.com

Dedicated to Judith, Margot and Valerie
and all the people in my stories,
many of whom are gone, but alive in my pages

TABLE OF CONTENTS

**PART 2 - Transplanted Without Roots
Edgewater/Bloomfield/Edgewater, 1951-1955**

Prologue

We are the sum of moments of our life.
Thomas Wolfe, Look Homeward Angel

...standing...on gray steps going down to a dark door...clinging to the iron rail...afraid...a cloudy sunken feeling in my body...waiting...afraid to go down... something bad happened there...something I can't know... standing...

I don't move... (1941)

Sometimes I remember a moment, look back, feel the moment and relive it – a woman's dialogue with the child inside. Do we really remember childhood or do we imagine these emotionally charged disjointed segments...a dim, elusive, but defining, moment from the past. How do memories happen in our brain? They recur from more than visualizing. They reflect ripples of someone's influence. They collide with my internal struggle to understand the world and myself.

My second memory takes me back to a cavernous railroad station swarming with dazzling uniforms...crowds of people...a sea of waists moves beyond my three-years of childhood...trains rumble in and out, caught like monstery snakes on an amusement park track...

Over the noise and crowds in the echoing train station, I yell "Bye, bye" to my big brother Bobby. Daddy tells his jokes to Bobby's new bride. Suddenly Bobby kisses all of us hurriedly, turns away, sprints up the three metal steps into the endless train on Track Nine already crowded with men uniformed in khaki and boots. The conductor winks at me. I wink back. Bobby appears at the bottom of a blotchy window and waves.

I giggle at his funny faces, giggle even more when he lowers the shade and disappears. Again, Bobby raises the shade, as he waves and smiles. The shade lowers, up, then down again, a game.

We all laugh on the platform as his shade goes up and down. I make funny faces back -- and Bobby always grins, like a smile mask. As the train gradually departs from the station, he pulls down the shade for the last time. When will we see him again?

Aunt Miriam's holding my hand too tight. I look up and see tears raining down her face.

"Why are you crying here where everybody can see?" I ask as her face crinkles.

She squeezes harder, whispers, "Diana, I have no window shade to hide behind." (1942)

Grandma, Aunt Miriam, Daddy, Bobby, Patricia, Eva, David and Diana

The dark staircase and Bobby's turbulent descent into wartime are my earliest memories. Now we leave the train station where my story gets underway, where the shadows of my past begin clearing. My early years reduce down to a few blurred semblances as I follow inner clues to connect to the peopled world I love. I bless these fragments that flash through my mind, shutting out the solitude of an older *woman. We live in the present, but the past lingers in our memory. Removed by many miles and even more years, our childhood remains, "permanent ghosts, stamped, inked, imprinted, eternally seen." (*Cynthia Ozick*).*

Children have the luxury of living in their head, aware of their surroundings when events get emotional or frightening, like being on and off stage. As I gather images from its edge, my make-believe world in the clouds drifts away, emptying into the immense deep blue sky. Yet my past still endures, removed by many miles and even more years, the magic places of childhood still exist. We merely need to look and never forget why we're looking. To retrieve that magic, I merge my thoughts, reflections and personal truths into my stories so they may resonate with yours and be kept alive. I will tell you about the places I have been and reflect on their influences, although these reflections may not be permanent. Nonetheless, looking backwards is still traveling since it drives a fresh perspective, purpose, celebration and acceptance. If you learn by observing people, as I do, join with me as I reach back to remember. Then I hug them tight and long before I say goodbye and let them go with my keystrokes. I love what was and long to cry for what was not.

PART 1 - Putting Out Roots
North Bergen, 1943 to 1951

'kol d'mama daka', the still small voice

Searchlights, 1943

Today, my throat is sore and my fever is high. I hate all sickness, but at least this time it isn't like chicken pox when I spent a whole week lying in my parents' bed in the dimness of their bedroom. Their room is shadowy dark already, so I stagger over to look into the brightness out the small window by the fire escape as our ticking clock chimes the quarter hours.

We live here now, on the corner. Against the sunless sky, the row of houses down 90th Street appears flat next to our gray apartment building. Sparrows perch on the power lines. Shouts from Sunday afternoon games tempt me. I poke my head out a bit further, seeking escape from my parents' bickering. Traffic flows constantly on the wide Hudson Boulevard. Noise and diesel fumes from the trucks hover on our corner, whether the light turns red, amber or green. Some cars from Hudson Boulevard venture down 90th Street, interrupting the boys' stickball game. Angry, the boys yell at the drivers or hit their fists against the cars' fenders as they pass through.

I hear the bouncy rhythm of Maureen and Carmella playing my favorite ball game, Russia, against our stoop. Onesie -- twosie -- under your leg -- over your leg -- turn around -- catch the ball, as it bounces off the bricks. The quick beats grow strong and enchanting.

The Good Humor man plays his tinkly xylophone song to announce he's coming. Normally, I have my dime in hand and run to catch him when he stops. But today, I yell out the window, "Please wait!" Mommy runs in and knots my dime in a handkerchief. I throw it out the window to Maureen Dunn, my best friend. In just a few minutes, she

1

brings my ice cream sandwich to our door -- creamy vanilla between soft chocolate cookies. Better than medicine…

I must have fallen asleep…fallen into the depths of my secret world. It was not as negative then. Simply unrevealed thoughts — do we ever really learn our secrets? We often write ahead of our own understanding. Then our task becomes to understand what we've written.

…I wake up, startled to be back in my couch bed in our living room. As dusk begins to darken the gray sky, I watch flies trapped on our windowsill. Upside down, but still kicking. Struggling to find the way outside where searchlights will soon track across the inked sky peering for enemy airplanes. I've never seen any, although I check for them all the time. Everyone follows the curfew rules. No lights or people can be spotted in the quiet emptiness of our street -- only our street's civil-defense warden in his hard hat. All the families are probably listening to radios behind their drawn shades in dark rooms, the sound lowered so no enemy planes can hear them. Mostly war news with Gabriel Heatter, Walter Winchell and Edward R. Murrow, my favorite.

Daddy sits in his knobby, green chair, smoking, listening to Walter Winchell's Sunday night war news on our Philco radio. "Good evening, Mr. and Mrs. North and South America and all the ships at sea. Let's go to press." February 1944, U-boats sinking ships…RAF bombing Berlin…our soldiers invading the Marshall Islands, fighting on the beachhead at Anzio. So much news. Where are these places? What does liquid-ate mean? What are ghettos?

As Daddy listens, he reads his small pile of letters by flashlight. They're on thin blue papers that came in the mail, folded into rectangles. The kind that have no envelope and every possible space filled with writing. They're from my brothers who are away in the war. I've seen newsreels of the war at the Embassy Theater in West

New York but can't find my brothers because Wally is on a battleship in the Pacific Ocean and Bobby is a prisoner in Germany. I remember the telegram and the hushed voices whispering "missing in action, then "prisoner of war". As though by whispering, it might not be true.

The paper crinkles noisily when Daddy puts away the letters, like scratching my fingernail down Maureen's chalkboard. Tears run quietly down his cheeks. His reaction to the music on the radio gives me clues. "God bless America, land that I love...." He doesn't talk, so I can't understand his secrets. My nose always runs, so it's hard for anyone to notice when I cry. But I don't like to see Daddy cry. It's so sad that I weep for him. I get up from my couch bed to peek out from behind the yellowed shade. I try not to let the dim red light from our radio get outside, so no one will yell at me. Searchlights circle the layers of dark sky and limitless air. I hope they find Bobby and Wally so they come back home "on a wing and a prayer."

Bobby　　　　　　Wally

Born into a world at war: So much death, so little time to be young. Big sky, searchlights exposing multilayers of unobstructed air. The clarity of seeing again...the little girl growing up. I don't remember my father's voice then, just his quiet sobs that I didn't comprehend. I listened, although I didn't want to hear. I felt my father's indirect presence with silence between us.

Clear, sharp, slow. Crinkling paper sounds against the background of soft music. Kate Smith sang ballads of love and loss to war, something I couldn't unravel. Everything seemed far away. Even my father's sobs receded into the room filled with his space in the late light. Light is distinguishable from darkness by degree only. Sometimes I don't understand my own quiet weeping either, but it helps me make sense of my father's sadness.

I didn't get to read my brothers' letters because I wasn't old enough. All their letters were gone by the time I could read. Children didn't know the adult world then. I would have had to get closer to my parents to settle the pieces into the frame. Instead, I escaped to play with my friends on the street.

∞∞∞∞∞∞∞∞∞∞∞∞∞∞∞∞∞

The Passing, March 1944

Daddy walks into our apartment, soaking wet from the pouring March rain. In his quiet, serious voice, he tells Mommy, "Grandma Krohn passed." I'm in our tiny kitchen with them, staring at a cockroach disappearing under the stove. He tells us about his flat tire on the way home from the hospital. His eyes look dark as his hair and his nose is runny, but he's still handsome as a movie star.

Grandma Krohn never lived with us like she did with her other five children. She seemed to belong wherever she was, but it was never with us because we don't have any place for her to sleep. Now, because of her heart attack, she never will stay with us.

What is death? An angel? Does it hide somewhere and then get you? Does death shoot you like the soldiers in the newsreels? Does it make the world bigger when someone dies? Where is heaven? Will Grandma be with Pop who didn't live long enough to be *my* grandpa? Does the sky turn bluer with more people in heaven? Do you really get to swing on a star? I look out the small kitchen window at the darkening sky. Is it heaven now or only at night when stars sprinkle across the sky?

Daddy takes my hand and says, "You'll never see Grandma again. Try to always remember her."

I think back to last month when Mom signed me up to start kindergarten and we stopped by Aunt Miriam's house across from Horace Mann Elementary. Grandma was living there, her fluffy white hair pulled away from her square jaw. She was serving boiled potatoes with sour cream to my cousins, Florence and David. She made me a dishful too. My mommy doesn't cook, so I don't get to eat this kind of food. Grandma sat me down at the table in Aunt Miriam's toasty kitchen. Her warm bony hands reached out to touch my shoulder. The potatoes tasted warm and solid and the sour cream added milky flavors.

My grandma was beautiful. Her voice softly murmured. Her hands moved like she was blessing us. Grandma never looked worried or confused like my mommy. Daddy always tells Mommy she worries too much. Grandma seemed calm, satisfied. I want to look like her and be like her. That good and that loved, but I don't want to die!

MY STREET

As Daddy lets go of my hand, he tells me that Grandma went to heaven. I think it's the same place where the stork comes from, bringing my brother Aaron to earth at the Margaret Hague Hospital. I wonder how you get to heaven. It's kind of far up. Maybe a truck... Trucks come down 90th Street selling hot bread with insides you can squish. When you put Swiss cheese inside, it melts into gooeyness. An old bakery man sells cupcakes, chocolate with cream in the middle. The back of his truck has drawers with pastries, brownies and eclairs. Another truck offers knife sharpening. The rag man adjusts his bandana and rings his triangle bell on his open truck piled high with ratty clothes. The ice man's truck is darkly wet. I watch him thrust his giant tongs around a big block of ice, lift and carry it into our building. He lets us take slivers of ice to suck until they disappear.

I imagine my grandma traveling to heaven like a white-robed levitating zombie rising off the hydraulic back gate of a delivery truck. Heaven must feel easy and open, like Bing Crosby croons on the radio, "...send me off forever but I ask you please, don't fence me in." I'll probably like heaven!

Sometimes you don't know the value of a moment, like tasting potatoes and sour cream, until it becomes a memory. Grandma Krohn, the shining star of those floating early childhood fragments, was 71 when she died in March, 1944. I was barely five. Yet she's remained my major female role model. She did the kind of giving that people accepted. My respect feels based on a sense, like an aftertaste I have of her, rather than any specific experience.

I've spent my life pushing to the head of the line, piling up successes. Di tsayt ken alts ibermakhn. (Time, it changes everything.) Now, with the leveling of age, I question what I have achieved. I believe Grandma Krohn had everything one could want out of life: good parents, a loving husband and children who adored her. She lived her last days with her children and grandchildren.

Today I pick up Grandma's photograph from my desk, the one taken before she died, the one with the wrong color applied to her eyes by the colorist. Her eyes were hazel green like mine, not blue. I remember Uncle Ted, her third son, being upset by the mistake. She wasn't tall or heavy, but solid, serene and lovingly beautiful. I resemble her, am some of her, and look more like her as I age. I like to reflect on the line that runs from Grandma Krohn to me and hope that she would love me. I wonder...do we create these connections ourselves or does some powerful presence in our midst fuse us into this moment of togetherness...

MY STREET

Wannabe Twins, 1944

Maureen and I are always together. Our apartments are on the fourth floor on opposite ends of the dumbwaiter. We play everyday. Sometimes we fight, like yesterday when she bent the neck on my Esther Williams paper doll. This morning in July, as always, she's at my door asking, "Can you play?"

We head outside, past the boxlike trimmed hedges that form a green wall as high as our chests. The hedges are a pretend boundary dividing our building from the concrete sidewalks and the short strip of dusty brown dirt beyond. The dirt becomes a place to find ant hills and make mud pies after it rains. Our knees have bloody scabs from falls on that cracked sidewalk.

We'd rather be on the street or in our lobby than in our apartments. Maureen's new baby brother cries. Her little sister, Cheryl, with curly blonde hair quietly watches us. My new brother lies in his crib and sleeps. My older brothers went to the war.

Maureen and I love each other. We're always saying, "I wish you were my sister." We really want to be sisters. Then we could play all the time, without having to ask. We sit on our stoop wondering how to achieve this.

"Maybe we could run away and be adopted together," Maureen suggests.

"Nah, the cops will just bring us back home."

"We could cut our fingers and mix our blood. At least we'd be blood sisters."

"Nah. Nothing would really be different."

As we sit on our stoop, searching for ideas, our old Irish neighbor from the bottom floor tells us, "If you die together, you might come back as twins."

Not knowing how to die, we put our heads on top of the boxy green hedges and hold hands. Nothing. So we wait. Nothing. Maybe it's because I'm not Irish. "How can I be more Irish," I think out loud.

"Let's hum 'too-ra-loo-ra'," Maureen urges. So, eyes closed, holding hands, waiting…waiting. "Too-ra-loo-ra-loo-ra, too-ra-loo-ra-li…"

The streetlights come on. We do not die. We will not be sisters. We go up to supper.

Children don't seem afraid of death. They just wonder. Do the dead rise with the pleasure of listening? Does their essence simply evaporate? Children don't understand the implications yet. Fairy tales and cowboy movies impart a skewed reality. I knew about death, but the older I get, the more I fear 'not living fully'. It's the only part I can control.

❧❧❧❧❧❧❧❧❧❧❧❧❧❧❧

My Promotion, April 1945

I'm far back in the line to get our glass inkwells filled. Today is special, our first day to write with ink. Usually first graders only use our thick black pencils. Miss Smith yells, "Hold your inkwell in both hands. Anyone spilling ink won't get to sign the poster we're sending to Washington."

Waiting in line, I remember my first day of Kindergarten last September. Mom brought me, pushing my baby brother, Aaron, in his carriage. We walked through the chilly concrete walled yard into the classroom. We must have been late because other kids were already there.

The room was filled with toys! Lionel locomotives with whistles and steam, red racing cars, a cardboard dollhouse with teeny furniture and little people, puzzles, storybooks, dolls with clothes. At home, I only have a dirty red yo-yo with a broken string that I found in our hedges. I started crying because it's too wonderful. But Mom thought my tears were because she's leaving. She turned around to stay, but the teacher quietly walked her out. I headed right to the pile of dolls.

In Kindergarten, every day at recess, we lined up and walked downstairs to the basement. Our class always arrived first. I gave the lady my dime to get chocolate milk, two Oreo cookies and a stamp to paste in my war bond book. I always tried to find a cold carton of milk from the tray. I hate warm milk. It needs to be cold or hot. Then we put on our coats and head out to the schoolyard where there's a real hopscotch that doesn't wash away when it rains.

Back in the classroom, my favorite toy was the small house with a kitchen that has cabinets, a play stove and refrigerator. I pretended to bake chocolate cookies and cupcakes like the old Dugan's bakery man sells from the drawers in the back of his truck. I learned to pronounce the alphabet from the cream-colored cards hanging around the room. The black letters printed in capitals and small letters had no pictures or aids. "A, aah. B, buh or baa, C, cuh..." Fun-etics, my teacher called it. Easy to memorize and so are the numbers...

Now I'm in first grade. I got skipped in January, just before my sixth birthday. Missed the second half of Kindergarten and the first half of first grade because my teacher wrote, "Diana is smart, quiet and well-behaved." We're having a special day. We're not going to print with our thick black pencils. Our classroom smells of ink. I breathe the scent deeply as my teacher pours the blue-black liquid into my inkwell. The strong odor hurts my chest. I carefully walk back to my wooden desk and place my ink into the hole in the upper right-hand corner.

I push my shiny nib into the wooden red pen and dip it. We practice by making circles that never end, until the pen's point runs out of ink. Then I dip it to start again. Finally, the teacher brings the poster around to my desk for me to sign in my very best penmanship. President Roosevelt died last week. Our class is sending this poster to Eleanor, the First Lady. Dad will be proud when I tell him. Even though we don't have Kindergarten toys, first grade at Horace Mann is wonderfully fun.

Today I have mixed feelings about President Roosevelt and am glad I wasn't born on his birthday. He could have ordered the bombing of the railroad tracks used to bring Jews to the crematoria. But getting re-elected was a higher priority. We all make mistakes. Alav Ha-shalom. (May he rest in peace.)

Poisonous dark clouds spill out from the untreated wounds of our past, putting a hole in our ozone layer. Wars, energy consumption, slavery, mass killings, partisan thinking and religious righteousness create people who milk the system. Most disasters are man-made. We've just ended one of the bloodiest centuries. Terrorism and anti-Semitism live in the margins. When morality is on hiatus, when guilt loses its meaning and when the conscience is cleared by indifference, cataclysm tends to creep into the center of the page. Anger from the past must be resolved or it will continue its violent discharge. This is not a sickness that time or whitewashing can heal. Its legacy has no statute of limitations.

∞∞∞∞∞∞∞∞∞∞∞∞∞∞∞∞∞

Home From the War, 1945

Wonderful news! The evil Hitler is dead. Germany surrenders. Like the song on the radio, our GI's "are home again all over the world." The newsreels at the Embassy Theater show blizzards of paper pouring from windows down onto Broadway's ticker tape parades. Bobby returned just after first grade ended. I wanted to see him, but Dad explained, "Bobby's too old to live with us now. You'll get to see him this weekend."

MY STREET

It's a warm June day. The scrubby lawn is greening and daisies are blooming in Aunt Miriam's backyard. Our family gathers, waiting to welcome Bobby home. I love this backyard. It's so different from our apartment with no signs of nature, not even a picture of flowers. Only low hedges in front of our building and the buggy dirt strip. I like standing in the open, grassy space of my aunt's backyard with yummy hamburgers grilling, sweet cabbage slaw and potato salad in glass bowls on the table.

Bobby arrives in his cream-colored convertible. I run to be the first to hug him. I feel his bones. He's stiff and crisp in his Army Air Corps uniform. He lets me and my cousins, David and Florence, sit in the back seat. He puts the top down and lets us play the radio. We listen as Joe DiMaggio hits the winning home run for the Yankees.

Diana, Florence, David

Mom holds my baby brother, Aaron. She doesn't let anybody else hold him. Everyone smiles and says how cute he is with his thick black hair and deep brown eyes. Both my parents have black hair and brown eyes too. My eyes are green and my hair is reddish brown. It doesn't make sense. I wonder how I got this way. I didn't get finished right.

12

Dad wears his dark blue Victory suit, cuff-less trousers and narrow lapels, but still with his ironed white handkerchief poking merrily out of his breast pocket. His gold cufflinks flicker as they catch the sunlight. His hair is pomaded with Bryl Cream but his tie can't hide his bulging belly poking out of his starched white shirt. He and Bobby have the same cocky smile. Bobby doesn't talk about his years as a prisoner in Germany where his plane was shot down. He smiles and smiles, even though this morning Dad told me a bad secret. He whispered, "Don't ever mention Bob's wife, Patricia. She isn't with him anymore. Only we are..."

Wally's coming home today, just in time for Labor Day. President Truman dropped atom bombs in Japan and the war in the Pacific is almost over. Wally broke his heel during the Battle at Leyte Gulf. He's been in a Navy hospital for months and months waiting for his foot to heal.

I can't sleep so I stare out the window as the lights come on in our neighborhood buildings, one after the other. I picture the men on our street starting their morning with coffee and a shave. Finally, Wally and Dad arrive in our black Pontiac. I run to be first at the door. Wally wears his Navy whites and sits right by me in dad's chair, a pipe between his teeth. Even with his cane, he looks like a blond, blue-eyed movie star, the Alan Ladd look. I stare at him and my weakness for good-looking boys starts.

Maureen knocks on our apartment door. "Can you play?"

13

I step into the hall. We sit on the stairs to the roof, looking at pictures of the Seven Wonders of the World in her View-Master.

"My brother Wally came home from the hospital," I tell her. We can see him. The windows in the hall look right into the windows of our parlor. He still sits in Dad's parlor chair. His bandaged foot sticks out from his white bell-bottom trousers.

"Please, I want to meet him," Maureen says.

I hesitate. "Not sure Mom will let me," I reply.

Not only do I want to keep him to myself, but I'm ashamed of our apartment. I know that Maureen shares a bedroom with her little brother and sister. They don't sleep in the parlor on a couch that has been broken in half, the halves against opposite walls.

"Please, please," she begs. "I've never been in the same room with a real sailor in his sailor's suit."

I still stall, hanging back.

"I'll give you this dime," she says as she takes a gleaming silver coin out of her pocket and puts it in my hand. A brand-new dime.

So we go in. We're both scared. We hurry through the parlor, past Aaron's playpen, to the tiny square kitchen. We take deep breaths, really seeing the green in each other's eyes. Then we bravely head back into the parlor.

"Wally, this is my best friend Maureen. She lives in 4A," I mumble nervously.

"Hi," Wally says to Maureen, giving her his biggest smile.

We quickly run out the door, but Maureen is happy and I keep my dime.

I shared this incident at Wally's funeral. Several hundred men wore bow ties to honor their "elder-elder". As he matured he remained dapper like my father, whether in his Navy whites or his formal bowties. Wish I still had his uniform in the duffle bag Mom threw or gave away.

When my brothers came home from their military service, my father's tears receded into the brambles of my mind. I didn't even remember my father much until years later. His cries eventually returned when he got sick, but they reflected agonizing more than sadness. Di tseit brengt vender un hails vunden. (Time brings wounds and heals them.)

◌◌◌◌◌◌◌◌◌◌◌◌◌◌◌◌◌◌

The Chicken Store, 1945

There's not much green in North Bergen, although it's late summer. I'm walking to the chicken store with mom. The heavy air touches my skin with warmth. Our worn-down streets seem less shadowy in summer.

Mom almost never cooks, but my brothers are coming to supper, a celebration. I hum, as I walk down Hudson Boulevard …bars of "Chickery Chick, cha la cha la, bollika, wollika, can't you see, Chickery chick is me…" I close my lips so all the vibration stays inside my mouth.

I've never been to the chicken store. It's around the corner from the fruit store. Too bad Mom isn't allowed in the fruit store anymore. You are supposed to tell the man how many pieces of fruit you want: six plums, three oranges and a banana. He chooses the ones to give you and puts them in a little brown bag. But she never wants the little plums he picks. The banana looks too green, or the apples have a brown spot that could be a worm. The fruit man yells at her for poking his apricots and she yells back. A line of customers waits behind us. Finally he yells at her, "You can't shop here anymore!" I slink out behind her.

Now Mom passes with her head down. The fruit man spits and looks at us as if we are giant worms about to attack his peaches and plums. After passing the bright, sweet-smelling stacks of fruit, the pasty red bricks on the chicken store appear worn and desolate.

We walk up the cracked steps into a large poorly lit room with three walls covered by chickens imprisoned in silvery wire cages. Stinky smells like wet dirt and old laundry water catch in my throat, limit my breathing. I've never been in a store with sawdust on the floor, just like the saloons in the cowboy movies. The chickens, in a flutter, are stirring and squawking – fun noises. So many hens to choose from.

"We want one that isn't too big for our family of five. We don't want one that's too old, so pick a perky one," Mom tells me.

The butcher is busy with other customers in the back, his dark curly hair visible over the top of the high counter. So we study the different chickens. It's difficult to tell them apart. Some have peppery feathers, but most are white. They start to calm down and I pick ours 'cause she seems peaceful and dignified. She settles down like a performer being observed.

We show the fat butcher man our choice. Then I detect blood on his apron as he approaches and opens the cage door. I've seen blood when I fall on my knees and elbows, but these are big blotches. My chicken really squawks when the butcher man roughly grabs her, easily overpowering her. He takes her quickly to the back counter.

By the time we get there, I realize the butcher man has twisted my chicken's neck. He reaches down, but I catch the movement as he chops off her head and tosses it into a large gray bucket along a scummy side wall. That thumping crack of his cleaver keeps echoing in my ears. It doesn't go away. I look at her tiny head floating in the gloomy colorless liquid. How can that be? Then he dips the rest of her in a giant sink and calmly plucks off her feathers with a

16

small knife. I smell her still warm skin. Is she still alive without her head? Can she feel the pain? I feel her pain because I picked her. It makes my body knot up into one place above my eyes.

The butcher man weighs her on a large scale hanging from the ceiling and wraps her in white paper. I watch as Mom hands him the money. A new truth sinks in. In that second, I know something now that I don't want to know. I grow cold with fear. I walk down the steps to warm up in the still summer air.

So many different ways to look back to this time when I felt connected to a caged chicken. I was too young to understand death, but there was still that instant of fright and loss of innocence. If we treat animals badly, why not their fellow humans next? Reality? The boys in Lord of the Flies who cannibalized each other. Brothers turning on brothers in civil wars. The inquisitions and Nazi genocide. We've learned from experience just how vile human beings can treat their fellow humans. Why can't we learn to respect that nothing is entirely separate from anything else.

Goodbye, Again and Again, 1945

Nothing moves in Indian summer. Birds are napping on the telephone wires. The sun fries the roofs and flies lay dead on our flypaper hanging by our windows. Mom tells Bob and Wally, who sit sweating in our cramped kitchen, "Take Di-ann to the movies with you. It's too hot here."

I know they don't want to, but she makes them. I don't know how, but she must make them feel guilty. They squeeze my fingers as we cross the street to Bobby's convertible. But it doesn't hurt. At the Embassy Theatre, I drop my can of new potatoes into the box for the poor people and a man in a red hat gives me a lollipop. Then, my brothers take me to the big glass counter and ask, "Which candies do you like?" I pick candy buttons, Hersheys with almonds, Beeman's gum, candy cigarettes, salt water taffy, Good n' Plenty and sugared orange slices. Enough to fill a whole brown bag.

They take me down to the very front row. "You'll see better from here. Stay in your seat until we return," they tell me. I know they are gonna sit in the back or the balcony where they can smoke and smooch girls. That's what big kids do.

The newsreels show General Eisenhower and piles of bodies found in Germany. The announcer says they are Jews. Horrible! What if the newsreel is true! How can this be? I need to get home quick because I think I might be Jewish. I'm scared, but don't know where my brothers are sitting. Suddenly I long for silence, for the news to stop. I eat all the candy in my bag, saving the chocolate for last, and enjoy "Anchors Aweigh" until the velvet curtain closes. The lights come on and my brothers show up.

"Bobby, did those bodies really happen?"

"Yes, Diana. The war office has been whitewashing the worst news. Now we're finding out many things that aren't pleasant. Don't you worry. The war is over and they won't happen anymore."

I'm so sleepy. I stop feeling scared when Bobby carries me home.

A few nights after the movie, I wake up hearing Wally's noisy gasping for air. Another asthma attack. Dad runs into the parlor buttoning his white shirt. As they quickly pass my bed, Dad says, "I'm driving him to the hospital." Wally's face is so pale and Dad is struggling to hold him up. The air from the hallway chills me and after I shut the door, I can't fall back to sleep. As I wait for them to return, I keep imagining what it must feel like when you can't breathe. It's already morning when they return home. No one talks. Wally tries to sleep sitting up in dad's chair. I watch his eyes drip a line of tears when the radio plays,

George Washington Bridge Park

"Peg O' My Heart." I don't know why he's so sad. Maybe he just doesn't feel good.

I head downstairs so Wally can sleep. By the time I come up from playing jump rope on Fifth Avenue, Wally left. Why didn't he say goodbye to me?

Two mornings later, Mom wakes me saying, "Bobby's coming for his last visit."

I wait, wondering where he's going. Aaron sits in his green vinyl high chair and bangs his heels into the back of the leg rest. *Thud, thud. Thud, thud.* It stops my thinking. *Thud, Thud.* It annoys me, but we're used to it. When Bobby arrives, he says, "Eva, you shouldn't let Aaron do that."

He takes the back of a butter knife and hits Aaron's knees when he bangs his heels. I grimace 'cause my mother and baby brother are getting yelled at. Then Bobby tells me to go get dressed for school. But my mom always dresses me. I get my skirt and shirt on, but I bring my socks and oxford shoes to her so she can put them on.

However, Bobby says, "Do it yourself."

"I don't know how," I whine.

He insists, "Do it yourself. You're a big girl. You're starting second grade and you still can't put your shoes on!"

"I don't know which sock goes on which foot."

"It doesn't matter," he explains. Then he shows me how you tell which shoe goes on which foot. I vow to always dress myself. I don't like to eat humble pie.

When Mom and I arrive home from school, Bobby's still in the kitchen. I sit at our little table as Bobby carries over the scrambled eggs and toast he fixes for me. While I eat every bite, he sits with me and picks up an orange from the fruit bowl on the table.

"Pretend this orange is the sun," he says, as he uses pieces of fruit to show me how the planets go around the sun. A potato becomes the earth and he sprinkles salt on it.

"This is us," he continues, pointing to two of the sprinkles. "We are only a small part of the universe. Remember that."

Then Bobby leaves too. I don't know why. I keep learning how many things there are to discover. My head grows when I learn new things. I wish I had asked Bobby more about the piles of bones in the newsreels. I wish I had asked him to show me where God is in the piles of fruit. Seems like he would know.

Someday I'll visit my brothers in Florida. Except Dad can't leave his job working on the government projects. He tells me, "Florida is too far!"

Even though the war is over, I'm losing my brothers again. I wish they didn't leave.

Both my brothers lost more than years in the war. Wally lost his girlfriend Peggy and Bobby lost his wife Patricia — neither woman waited for their return. It's hard to wait when there's too much death, so little time to be young. When the lessons hurt, we change faster.

Diana Ruth Krohn

My Last Grandparent, 1946

I stand alone, far back, at Grandpa Steinberg's funeral, picking scabs on my elbows, uncovering the slick red skin underneath. The trees overhead are full of leaves, the same as in the lot across from our apartment. I imagine climbing them, way high like fearless boys. Most of us seven-year-old girls just climb the easy places, especially me, since I'm afraid to get too high. I don't know many of the people here in the cemetery, too many raisinette faces. Only Mom and her sisters stand by the coffin.

Just a few months ago, I remember waiting in the narrow hall of Grandpa's apartment in the Bronx. It smelled like food cooked in old oil. I would have rather been playing jump rope on my own street. "Teddy Bear, Teddy Bear, turn around…Teddy Bear, Teddy Bear, touch the ground…"

Mom brought Aaron with us so Grandpa could see his grandson. We traveled on two crowded buses with no empty seats and then, the subway. I stood in the quiet, dark hall, curious about my grandpa and what was behind all the doors. I closed my eyes, trying to remember parts of him before he got sick – bits of fuzzy hair so his ears showed too much. He used words like *tsores, bisel, farshtais.* He called me *"Gelibteh Badana."* When he sat in his faded flowered chair, I could see the bare top of his head and study the different colors. Does everyone have those pinks and whites and brown spots under their hair? There's no way to see under my hair because it's too thick.

On that last visit, he didn't come out, even though I waited a long time in that hall. I hadn't been told to sit down. I felt hungry and didn't want to ask for food because it might be strange stuff. I don't trust Grandma Steinberg 'cause she's really my step-grandmother and I know what happened in *Cinderella.* She doesn't even ask grandma-like questions like what grade I'm in. She and Mom don't talk either.

I couldn't see Mom anyplace or even hear any talking. Then, she came out of the bathroom carrying Aaron. She grabbed my hand, jerking me up, and took me down the hall to the bathroom door. I could see that Grandpa was sitting on the toilet. Why couldn't he get up, I wondered nervously. He handed me out a big, cold, worn fifty-cent piece pinched between his callused fingers. We left quickly, before Grandma Steinberg could take it away. I never saw him again.

Men in overalls use thick ropes attached to Grandpa's brown casket to lower it into a hole. I picture Grandpa in the ground and wonder if he feels lonely. What can he feel? I know that when you're dead, you're dead. But maybe it's possible to be dead, frozen silent, but still realize it? Mom and her sisters kneel on the ground sobbing, clawing at Grandpa's coffin as the men cover his grave with dirt. Maybe we shouldn't put him in there. Maybe he doesn't want to be buried in the ground with damp dirt thrown on top of him. Is this where Grandma Krohn went too, hidden away under the ground? Maybe heaven is merely a lie our parents tell us, like the stork flying around delivering babies. Otherwise, why are they down on their knees as dirt covers over the grave? They don't leave, just cry and cry. I stand in the back feeling the air around me darken, my body grows cold and I'm so afraid.

At least I have these memories of my quiet Grandpa Steinberg, his kindness and my fifty-cent piece. He was too gentle for the shrill world of his second wife and stepdaughters. He never spoke of the home, work, relatives and friends he left in Bialystok. Badana, his dead wife, took on a different scale like the minor keys of Yiddish melodies in the dark shadows of his past. The poverty he fled in Europe remained with him in America. His streets weren't lined with gold, but he loved his daughters, Estelle, Eva and Molly, and they intensely adored him.

Diana Ruth Krohn

Visiting the Fleet, 1946

It's a nippy day. Dad's taking us in our Pontiac sedan to see President Truman. He's visiting our Navy carriers on the Hudson River. Dad likes Harry almost as much as FDR. On the way, I read the billboards out loud to everyone until we stop at Hiram's for frankfurters. Dad gets in line at the counter. Aaron and I watch him through the car windows. Many people crunch gravel walking to and from their cars. Everyone's enjoying being able to get gasoline for their Sunday drives. I breathe in greasy smells of beef and mustard as Dad returns with our bag of treats. I divide the French fries between Aaron and me and then taunt him by eating mine extremely slow. By accident, we drip ketchup on Dad's road map, so we hide it under the seat.

We don't wait too long for the Hudson River Ferry. The sign says it's been operating since 1658. That's 288 years ago, a long time, but the ferry doesn't seem old. As we cross the Hudson River to Manhattan, a lady in a real fur coat walks over to me. "I found this doll when we got on the ferry. Perhaps you would like it."

The lady has thick mascara covering her curled eyelashes and a reddish blush on her cheeks like a kewpie doll. She's beautiful, her long, dark hair captured in a hairnet to protect it from the wind. I look at the little rubber doll in her hand. Not pretty at all. A hard little unmoving doll with hair and black eyes molded into its head. Only its neck turns. It has a painted-on face, but the eyes and lips are worn down from being rubbed. Its hair is painted, too, and the blonde is streaked with black grease. Her fingers are perpetually drawn apart. I never had a doll, so I take it saying, "Thanks."

Dad tells her, "Thanks," too.

"Give her lots of love," the lady says as she turns away toward a white-haired man in a black beret.

All across the river, I clutch that little rubber doll. My first doll ever, my first toy. It's only about eight inches, but

I'm almost eight years old so it's perfect. I can't wait to show Maureen my very own doll.

The Navy ships are huge and gloomy gunmetal gray. We walk to the end of the line on the 129th Street pier. The line moves so slowly. I'm cold even though the sky is turning blue and the sun is starting to shine. Finally, we step into a boat that takes us from the dock to the ship's ladder. I'm so scared when I look down and see the water through the ladder, but a sailor holds my hand and tells me, "Nothing will happen to you, missy." I want to thank him, but I'm not sure who gets called "Sir." So I clutch my doll with no name. She needs to be held.

From our place on the deck, we see President Truman on another aircraft carrier. Dad says, "See, Diana, how much all these people like Harry. That's his wife, Bess, and his daughter, Margaret, waving."

I see their black hats and fur collars. Their faces smile like real people. I feel safe and warm even though my coat is only made of lightweight cloth and I have to wear a kerchief to keep the wind away from my ears. I put my doll in my pocket with her head out so she can be warm and see too.

The loudspeaker announces, "President Truman has proclaimed November Eleventh, 'Armistice Day', to honor our fellow countrymen who fought across the seas." There's a long silence for the dead soldiers. The band plays "Oh, Say, Can You See" and "God Bless America." Everyone cheers and salutes, including President Truman. Men take off their hats and raise their left hands to their forehead and women put their right hands over their heart. I'm uncomfortable doing this, never sure where my heart is and not wanting to touch my breasts, in case they start to grow. I wish I could salute the men's way.

Funny how we coin words with images relating to ships: relationships, friendships... Yet real relationships and friendships are sometimes as rare as happy childhoods. What is their antithesis? When is the right time to say "Sir"? Ceremonies leave us accepting ideas that make us feel that the problem is solved; we have nothing more to fear. We accept the illusion because it's too difficult to deal with our dangerous capacity for self-delusion.

As for my gift, I never named that ugly doll and she never had any clothes except for the blue skirt, yellow blouse and brown Mary Janes painted on her body. She became my only real toy for many years. Something of my own. Of course, I had my paper dolls, but their necks were bent and the tabs were tearing off their clothes. I didn't feel as ashamed being with the other girls because now I had her, my worn paper dolls and many tempting pictures of toys circled in our Sears catalog.

MY STREET

A Vague Presence, Spring 1947

She's okay, Miss Sauer, my third-grade teacher at Horace Mann Elementary. She's nicer than Mrs. Rash who left to have her baby. School is nothing special. Something I do 'cause I'm supposed to. My real friends are the kids on my street, not the sought-after kids who live in elegant houses closer to the school. The girls that go home for lunch are never mean to me, but I'm not invited to play with them after school. So, school is a place to go and, to me, it seems a long way. Our street is one of the farthest from the school. We live in tenements on the other side of the sinful lot, like the other side of the track. Yet, our street is where I learn more important things than getting "Outstanding" and "Satisfactory" on my report cards.

In the warm air of this spring afternoon, I leave the cyclone-fenced schoolyard for my trek up the hill to Hudson Boulevard, my route home. There's a man waiting at the gate, a vague presence, familiar but hard to see. It takes a few seconds for my dad's features to come into focus. Weeks would pass when I didn't see him. He's still on the road installing shades at federal housing projects, so he's rarely been home in our apartment. However, Mom whispered that he got a pink slip, but he'll be starting a new job at Alcoa Aluminum. Why is he here – in this place, so out of place?

"I came to walk you home, baby face," he says.

I'm startled, shocked to see him. I don't answer 'cause I don't know how to react. Nobody I know walks with their father. I'm so embarrassed. I make my legs take extra long steps.

Sometimes Mom still comes to school to pick me up. Everyone knows she's different. I do what she says so she won't make a scene. She takes me to the malt shop, always trying to fatten up my bony body. Mr. Geneta, the owner, stands behind the big cash register. I love the burnished cool feeling of the long counter at the soda fountain. I twirl on my stool. Above me the fans turn like slow clocks ticking the lazy time of afternoon. I hear the clink of coins on the counter, to pay for the milkshakes, cherry cokes, ice cream sodas and bacon, lettuce and tomato sandwiches.

But this is my f-a-t-h-e-r! We don't stop for a thick strawberry malt. I feel him behind me. His presence invades my homeward territory. I walk fast, trying to see no one, so no one will see me. Across the boulevard, past the Italian bakery with chocolate donuts, past the deli with great big pickles for a nickel, past Zarretts' Pharmacy – all the way to the lot. Even at the empty lot, a long way from school now, I pretend he's not with me.

When we arrive home, he doesn't say anything. But I don't think he'll ever meet me again. I don't feel good. I study him quietly sitting in his chair, a way to hold on to him. I wish I had taken his hand … and walked together with him.

This remains one of the most regretted moments in my life. Yet I never discussed it with my father. My stupidity haunts me, but made me sensitive to try never to hurt someone again. Now when someone reaches for my hand, they touch my heart. Sometimes when I'm alone outdoors, I hear my father's voice say, 'Diana,' and I don't ignore it. I feel him in the silence that follows.

ⁱ⊙ⁱ⊙ⁱ⊙ⁱ⊙ⁱ⊙ⁱ⊙ⁱ⊙ⁱ⊙ⁱ⊙ⁱ⊙ⁱ⊙ⁱ

The Dumbwaiter, July 1947

On our muggy, mosquitoey New Jersey summer nights, Dad and a few of our neighbors buy pitchers of Ballantine at the tavern across Hudson Boulevard and carry them to our stoop. They sit in their chosen spots in their undershirts, handkerchiefs knotted to stay on their heads and collect their sweat. Dad claims, "Drinking together is acceptable. Only drunks drink alone." The men, fanning themselves with their copies of the Jersey Journal, all laugh.

But it's rare to see adults on our street. Most families remain inside their apartments. During daytime, the street is filled with silence until the kids come home from school or finish their chores. The men work long hours, sometimes away from home like my dad. Occasionally the milk man, mail man, fruit man, ice man, bakery man, rag man, or scissor and knife sharpening man break the silence. The parked cars are gone. Women stay inside. In our building, the women only interact with each other in the cold hallway when they take the garbage out.

Each evening as the light fades, before the smells of onions and tomato sauce and sauerkraut disappear, a short, shrill buzz sounds in our apartment. The unseen super's bell calls us to bring our bags of garbage to the dumbwaiter. Tonight, the smells of Friday's fish dinner are overpowering. I follow Mom, invisibly attached, hoping to see Maureen.

Along our hallway's center wall, the dumbwaiter's shaft goes through each floor of our building. Inside it, a set of pulleys is attached to a heavily stained 2'x3' plywood board. A primitive, motor-less, miniature elevator. The small scuffed door sits midway up the wall from the tiled floor, disguised by nondescript paint that matches the faded walls. The grime left on the door appears heavier than the grime in the rest of the hall.

The fourth-floor women come out of their apartments to the call of the dumbwaiter buzzer. They never laugh, even at or with each other. They wait together in dead time, still in day clothes, with flowered aprons or sweaters. Only my Mom wears a flowered housecoat, faded from her overuse of Clorox. Remnants of Ponds cold cream drip down her cheek as I listen to the shrieking sounds from the loading on the floor below us, the pushing, pulling and gliding of the pulleys, going down to the cellar and back up to our floor. I know the super, Victor's dad, pulls those

ropes in the cellar, but I don't remember what he looks like.
He must smell awful. I've never see his face clearly. The
murky cellar is dark and indistinct, with a huge coal bin and
furnace and piles of flattened tin from our canned foods. I
don't know where the garbage goes or why someone would
take this job. Who would want to smell the stink of other
people's garbage?

Then the loading board stops its creaking at our floor.
When Mrs. McNaught pulls the tarnished brass latch to
open the dumbwaiter door, the board is askew. The women
shout down to the super, "Too high!" "Bring it down
lower!" "It's not right yet!" Their voices sound loud, sharp
and harsh in the cold, unwelcoming hall. Finally, the
women take turns placing their full brown paper bags,
dripping with grease, on the board. It's hard to make them
all fit. The sour aromas mix with the lingering supper
smells. The ever-present odor of pee makes me gag. Mostly
the women don't talk. This is one more chore in their long
day and they want to hurry back to their apartments. Sort of
like the quiet before the storm.

The neighbors don't like my mom. But she doesn't
seem to worry, like I do, about what people say or think.
She's often late and last, her trash usually wet and in a
variety of bags. She pokes through them to find things she
might have lost, like our keys. My mother has trouble
letting go of stuff. On nights when she misses the
dumbwaiter's deadline, her banging on the closed door
never brings the dumbwaiter back up.

The platform isn't sturdy. You have to load the bags so
they won't fall off. Mom becomes pushy and abrasive
when the women get impatient with her. They shout threats
at her. Tonight, her wet bag breaks as she lifts it onto the
board. Cantaloupe rinds and seeds scatter all over the floor
and the women's clothes. Mrs. Anthony sharply screams,
"I'll sweep the streets with you, Eva!"

Mrs. Dunn, who looks like a grown-up Shirley
Temple, harshly proclaims, "My daughter won't play with

your daughter ever again."

Mrs. Murphy shrieks too. I'm shocked by the impact on Maureen and me. I can't stop crying. I stop listening until I hear my mother loudly yelling back, "You louses! You louses!"

Not quickly enough, one of the women shuts the dumbwaiter door and another turns the small latch and the noise is over. The final sounds in the corridor come from the pulleys lowering, lowering, and our retreating footsteps.

I'm shocked when I recall that storm-like noise and my tears. With hindsight, everything sharpens as I see what was wrong. This wasn't how it was with us kids on the street. We knew we had to get along with each other because it could be too difficult to be an outsider. Other than taking out the trash, I rarely saw my mother with other women. Why did these women stay in their apartments all day? Their husbands sat together on the stoop and shared pitchers of beer. These women lived in a sour blend of loneliness and fright -- unhappy, the same as me when I stayed in our apartment. Fear is when you know what you're afraid of and anxiety is when you don't. Is this what caused Mom's nervous breakdowns? Maybe if grown-ups played games together like us kids, they'd be happier.

⟨⦿⦿⦿⦿⦿⦿⦿⦿⦿⦿⦿⦿⦿⦿⟩

Our Fourth Floor Incident, 1947

I've lived in this colorless building on this narrow street for five years. Downstairs, the marble entry is too small to be elegant--the six vestibule steps stained and worn in their center. On the wall over the steps, each apartment has a mailbox and buzzer. Visitors are buzzed in from our small vestibule to be let into the inner building. Gabriel, Carmella and I sprawl on these cold steps reading comics because it's raining. But Rosemary yells through the lobby door, "Time to come home. Zia Adina's arrived."

30

Diana Ruth Krohn

Disappointed, I climb the flights and flights of stairs of our five-story walk-up. Our stairway isn't busy, especially as I get past the short second floor. I've only visited two other apartments on our floor. 4D with Mrs. McClanahan's lumpy couch and 4A where Maureen and I play paper dolls, 'Monopoly' and 'Go To the Head of the Class' in her parlor. She's not home today. Above our floor and through the half door is the roof. We don't play there. It's where we hang our laundry to dry.

Most floors have five tenants. Closest to the stained, chipped stairs with their iron railing, the door marked 4A leads to Maureen's apartment. She and her sister are the only other kids on our floor. Her baby brother died of a fever last winter. People with kids prefer to live on the lower floors, although the women still have to carry their laundry past our level to the clothesline on the roof. The two working couples, the Anthonys and the Murphys, aren't home much. Once, I peeked in the Anthony's apartment, 5B, when their door was ajar. Over their stuffed green sofa and dark wood table was a shelf with a cross. I heard Jack Benny yelling, "Rochester. Oh, Rochester," on the radio.

Our apartment has an unusual feature. People can look through the one hall window across a small, atrium-like space, into our parlor. We usually keep our window shades pulled. I love to spy through that window when I can't be outside. Smells of beef, cabbage, beans, garlic and sweet cakes from other apartments overpower my air. No cooking smells in our kitchen, so I grab a piece of pound cake and peek through the opening at the bottom of the shade. Dad takes his newspaper into the bedroom. Not much to observe. Mrs. McClanahan huffing up the stairs in her gray coat, quickly turns her key and shuts her door.

The McClanahans live next to us in 4D. Monochromatic, that describes Mrs. McClanahan. Like a photograph that faded even before it faded. Her short frizzy hair blends with her skin. She never appears happy or sad;

31

her personality seems to have settled and become one with her apartment – a blending of used things like ours. Her worn house dresses, carefully washed and ironed, hold her short body intact. No one ever visits her. She's home alone while Mr. McClanahan works – something with bricks. She talks to Mom sometimes, but not to me.

I doze off for a few minutes until Dad walks back in, sniffing the air. "Do you smell anything? he asks me.

'Maybe', I think as I sniff the air around me. Before I can even answer, Dad is running out our door to Mrs. McClanahan's apartment, yelling "Open the windows, Eva."

I follow him. He bangs on her door, 4D. She doesn't answer so he breaks the door with his foot. He runs in and sees Mrs. McClanahan with her head in the oven. He pulls her to her entry and lays her on the floor. He yells at me, "Cover her with a blanket!"

Staring at her pale face and blue veins, I cover her quickly with my bed blanket while Dad calls the police. She doesn't move. She just lies in her doorway sometimes making soft sounds that make my head whirl. Dad turns off the oven and opens her windows wide.

Everyone on our floor hears the banging and smells the gas. They stand in their doorways, waiting. I don't ask questions because everyone is quiet. But I wonder so many things. How can a person hold their head in a gassy oven? What does it feel like? What was Mrs. McClanahan like as a little girl? Did the other girls play with her? I try to picture her as a young woman in love with Mr. McClanahan. Does she miss her family in Ireland? I wonder what she does all day; she has no children. What are her dreams?

Dad isn't an 'at home' person. He always wears white shirts and proper ties. Simple and familiar. Yet, Dad rescues Mrs. McClanahan from an attempted suicide. All the neighbors tell him that he's uncommonly brave, but he says he could go in because he has a poor sense of smell. A doctor and, finally, two police officers arrive and take Mrs. McClanahan away. And then...silence.

Mom and Dad go to the hospital. I'm alone, but it feels good to just lie in our parlor, surrounded by the sense of the other families in the building. I'm engrossed in a library book about an adventurous emu named Karrawingi. But it's hard to read when the neighbors bang on their radiators demanding more heat from the super.

Alone in bed, I put down my book and look up at peach walls with the white molded trim below the ceiling. I study the chipping paint below the dirty white trim. As I doze on the sofa, waiting for someone to come home, music drifts through the windows and I remember my dream last night. I have this dream often.

All the people living in our building hang around me, even people who lived in this room from another era. The shades are drawn and shadows play on the walls. Shadows get in wherever the shades are ripped or don't fit. The peeling paint chips start to fall, like new snowflakes at first. Then they get bigger and heavier and hit my body until I'm buried in paint chips. My tattered blanket does not protect me.

Mrs. McClanahan returned home from the hospital a few days later, but she never revealed anything. I never saw her cry or laugh. Everything just seemed the same. Our neighbors in our building and on our street were back behind their closed doors again. These Italian and Irish immigrants associated freedom with privacy. If they didn't talk, then they couldn't make mistakes. Old people, especially, were silent and patient as a rock. They didn't even look at my mother and me when they hung their family laundry. They never came to our door. Their isolated lives were so different from us kids on the street. They felt something their children had not experienced, the deep sadness of leaving their homeland behind.

MY STREET

The Squigglies, October 1947

First the goldenrod, then the leaves turning color, as we start wearing sweaters and coats. It's October, the time of year when fuzzy seed pods fall from the big tree beyond our apartment building. Soft, furry, annoying little crescents that make me shiver. For days, as I walk down the sidewalk, I avoid stepping on those squiggly pods, in addition to cracks, gum and spit. Not much space left for my big feet, but years of playing potsy help me keep my balance.

Saturday, the start of the long Columbus Day weekend, I step outside to meet my friends. They are waiting for me, surrounding me in a semi-circle. Something is wrong. Their faces look different -- broken. They have ganged up on me. I cannot believe it. I'm a quiet, shy girl, the kind they call sensitive. I bite my nails and blush when the teacher calls on me. I don't make trouble. I just like to play.

I see their fiery faces, their dark jackets with slouchy hoods. They appear so big as they watch me come down the brick step from my building. Seeing them all together, I instinctively freeze and flinch. They start throwing squigglies at me from piles they had gathered, hitting me all over my body. It feels awful. I don't know how to stop them from hitting me. They yell, "Cry-baby! Brown nose! Jew-baby!"

My breath leaves me, as I enter the hole of a new space. My mouth opens in astonishment at the swiftness of their swirling actions and the meanness of their taunts, "Scaredy cat. We're gonna get you, Jew-ba-by."

My hands cover my face, but nothing can protect me from seeing my friends turn on me. Why is Maureen with them? I don't understand. I close my eyes as they throw their stash. The shock of their attack smacks like an unfamiliar food, difficult to taste because of its newness. I feel the damaged space in my chest. The hole is growing bigger. The air in the hole has the prickly chill of night. My mom, with all her protective warnings, never mentioned this horror.

A new thought comes to me. This is the way the women in our building treat my mom. But I'm not like her. In war movies, they talk about 'knowing your enemy.' Now I know my enemy so well. They are the friends I play with everyday.

I run upstairs. No one follows me. No one talks to me. I don't go outside. I don't even look out the window. I always sense that no one understands the family behind the front door of my apartment, other than Mom being weird. I'm not sure about the Jew part, but I don't think it applies to us. Yet, it's different now. I don't tell anyone else what happened.

I pick the skin around my fingernails till they're bloody and suck the blood till my skin gets wrinkled like a prune. My fear of the squigglies turns into a powerful surge of anger. I especially can't bear that Maureen was in the pack. She has been my best friend since I was two years old. I don't know why! Why me? Why now?

Days of silence. The world stops. I have no toys, except my rubber doll, not even a ball or a game. The hole in the center of my chest becomes hard. Playing endless solitaire on my couch bed, I notice the rain start to hit our parlor window. Two flies are sitting on the windowsill in their 'in or out' predicament. If I were those flies, where would I rather be? Probably outside, even in the rain. Without my friends, I have nothing.

After three days, I hear Maureen's voice at my apartment door, asking Mom, "Can Diana come out to play?" That's what she always says. But Mom never speaks to her. She just calls out, "Di-ann, Maureen's here."

I hesitate. I don't want to stay angry, especially over the name-calling. I know it isn't true. People yell bad names, like barbs, when they are being mean. It doesn't take me long to decide. I run to the door, happy to go back out to play. "Let's go," I murmur. The squigglies don't even matter anymore.

"Jew-baby." Velcro words. What a massive amount of data in the blink of an eye. It's said that you have to know where you're coming from to know how to move forward. Without knowledge of Judaism, I lacked supporting structure to stand on and not enough understanding to defend myself. My immediate feeling was shock (these were my friends) and a glimmer of fear. We all have certain fears that drive us.

With time, I learned you're a Jew whether you practice your religion or not. For those three days, I became vulnerable to the effects of hatred, pain and grief. As a result, the word 'Jewish' became a root word for me. Roots don't merely hide in the ground. They are born to multiply, subdivide like rivulets of rain water hitting the desert hardpan, sending shoots of water branching far from the original erosion.

Now, my Judaism insulates me, offering a mantle of safety, connections woven together into an invisible fabric labeled 'belonging.' And, as for the squigglies, on my overnight trip to New Jersey to bury my mother, I picked up a handful and laughed at those memories. Another example of something I didn't understand which gained perspective with time. Perhaps the hurt you experience as a child toughens you up for life's blows.

◌◌◌◌◌◌◌◌◌◌◌◌◌◌◌◌

Humor, 1947

On weekends when Dad's home, we listen to Uncle Don Carney read the Sunday morning funny papers on WOR, the Newark radio station. We like Dick Tracy, Little Orphan Annie and Prince Valiant, although his warriors confuse me. I spread out the colored pages on the parlor floor and lie on my tummy near the radio. I try to keep up with Uncle Don, who moves from Blondie to Mrs. Worth to Dennis the Menace, not in the same order as our New York

Daily News. Dad sometimes has to put down his sports section of the paper to help me as I try to find the right place so I can read the words recorded in balloons. But our funny page sessions end when Uncle Don goes off the air. Dad told me that Uncle Don slurringly stated, "There, that should take care of the little bastards for another week!" Those brief seconds cancelled his radio career.

Dad stays home more frequently now that he's working at Alcoa where he makes things out of aluminum. He brings them home to show me. Toothpaste containers with screw-on caps. Pieces of machinery. Shelving for aircraft. He makes jokes about how they're used. Last week, he brought home a juicer that looks like a water pump. I'm so glad he's back.

The tubes in the back of our Emerson radio glow red most evenings. The two of us are glued to the news. Great events take place and we sit in our parlor and listen to them on the radio. We hear stories of the Jewish underground and the difficulties of emigration to Palestine. The Marshall Plan, Bugsy Siegel, Jackie Robinson, Chiang Kai-shek...

Mostly we listen to the funny shows since Dad loves jokes. Our nightly lineup favorites are Amos and Andy, Abbott and Costello, and Baby Snooks. Dad calls me "Baby Snooks." I breathe deeper when he pays attention to me. He fancies Duffy's Tavern, "Where the elite meet to eat." "Well look who just walked in, folks! It's Jack Benny, Henny Youngman, Red Skelton, George Burns & Gracie Allen..." Dad says, "Bitterness blinds men and humor brings them together."

Dad is starting to tell his jokes to the neighbors in front of me. It makes me feel so grown up. He's a magnet in the neighborhood. I think he knows ten thousand jokes, long ones. They always start: "Have you heard the one about..." with some twist on the Pearly Gates, the farmer's daughter or things done in the bathroom. Dad loves when men ask, "Tell us a story, Irving," and he always has one. He should be on the radio. I want to make people laugh too, so I keep a notecard file of his jokes with the lead-in, setup and punchline. However, there are so many versions and too many stories. I don't know how he does it!

But many of his inside jokes, imitations and monologues expose Mom's family. They're 'mean' funny. Jokes and Not Jokes. His barbs and nips are so amusing that I can't help agreeing with him. Dad convinces me that Mom's whole family is stupid and not worth emulating, and he does it with laughter.

Mom is "Poor Eva/Little Eva." Her older sister Estelle is a Christian Scientist who had been put in Bellevue, but her husband signed her out. Her husband, Uncle Arthur, fills his plate first and eats by himself in the kitchen, like a death wish, messily forking his food as fast as he can. He eats with an energy that rules out any conversation.

Mom's younger sister, Molly, is shorter than me. I like standing next to her. She married Irving, with the same name as my dad, but with lips that lisp, "Where is my kisth-sss?" whenever we arrive at their Bronx apartment. I hate kissing his bald head. My parents never kiss or touch me, except when Mom removes worms and fleas and lice from my body. I go into the bathroom to clean my lips from the taste of Uncle Irving's head. "*Oy, vey iz mir,*" I mutter to myself. That's the way people talk in the Bronx.

Dad never joins us on our visits. Mom's sisters never come to our house. I don't know the reasons for his hostility. I don't question him. My brother and I wear our cousins Barbara and David's hand-me-downs, even though they're shorter and chubby and we're tall and skinny. I'm barely above death-camp weight. My sweaters are unraveling, my skirts have safety pins to tighten the waist and my pants are too short and have a saggy butt. At least I don't wear hand-me-down shoes. My feet, especially my heels, are too narrow, so I always wear brown high-top oxfords.

What is humor? "Oh, I don't want her, you can have her, she's too fat for me..." Even as I sing along with

Arthur Godfrey and shriek with laughter, I have doubts. What is the starting point of doubt? Uncle Don's words linger in the air with my Dad's. My smile diminishes, turns into grimness. I want to ask, "Why?" But I don't.

My father hid in jokes. He pushed for the humor, even though it often bordered on degrading. He didn't talk about his childhood, his parents, the army, his illnesses, why he lost the store or why he wouldn't go to the Bronx. His humor left me uncomfortable and afraid, intensifying the emotional weather that hovered over our apartment.

Every time I hear 'mean funny' or 'negative cynical' or 'self-deprecating' jokes today, and there are too many, my childhood discomfort returns. I love to laugh, but not at someone else's expense. Such a fluid boundary to overt and covert messages, but they all eventually lead to pain. Now, my sensitivity to derogatory humor and arguments, especially if someone in my family is the target, leads me to find the closest exit.

My mother hid in fears. As I've grown older and discovered the vulnerability underlying her anxiety, I realize my view might just be a factor of my level of naivety. Whether humans, nations or societies, we eventually decide our own truth, often arriving at warped conclusions. Its pursuit is challenging, requiring concentration and silence. Nothing is gained by rushing to figure everything out at once. Very few principles survive the test of time. What if I doubt myself or don't like the results? Do I still believe it? Or does it become fact because I believe it?

MY STREET

Insomnia, January 1948

It's hard to sleep in a parlor with no doors for privacy. I'm upset about my shorn hair from our trip to the barber shop this afternoon. In the window I see the reflection of my head, stripped of its hair. I was the only girl in the barbershop. In the mirrored blackness of our bare window, I can see Mom, her hair randomly pin-curled, scrub the hall floor in our apartment with a gray rag mop. I'm trying to sleep. Electric light bulbs shine in. Red spots free fall behind my closed eyelids.

The only way I can be alone is to close my eyes tight, hold my breath and feel my mind tightening, growing smaller, just like my closed eyes. I try to pretend I'm alone in a cozy bedroom. I don't want to let everybody back in.

Dad arrives home. He tosses his fedora and overcoat on his chair, not saying hello. He stumbles past my couch bed and trips over the water pail in the hall. He yells at Mom, "Dammit, you're as stupid as the rest of your family."

I pretend to sleep, hide my face under my pillow, in the place before tears, trying not to twitch or scratch my mosquito bites. Dad turns on *The Shadow*, a radio program I'm not allowed to hear because I'm only eight. "Who knows what evil lurks in the hearts of men," the announcer taunts, before Dad lowers the volume to keep the sound to himself.

When Dad's radio goes on, Mom usually goes into the kitchen and sings. They don't talk much. Both do their own thing. Grown-ups don't seem to play together. I lift my pillow to try to hear *The Shadow*, but only hear my parents shout bad words at each other. Mom sings her anniversary waltz, her black hair falling from its pins. "Oh, how we danced, on the night we were wed..." She forces her voice to be loud. "We vowed our true love, though a word wasn't said..." She pretends not to hear Dad's nasty words, like I pretend to be sleeping.

Mom vacuums dirt spots off our parlor rug. Her dark eyes don't look at me. Once I asked her why she cleans at night. "Ssssh, go to sleep," she answered.

She jerks that vacuum around, leaves it in the middle of the floor as if broken. I bump into it on my way to the bathroom.

Down the hall in our narrow kitchen, Mom, in her flowered robe and scuffs, is bent over the washboard. She sings that song again, …'two hearts gently beating and murmuring low, my darling, I love you so.' She rubs our clothes and sheets with Fels Naptha. She squeezes until the dirty water circles down the drain.

I lie here listening to my sleeping family, their snores reverberating off the walls. It sounds like the barber's scissors whistling mean tunes in my ears. I felt cold then too, like I feel now, in this cold room. My fingers fidget with the ripped binding on my cover. My doll feels so hard. If only I had a teddy bear to love. I could show him the piles of white snow accumulating on our windowsill, locking us in, to inside noises. Fires, explosions and the shadowy face of a man lurks beyond the room, waiting to hurt me. I can't talk or scream or defend myself.

The nights grew longer, our apartment grew smaller, lying alone in my narrow bed, blemished like our rusting tub, windows closed in the hours till the traffic on Hudson Boulevard stopped. Sometimes I'm still afraid to sleep— afraid to let go because if I let my mind free, it might reveal some awful truths. I keep analyzing, not leaving room for the present to unwind. However, I've learned that when you open your mind, it's easier for things to fit. At least I now understand the difference between being alone and being on my own. No more oscillating or spiraling into an abyss. No more being deluded by the system. Courage has to be assessed differently in spite of struggle, malnutrition, disease, imprisonment by external factors. I paint life in a watercolor way with the past in light washes and a strong statement at the end.

MY STREET

Arithmetic, spring 1948

Fourth grade is so different. The boys are in separate classes from the girls. I hardly noticed the difference that first morning because there were still boys in the morning courtyard, at recess and in the pea green halls. Quickly the silence, the lack of noisy energy and boy naughtinesses became apparent. The girls spend more time glancing out the door to the hall. More girls raise their hands to gain permission to go to the bathroom. When Mrs. Christiano approves, we write our name and the time we leave on the blackboard. We erase our name when we return.

I dream of growing up to be a teacher. There's so much information in the world that school should never end. Even when I'm not at school, I love to play school, mostly with Aaron. I'm the teacher so I set the schedule, allotting time for each subject, but leaving extra time for vocabulary and Webster's dictionary. I'm up to "s" -- the joy of columns of words. My goal is to learn lofty, unusual words like *sufferance* and *melodious*, so I speak beyond the confines of ordinary language.

My favorite subject is arithmetic. Nothing seems hard, and if it is, I simply guess. Memorizing tables is the easiest -- singsong, like jump rope rhymes.

> Down by the ocean
> Down by the sea,
> Johnny broke a bottle
> And blamed it all on me.
> I told Ma, Ma told Pa,
> Johnny got a spankin'
> So, Ha! Ha! Ha!
> How many spankings did he get?
> One, two, three…

Multiplication table games are my specialty. I'm even faster than Barbara Zaretsky. The rules live someplace in my head, like a skeleton holding me together. I love seeing my bones in the X-ray machine in the shoe store. The salesclerk lets me view my toe bones as they wiggle and move, even when it's only my mom or brother buying shoes. My toes turn into ghostly mysterious shadowy lights. Seems like seeing the invisible, knowing that the world is full of invisible hidden structures. The bones I see are alive and there all the time. So is my understanding of arithmetic in my brain, even when I don't think about it.

I multiply and divide in any order like a whirlwind. I even love number problems and their proofs at the bottom of the page. Most of our books have answers in the back. After a while, I stop checking. Getting the right answer is so freeing. No work or worry.

Mrs. Christiano announces a tutor program and I raise my hand to volunteer. She hands me a yellow piece of paper with Victor Fusco's name. I'm so relieved to get someone I know, even though Victor lives in the basement and his father cleans our building. I head to his classroom, all boys, with the paper in hand.

Victor's teacher gruffly questions, "What do you want?" like he doesn't know about the program. He reads the slip and mutters, "What makes you good enough to tutor?"

I feel suddenly stunned. What should I say? The air in the room turns to night air. I glance up at the worn paddle hung over the doorway. Victor's teacher starts asking me tables and my answers come quickly. The room is so quiet, rows of boys' faces. Only his gruff questions, "79 x 4" and my shy, but quick, "316." I pass his test with all the boys staring at me. What a relief, that feeling of 'escaped again!' I start to tutor Victor. He's likable. We become friends.

Time holds us and molds us. One, two, three… Just like arithmetic rules living in our head. Four, five, six… We turn the page and learn more each day. But each of us goes through time in a different way. Seven, eight, nine… As

43

*years go by, it feels like time speeds up to an invisible
pulse, putting a damper on my day. But maybe the tease of
time and discovery can slow life down. Who doesn't want
life to slow down? Its mystery, like death, adds value to life.
But time doesn't stop to ease the undecided or assure the
chimerical answer from our certainties and impressions.*

ↃↄↃↄↃↄↃↄↃↄↃↄↃↄↃↄↃↄ

Bumps, spring 1948

The tavern is across Hudson Boulevard. This spring,
Dad sometimes takes me with him now when he goes to
have his 'coupla' beers. I meet boys my age who are there
with their fathers. We play shuffleboard on the long table in
the side porch room when the men are done playing. I like
the feel of the metal puck in my hand, running it on the
smooth shiny wood table and the sawdust, like the sawdust
on the floor, that helps the disc slide farther. There are
numbers at each end for scoring. I slide the disc with much
more control than I ever manage with a pool cue. My puck
lands on these numbers, not into the gutter. Hubba hubba!

We stand around the people at the bar and stare at their
burning cigarettes. The cylinder of ash grows and grows
like a shriveling man about to fall. We don't want to miss
when a piece falls off, into their ashtray or on the floor.
When the men aren't looking (they probably turn the other
way on purpose 'cause we aren't that clever), we bottom
off their not quite finished highballs and beers. Liquor
makes my face red, but "Yum!" The juke box is playing,
"Buttons & Bows. "When Dinah Shore stops singing, I
hear Dad brag to his friends, "Diana had her first beer in
her bottle." He's the most popular man because every joke
reminds him of another joke.

It seems to me that the tavern is to the men what the
street is to us kids. For us, a place to escape our apartments
and our mothers; for them, to escape their wives. Mothers
and wives are always telling us what to do. How can my

44

mom stay home all day? No wonder she wants to come to school. It gives her a place to go. I won't ever get married and stay at home with nothing to do. I will drink liquor and laugh like the men in the tavern.

We finally leave for home. Down the block, wait for the light, cross Hudson Boulevard while the rumbling noise of impatient car and truck engines threaten. Maybe those drivers are trying to break the sound barrier, just like Chuck Yeager did two years ago. I don't blame them. Being that powerful would be amazing. No pedestrian laws protect us. I lift my head to scan the late afternoon sky, its layers of gray barely visible beyond the buildings. The clouds are not moving or separate enough to observe shapes. No omens.

Do you believe in omens? I don't, yet I start thinking about them. Even though I don't accept them, I always welcome a good one like a penny in the street or an empty stool at the soda fountain. I continue down the sidewalk with Dad and Mr. McNaught, focusing on not slipping in the mud and not stepping on cracks or spit or gum. So many cracks dissect these crumbling sidewalks. Mr. McNaught is roly-poly, with a round belly like mom. He's one of those burly, strong torso, short-legged men. His puffy face is covered with red freckles and his nose is red with blue veins.

I want to get ahead of both men, dragging on their cigarettes, who are moving exasperatingly slow like old people do. But Dad doesn't see me move out in front and he walks right into me. I fall forward, forehead first, hitting the sidewalk. I lay there. My head feels weirdly large and full of pain. Lost in a loop of time, I can't even think about getting up.

Dad carries me up the stairs to our apartment. My whole body feels open and icy. In the kitchen, he takes a large butcher knife and pushes it hard against the bleeding and fast-growing bulge. The cold steel hurts more than the pressure. We don't even think of going to doctors. No dentists either. Dad simply says, "You'll be fine tomorrow.

You've got a thick skull." That's what you do for bumps!

When I arrive at school, Mrs. Christiano looks at me and writes a note to the other teachers. They send me from classroom to classroom to make me show my purple protuberance. It sticks way out. My forehead and right eye are black and blue.

The kids stare at me. I hate it. It hurts and I blush. After school, I go to Maureen's apartment and beg her to cut bangs to cover the bump that I'm afraid will probably never go away. She cuts and cuts.

I remember my clipped hairs falling into Maureen's bathroom sink, snippets of hacked away pieces that didn't belong to me anymore. As I raise my fingers to feel the bump that still juts out of my right forehead, I suffer again the shock of that broken hair in Maureen's white sink. Broken, like the bits of shells my brother and I found at the shore. Shattered chunks not good enough to be picked up. Those splintered slices of hair still call out to me, like shards coming in with the tides — even after I've walked too far to turn back. Maybe the only keepers are words.

◦◦◦◦◦◦◦◦◦◦◦◦◦◦◦◦◦◦

Aaron's Coma, June 1948

I sit on our apartment steps, waiting my turn at hopscotch, when it happens. My little brother hurtles headfirst over the handlebars, as the front wheel of our neighbor's trike he's riding hits a rock. He hits his head on a monstrous pointy rock. Mom rushes to him, picks him up and carries him up to his crib. He lies there, not moving, like he's never been alive for the past five years. Dr. Friedman comes with his black bag and examines him. Mrs. McClanahan comes. Finally, Dad joins us after his swing shift. We stand, looking at Aaron, but he always looks asleep. He's sleeping on his back with his arms spread outward. His pillow isn't even wrinkled. I wonder if he's dreaming. My fingers grip the cold rails of his crib.

Aunt Miriam, Uncle Dan and Aunt Jean, come to visit over the weekend and so do four work friends. It's the first time I remember having visitors, sort of a party for my brother's coma. They sit in the parlor on my bed, the blue couch that's divided up on opposite walls. I can't sit on any furniture because I have Unguentine ointment on the rashes on the back of my knees, scabs on the front of my knees and ringworm on my arms. Very annoying! I stand quietly in the back, scarcely looking at anyone.

After they stare at Aaron for a while, they sit in the parlor under their canopy of smoke. The smoke lifts away as I listen. They talk and flick ashes like nothing is wrong, seesaw speech and mingling smoke. Something makes me focus on one woman who came from Dad's work. Maybe her permed hair, the softness of her beige-flowered dress with its matching covered buttons, her straight-seamed stockings and sling-back shoes, or the very red lipstick. She's called Christine. I watch her and wonder. I think I'm not the only one distracted by her. She seems more alive than anyone else. However, if anyone is Dad's sweetheart, it is Virginia, our divorced neighbor across Hudson Boulevard. I love Virginia's husky voice when she teases me. She acts like Mom's friend, but flirts with my father. Maybe nobody is Dad's girlfriend, but then why is he gone so much?

When everyone leaves, I hear Mom make a comment about Christine, "So that's your woman friend!"

Dad explodes and roars, "You crazy bitch. You don't know what you're talking about."

He doesn't stop yelling. He slaps her face. Violence happens so fast. I didn't expect it. I walk past the bathroom to see if Mom's okay. She's moaning. There's blood coming from the side of her head. She cries, "Irving, you shouldn't have hit my ear." Those words stay in the air. '*hit my ear...hit my ear...*'

I don't like this at all. I move towards Dad whose yelling makes no sense, and I assert as loud as I can, "Stop hitting Mom!" He throws a sofa pillow at me. Hard. I'm stunned, speechless. It's the first time I'm ever hit. No belt or flyswatter or brush was ever used to punish me – until that pillow.

Dad leaves the apartment, slamming the door. I wait. Mom's mantle clock chimes eleven times and still he doesn't come home. I listen as the resonance of the chimes fade. He doesn't return until very late. I never hear anything more about Christine.

As daylight filters through the window, I hear a moan in my parent's bedroom. Mom is talking softly to my brother. I run to his crib to see Aaron with his eyes open. She offers, "Want a bowl of Cheerios?" I hope that by his birthday, he'll be able to get out of the crib and play again. I feel lighter and my secret fears stop breaking my sleep.

Old people get left alone with their memories. They become unseen, unscrutinized. I wonder if that's how Aaron felt in his coma. If you're not noticed, are you alive? It becomes important to know how to self-soothe and be confident of other people's love, even when they're not there in front of you. I know what it's going to take for me to be satisfied with my life — the answer is the 'real' me. I discard the distracting activities or file them in a box on the crowded top shelf of my closet. Then I have space to surround myself in an environment to reach my dreams.

Several years ago, in a small cafe in Venice, I asked our waiter for 'fresh' orange juice. He just looked at me. So I asked for 'real' orange juice. He continued to stare at me. "Nothing is real; it's all an illusion," was his answer. Then he joined my daughter and me and we spent twenty minutes talking about life, memories, violence, peace. And we had a 'real' delicious breakfast.

Diana Ruth Krohn

The Rules of Voting, 1948

Summer isn't very noticeable in our noisy, densely packed neighborhood. Except the heat quickly turned our few wildflowers and weeds from green to brown. We know little about birds or any animals who live by following their instinct. Birds swoop quietly, but frantically lift off when seeking refuge. Our instinct is also to seek safety, but we have different rules than the birds. I know the rules to Hopscotch, Red Rover, Mother May I, Hide and Seek, Dodge ball and all our games.

In fifth grade, Mrs. Janpole has so many rules. School bells and teachers' whistles regiment our day. Mom never gives me rules. I make them up to be like the other kids. I say, "I have to be home when the street lights go on." "I can only play in the vestibule when it rains." "My mom won't let me trade comics." "My mom won't let me go in the lot." It's really best to make your own rules because then you can change them whenever you want.

Jersey residents are familiar with our Democratic stronghold headed by Frank Hague. Dad knows him from the eight years he was President of the Elks Club. If we need anything, the rules are that you **never** go directly to a government office. Someone in 'the party' takes care of it for you. When Mom changed her name from Rebecca to Eva, the party completed the legalities. When she decided to become a naturalized citizen, the party arranged it. There was a question whether this formality was necessary, since she arrived at Ellis Island when she was six months old. But she wanted to be sure.

A few weeks before today's elections, a ward heeler in a dark suit came to our apartment door to ask my parents, "...things okay? Need anything?" From the corner of the room, I watched as he silently slipped a ten-dollar bill into Dad's hand. Two days later, Mom also took bribe money, but from the ratty Republican guy who represents Dewey. She gave it to old Mrs. Sinagra down the street. "She needs help bringing her grandson's over from Italy," she explained.

Today, on Election Day, Dad grips my hand saying, "C'mon, Diana, we're going to vote for Harry Truman."

Dad knows everything about events in our country and the world because we listen to the news on the radio. We were so excited during the countdown of the United Nations vote on Israel in May. We heard stories of daredevil pilots flying into Berlin and learned of the far-away assassination of Mahatma Gandhi.

We meander down Hudson Boulevard together. Dad looks dapper in his blue suit with a fresh handkerchief in his breast pocket. He wouldn't be caught dead buying one of those Robert Hall suits with two pair of pants. He tips his hat at the ladies as we pass them. We come to a street corner I don't recognize, crowded with men standing around. I see the same ward-healer, the one that came to our door, with his thick black hair Bryl-creamed into place. I don't like that man. I bet he's a bully like big Michael Flaherty in fifth grade. They both spit frequently, as if they're daring you to challenge them. He watches us and nods at Dad when we enter the building to vote. He's with other men in suits, standing like they're used to being the victors in Bergen County elections. Dad told me they know how we will vote because "They're tough and shrewd. We are putty."

With no other children at the voting place, I get a lot of attention. I don't see any ladies either. I'm very shy and don't talk, but the men don't care. They're excited because it is the first election using the new voting machines. Two grossly fat men demonstrate how to pull the levers. I wonder if I'll grow that fat and limp. "Pull the small levers separately to vote on each candidate and ballot issue. Or better yet, pull the big lever that moves all the small levers to vote a party ticket."

The names on top are Harry Truman, Thomas Dewey or Henry Wallace. The man calls to me, "C'mon up little girl. You can demonstrate how easy it is." Dad lifts me on to the platform, saying, "Go ahead Diana, grab the black ball and pull it all the way down." The man helps me reach up and pull the big black lever for Harry Truman. The demonstration is over. The men clap and whistle. I'm so proud. I love voting and I've learned the rules.

Maimonides taught that truth is in the middle. But the rules keep changing with the seasons, having little to do with religion or justice. I've voted in fifteen U. S. presidential elections since Harry Truman's. People still opinionate, often simplistically or bombastically, avoiding the task of determining reality. They don't foresee that unity can develop from harmony. Some election years it's hard to believe in a country of almost three hundred thirty million people (more than double 1948), our candidates are the most effective and experienced leadership we can find. Add the harsh divisiveness of partisan politics and we risk becoming a crumbling country with a fading future these candidates cannot fix. What use do we make of history, or instinct or memory?

Betrayal, November 1948

I wake up to a sweet, yet sour smell, the kind that makes you not want to eat. Mom is rubbing gobs of mustard on my chest and popping Pyrex custard cups over the mustard, doing her utmost to get suction in spite of the scalloped edge.

"Don't," I try to yell through my hoarse dry throat, but it doesn't even come out a whisper.

"Stay still," she says. "Be a good girl." Her strong arms are focused on the cure. Muscle prevails over gentleness.

"Get away from me," I try again to wail, but coughing

takes over and some of the cups roll off my still flat chest.

You don't want to get sick at my house. It's like being under a she-devil's curse. This year I've already had measles and mumps. Aaron got mumps too but Mom seemed glad rather than mad.

Today Mom looks more tired than angry. Dark hairs dangle from her pin curls. Mustard spots have spilled across the front of her gray and white polka-dot housedress. She stretches back on the easy chair next to my half-couch bed and lights a cigarette. Smoking makes her look strange, like it's her first time. She holds the cigarette with the tips of her fingers. Her lips exaggerate the motion when she blows out the smoke. She smokes more, and worries more, when my father is gone. I usually don't know where he is and maybe she doesn't either. But this time he's in Cleveland at Bobby's wedding to a girl named Dorothy.

"Mrs. McNaught says mustard will stop your coughing," she explains, without apology, as she returns to reapply the cups that usually hold Jello.

Felled by my usual case of bronchitis, the plight of Jersey girls with ever-drippy noses, I don't stop her. This is the spring version and, in addition to the mustard, my mother crushes powdery bitter aspirin in Mott's applesauce. She has a perverse fascination with sickness. Fever is not to be taken lightly. Her mother died from fever when my mother was a little girl.

I wriggle a cup off as Mom stubs out her cigarette and leaves to get me juice, canned juice, the liquid cure. Like the applesauce, the juice is warm, flat and spiked with aspirin and cod-liver oil flavored stuff. I usually take pretend sips and then pour it down the sink when I go to the bathroom. But today, I drift into studying the rise and fall of the remaining cups and sleep returns…

A cold washcloth wakes me up. I don't mind getting my face and arms scrubbed, but the cold alcohol on my tummy and legs feels too severe for my feverish body. The morning light comes through our hallway window. Uneven patterns drift across the ceiling. My chest feels like gravity is settling in heavier than usual. My head is connected to too many places. Feels like I'm coughing up my lungs.

Alone again, in my bed. My dream lingers. In it, a letter from my dad has disappeared from our mailbox in the marbled lobby. I panic, wander up and down the stained vestibule steps where we trade comics and baseball cards when it rains. I look all over, feeling isolated in that cold place and not knowing what to do. Helpless, unable to reach out across the vast space that separates me from him.

I glance around the room as I awaken. I don't think my little brother is home. At least he's not sleeping on the other half of the couch on the other side of our parlor. The small room is dim with drawn window shades and shadows where the ripped shades don't fit.

My sickness carries me in and out of sleep, daydreaming, real dreaming... "I'm looking over a four-leaf clover, that I overlooked before..." drifts through the open window, along with traffic noises and crashing sounds from some boy chugging his toy car in the dirt. My eyes and thoughts focus on the room behind the shadows. It was built in another era with high narrow windows, a fire escape, and peachy walls with a molded trim below the ceiling. The chipping paint threatens, ready to fall and smother me. I give up to the inevitable...

Mom walks in the front door. I can always tell it's her without looking because of the way she struggles with the keys and door lock. "C'mon. We're going to the Sinagras." She shakes her head at me like she does sometimes and pokes my arm. "Old Mrs. Sinagra will help you get better."

'Yay!' I think without saying anything. Mostly I don't talk 'cause I'm not sure what to say. After Maureen, the Sinagra kids are pretty much my closest friends. Carmella and Gabriel are close to my age, and I like Rosemary who has a home perm and doesn't play as much now that she's in high school. The Sinagra kids sometimes get to stay in the street even after the streetlights come on. But none of them can play on Saturday until they finish waxing all the furniture, even the holy crucifixes on the walls.

Their mother sews in the basement, seaming black skirts that get sold in clothing stores. After his regular job, their father repairs shoes in the back corner of their basement where it smells like rubber and shoe polish. He uses an upside-down shoe rest to replace soles and heels. The friendliest one is old Mrs. Sinagra who cooks the spaghetti. We don't see many old people except when they hang laundry on the line. But all us kids like old Mrs. Sinagra and she likes us. She takes care of the boy cousins who come over from Italy and live there for a while. Once she made a birthday cake for Gabriel and she gave me a piece. It had layers of cream, like pudding, with canned peaches hidden in the middle layer. So-o-o yummy!

"Don't tell anyone where we're going, or why," Mom says as she buttons my winter coat over my nightie. "We don't want the neighbors to know about your fever."

She holds my hand and we walk down the worn steps, through the vestibule that is too small to be elegant. No one sees us. We head down the street. Mom makes a clicking noise in her throat as she gulps the warm air. It feels like we're moving fast, hurrying. Too bad Dad is gone again. He could tell her not to worry.

I don't see any kids. Maybe they're at school. We pass the weedy dirt patch at the end of our apartment building, just past where the delivery trucks stop, but there's still no green coming up where Maureen and I used her mom's soup spoons to bury our peach pits. I wonder when they will grow into trees. I look into all three houses we pass, but there are no distractions.

At least I don't see the cruel Joan who lives in the wood house past the Sinagras. She's in my fifth-grade class and always stirring up trouble. She walks to school the same route I do, in the same cluster, so I always pretend to be her friend. When I'm home sick, I worry about the bad things that could be coming out of her evil mouth. I would be very unhappy to run into her with my nightie pants hanging out of my coat.

We step carefully up the concrete stairs into the Sinagras' entry hall and wait. I've stood in this hall before waiting for Rosemary and Carmella to finish rubbing their furniture with oil before they can play. They wax dressers, tables, crosses and their buffet that holds old family photographs with people in starched collars, tight clothes and unsmiling faces.

I hear old Mrs. Sinagra in the kitchen. She doesn't come out and look at my throat or feel my forehead. But then she's walking toward me, dressed entirely in black, carrying a filled whiskey shot glass.

"Drinka dis," she says, looking straight at me.

And I do. Immediately, I know this is the most revolting thing I have ever drunk. Garlic juice! Oh, jeez, I wish I could take back what happened and not drink it. I gag and retch and shudder. That nasty stuff has gone down too far too fast.

We're out the door and in the street before I know it. I cry in despair at the awful taste of garlic juice trickery. If I die of fever right now, I'll be better off, but I don't think I'd get into heaven with this awful stuff pressing into my body. Mom says nothing. I will never trust her again.

As we reach the sidewalk, old Mrs. Sinagra comes running after us, her stockings not quite rolled up high enough to cover her blue legs and puffy knees, tying her widow's black kerchief tightly under her hairy chin. "Heah, sweedie. Chocolatte make da tasta go avay."

I should know better, but I still don't fully understand the connection. My heart is thumping away in my chest and the garlic is making a straight shot down through my tummy. Without thinking, I put the round piece of chocolate in my mouth. The inside is mushy, soft and sweet. A chocolate-covered cherry, another unpalatable first. It is too much to go down. I have to keep chewing it.

I know this candy cannot make the taste go away. I stay quiet. Mom's chin begins to quiver. I think she's still afraid. She's always afraid. I walk home with her, burping up garlicky chocolate cream. I curl up in my half-couch bed, a skinny ball of sweaty sickness, my fevered brain tainted by garlic, promising myself that if I don't die, I will never tell my mom when I feel sick -- ever again.

Mom and I remained close after all. I can't seem to stay angry. Yet I've spent my life avoiding garlic, or at least foods where garlic leaves an aftertaste. Because of those whiskey glasses of garlic juice, for over sixty years I've scrutinized menus in restaurants avoiding any items with garlic listed as an ingredient. Imagine the impatient white-aproned waiters dealing with my perusal of the fine print, especially in Italian and Mediterranean restaurants. Neither common sense nor hypnosis worked. My children warn me when they've used garlic in their dishes and sometimes go to the trouble of creating separate dishes for me. When I have company, I put heavy doses of garlic in the fattening foods so I'm not tempted to eat them. A few of my friends think it's a joke when they try to serve me garlic soup. OOPS!

◖◦◖◦◖◦◖◦◖◦◖◦◖◦◖◦◖◦◖◦◖◦◖◦

Rheumatic Fever, winter 1949

I still get sick, in spite of Castoria, and Mom mostly finds out. Now I have rheumatic fever. I'm not sure what that is, something about rheumatism which sounds like a disease old people get in a drafty English cottage in a Charles Dickens novel. I've been in my parent's bed since August, three months, taking handfuls of aspirin and stuff. I mostly sleep or daydream, longing to be somewhere and someone else.

Dr. Friedman comes and takes my nighty off so he can hook up his tubes, from a special black bag, to my chest and arms. I feel naked and cold. He never says anything to me and I never say anything to him. Sometimes he brings another doctor and they whisper in the corner of the bedroom as they look in the black box. At least Dr. Friedman is a real doctor, and a Jewish one. Mom says Jewish doctors are the best kind.

I'm not allowed to do much. I can't even read because the doctor doesn't want me to get "e-motional." Mom doesn't read. She's not a good reader. She says she can't read without glasses, but she never buys any and they won't help her learn the words. She says, "Di-ann, you're reading too much. You'll go blind." I'm not sure if "no reading" is her rule or Dr. Friedman's, so I hide my comics under the pillow.

Sleeping in my parents' bedroom is comfortable. Before I got this rheumatic fever, I hardly ever went into my parent's bedroom even though my clothes are stored in one of their drawers. Their drawers are full of pack-a-way places. Stuff Mom saves, but doesn't seem to use.

I wonder where my parents sleep. Maybe in the parlor where they moved Aaron's crib. I don't see Dad much, but Aunt Miriam visits and teaches me to crochet squares to make an afghan. It takes eighty squares to use all the wool, but now I don't know how to put them together. So Mom stores them in a bag in the hall closet, keeping their warmth for themselves.

My fever is gone now, Mom says, as she brings me her button jar. I don't want to play with the buttons, but she says I still can't play games in the street. I have something called a heart murmur. Another sickness triggering her fears. I can't hear it mumble, or gurgle, or mutter. I imagine my heart trying to tell me something that I can't understand. And I play games with buttons.

You don't see as many clothes with creative buttons anymore. On 90th Street, every home had its glass button jar, like EMT for our clothes. Uncle Arthur was a button salesman. He carried a suitcase full of button cards, samples for garment manufacturers on Seventh Avenue and fabric stores in all five boroughs of New York City. Buttons were a profitable business. Uncle Arthur provided my cousins with their own bedrooms, new clothes and books. Aunt Estelle had a piano and their apartment was across the street from the tree-lined Grand Concourse Park where they met.

I still have Mom's button jar, although with so many moves, I discarded the boring ones. But I've kept my favorites, especially the brass anchors. Since my daughters left home, I rarely sew on a button, but who knows! Just another treasure diminished by the inevitable pulse of time.

<><><><><><><><><><><><><><><><><

The Library, spring 1949

On my first Saturday outside after my rheumatic fever, Maureen and I are allowed to go to the library. Saturday is our library day since it's a farther walk than going to school. We head to the other end of 90th Street, wearing car coats and kerchiefs, past the scary walled-in haunted house on the corner. I'm always intrigued by its wall, the only house with a stone wall I've ever seen. The house hides way back from the padlocked gate, with bushes and vines obscuring what we keep trying to sneak a look at. We heard an old lady lives there, a strange old lady, different from us. Joan says her house is haunted. She's seen her walking around her garden, a ghost lady with pale skin and white hair. She doesn't like people and does evil things to keep them away. We believe she kills animals too. Even teenage boys are afraid to climb that stone wall.

For two more blocks, all we notice is a cat sitting on a window ledge and a mangy brown dog barking against the cyclone fence. Then we reach Bergenline Avenue and cross to the park. We take turns carrying the heavier books. We stroll and talk along the gravelly path until reaching the end where the big sycamore tree spreads its roots into the grass. Our library sits across the street near the West New York boundary.

Inside are two rooms stuffed with books and a desk for the librarian, Mrs. Bauer. The rooms smell like the cloakroom at school at 4 o'clock. You know that dark place behind the back wall where our coats, galoshes, crumpled gym suits and leftover lunches are kept among the boxes of old textbooks and art supplies, covered by extra pencils, bottles of ink and bulletin board cutouts.

Mom still yells at me for reading too much. I've read all the children's and young adult books, from *Aesop's Fables* to *Zorba the Greek*. Characters in books become so very real to me, more than most of the people I know, more than my relatives that I see only a few times during the year. There's magic inside books and pictures living inside my head. I live in the world of my books.

Sometimes I wish for a different family like the March family in Little Women. My cousin Barbara gave me the book and, so far, I've read it eleven times. I long to be Jo with her wise and loving Marmee. Mr. March is gone, like my dad. He's fighting for the Union in the war. When he comes home sick, everything's still simply wonderful. The March's eat together and have holidays with presents, even if they are homemade. The radiator hisses in their cozy house. Our parlor sits silent except when the neighbors bang on their radiators to get the Super to turn on the heat. I long for sisters too, instead of brothers who live in Florida and a little brother who poops in his playpen, bangs his feet in the high chair and only eats cereal.

Treasure Island is another favorite because so much happens. I've read it enough times to picture every scene. I love the fight at the Alamo, Daniel Boone and Davey

Crockett. I gobble up everything about the Civil War. I've read the Bobbsey Twins and the whole shelf of Nancy Drew. I'm bewitched by fairy tales with knights and dragons, Greek gods' grief and gory ghost stories. Books add new circuits to my brain and change the way I think about the world.

Miss Bauer made me bring my last report card to her. Now she lets me use the adult section, as long as she approves the books I check out. I plan to read every book. Marjorie Morningstar replaced Jo March in the silent shelves of infinite authors: the Bronte sisters, Edgar Allen Poe and Mark Twain. I read the juicy parts of *Lady Chatterley's Lover*, hiding back in the stacks, when that prissy librarian isn't looking. The gardener kissing the flowers on the lady's body. Wow! That's what my life will become when I grow up. I can't wait.

We check out the max, four books, and carry them to the park. We try to read at least one book in the park, so we can return it and bring new ones home. We sit under the sycamore tree as its shadow lengthens, reading and sharing the peanut butter and apple sandwich packed by Maureen's mother. What a wonderful spring day! The blue sky seems infinite, clouds hover on the horizon, forming mountain ranges in the sky, and sunlight bounces among the green leaves. What limits them? What limits me?

E-books, today's rage, can't duplicate my library experiences in those wondrous rooms where books marched to the ceiling, undusted. They drew me into their net of beauty and history. When I read children's stories, evil was clear and good was without doubt. Problems led to adventures. Disaster seemed inevitable until noble sacrifice allowed the hero to win. Life proved fair after all.

Adult stories, with their giant obstacles, elicited worries that I wasn't good enough to overcome my flaws. Maybe I was nailed to my failures. They danced through my head, uninvited. I needed Tolkien to turn my mishaps into adventures, Dickens to reveal my character and Hemingway to keep me on the path. Certainly, Maureen and I shared a passion for books, one of the strongest bonds that can spring up between people. A path of endless association…and I still enjoy walking that path.

❦❦❦❦❦❦❦❦❦❦❦❦❦❦

Jump Rope, summer 1949

The summer heats up into days of doldrums. "Eat something," Mom nags.

I don't want to go in our kitchen to eat the same old Swiss cheese. I grab *Treasure Island* and sit in dad's chair. But Aaron's banging on his playpen sides. He's always stuck in his crib or playpen. He wants to get out but Mom ignores him. He needs toys, but we don't have any. I can't play the radio because Dad isn't home, seems like he never is. I can't stand it.

I run down the worn steps, through our marble vestibule, through the heavy double doors to our street. Since we live near the top floor of our building, no matter where I go on 90th Street, Mom can still see me from her bedroom window. No kid wants to stay inside their dark crowded tenement rooms. Sitting in school all day gives me pins and needles. It's crowded and mediocre. Church is too disciplined and scary and it hurts my knees. In the street, we're free to play ball against the stoop or be on a team. We find caterpillars and grasshoppers. Before dusk, we play hide-and-seek. It's swell!

I'm free, ready to check out all the stuff going on, I look for my favorite kids. First Maureen. Then Carmella, Rosemary and Gabriel Sinagra who usually play stickball. I like stickball best when Carl is pitcher because I can hit his pitches. He doesn't throw easy to anyone else, so he must like me. His mom's a teacher, so he can't play until his homework is done. Victor is fun too, but he doesn't say much, even though I taught him arithmetic tables. He's the son of the superintendent of our building and I think living in that dark basement sometimes makes him act weird.

No one's here, so I'll have to find them. They're not playing Russia or dodge ball or just catch right now. Maybe hopscotch–no. Ah, here they are–around the corner on Fifth Avenue playing jump rope. I hear the rhythm as I get nearer.

"Cinderella, dressed in yella
went downstairs to kiss her fella.
How many kisses did she get?
One. Two. Three..."

Ooh, Joan! I need to be careful around her. She whispers secrets and when she turns the rope, she wiggles it. I know she does. We never admit we like performing for the crowd, and we never admit that girls like Joan want to trip us up. Rosemary calls, "Jump in Di," so I do as Rosemary jumps out. Maureen replaces Joan and turns with Carmella. Everyone's watching me jump. I feel the rope encircling around me.

"Ice cream soda, lemonade tart,
Tell me the name of your sweetheart.
A, B, C, D, E..."

I love the tease of anticipation in this rhyme. I twist my apple stem with the same big question. All us girls know we'll be getting a boy to marry and I want a clue.

Whoops, it's Victor's turn to turn the rope. Boys are undependable. They don't focus on the turning. I also hate to jump when the Fifth Avenue girls are turning. They're mean to us 90th Street kids. We're stuck with them because we have to jump on their corner. Otherwise we're in the path of the stickball game. I love the airy feeling of jumping, flying so lightly over the moving rope.

We get tired as it gets dark. The streetlights come on and everyone heads home for supper. I hate the night.

Sometimes I think about hiding in the lot across the street, but I never do.

Life on our street was one long ongoing conversation. The only times we weren't there were during school, church, if we had a fever, or after the streetlights came on. Weather hardly stopped us, although summer's heat and mosquitoes slowed us down. Snow was fun. We didn't care about cold, even when it caused snot dripping down our upper lip to freeze in place. If it rained, we traded comics and baseball cards in our lobby until that sweetened chill arrived in the air, signaling clearing skies. We played, and we played out all our emotions. Anger in dodge ball, fear in hide and seek, joy at the xylophone tinkle of the ice cream truck, silliness in the nonsensical words of jump rope and challenge in stickball. Absorbed in play, we experienced childhood's presence of infinite days -- no sense of time until the streetlights came on, stealing the first evening stars from view.

My apartment lacked toys. I couldn't play the radio unless my father was home and he was gone most of the time. My mother was weird and afraid. Aaron sat in his playpen in the middle of the parlor which was my bedroom, so I never had private space. No one wanted to stay in their dark crowded tenement rooms with their aura of absurd hopelessness. Our only hope was the street. Space to breathe and think openly, fresh air, fresh thoughts, escape, someone to play ball with, whether we ganged up on a team or played in twosomes by the stoop. My street symbolizes where I formed my identity, providing the reality I needed to keep me sane. I don't know who I would have become without my street.

We didn't appreciate our inheritance from previous generations of dreamers, courageous immigrants, builders, philanthropists, religious and political leaders. We were children who lived in the present as if all the time in the world held still. We just played our games in the street.

Such mesmerizing rhythms that linger, defining my life long after my years of childhood. Always someone to talk with -- always so much to talk about. Our lives connected by those games, especially jump rope. My grandchildren laugh when I jump rope, but they think I'm fun. The confident rhythm, cadence and lilt of the rhymes led me to my love of language. The unwritten street rules taught me to get along. It started me on my lifetime search for friends that bring meaning to my days. With rare exception, I prefer being stimulated by everything 'out there' rather than being a homebody. Staying home implies 'old on hold.'

In spite of my mistakes, I'm glad to be myself, unburdened by rules, expectations and images. I know where I'm going -- it's still downstairs to play, whenever I can -- especially now, in my playing time of life, my dotage. Today, a larger street calls to me, with my friends in this world that want to play. My many moves have made closeness a challenge, but not impossible. Please knock on my door, call, text, e-mail and I'll come out and play. We'll find a trail, a beach, a movie or book to be dissected over Dubonnet, any excuse to party, memories to share... I wish I could gather all the people in my life, my loves and lovers, my heroes and heroines who taught me in a way that significantly changed my perspectives. People who enlighten you must love you.

∞∞∞∞∞∞∞∞∞∞∞∞∞∞∞∞∞

My First Vacation, August 1949

As the summer of 1949 heats up, outbreaks of polio produce panic in our neighborhood. The Jersey Journal's headlines cite over thirteen hundred cases of polio in Jersey, more than any other year. The article mentions the tainted air thickening with the suppressed desperation of parents attempting to protect their children. The street's empty, but I'm lucky. We're invited to visit Mom's cousin for nine days. She owns a boarding house on ninety acres outside of Monticello, New York. Mom says that families go there, to this cleaner air, to decrease their risk of getting polio.

As we leave the densely populated Hudson County with its derelict smokestacks and fading factories, our black car rolls through the scents of pine in the forested hills and wild flowers in the meadows. Nature seems to present itself somewhere outside the city limits. Now I know where summer breezes live. Every breath cools me down. Arriving at this new place feels filled with discovery.

Most of the boarders here, maybe everyone, is Jewish. I know I'm Jewish. I think it's a race, because we're not religious. Many Jews or Hebrews go to a temple, shul or synagogue. I'm not sure which words are right. At school, we fill out forms asking for race and Hebrew is one of the choices. I'm afraid to "X" it because so many were killed by Nazis. No religion gets attention in our apartment in North Bergen, except for the priests and rabbis who are the subject of my father's jokes. However, I've visited churches with my friends, attending Mass or praying at the Stations of the Cross on our way home from school. Sunlight passing through the stained glass gilds the people on their knees. Churches feel safe. People who go to church have a right to feel sheltered.

I envy my friends who wear crosses on chains around their neck. I don't have any jewelry. My brother and I don't get birthday or holiday gifts. But, after Dad dropped us off at the boarding house, as he's leaving to drive home, I'm totally surprised to hear him ask me, "Would you like me to bring you something next weekend?"

I have a ready answer, "A Mogen David."

He laughs, "You mean a Star of David?" He keeps chuckling as he heads down the path to our car.

Now Mom, Aaron and I are on our own with the other boarders. Dad has to work at Alcoa and make his boat covers on the side. We sleep in a real bed in an unpainted, wooden building, like a wrangler's bunkhouse. Our family's room has an outside door similar to the others all around the knotty building. The outhouse is a short way down a muddy, mosquitoey path of boards under the trees. We wash up and shower in the community building.

I hang out in that community building, a gathering place like my street in North Bergen. To get there, you walk through the large kitchen with lingering smells of brisket, chicken, cholent and baked desserts cooked with cinnamon and ginger. Each boarder has their own two-burner gas stove and icebox. Just beyond the kitchen is the dining room where families bring their food to eat at one of the tables. No one shares tables. Grown-ups don't mix much. One of the old women, Mrs. Gold, is teaching me to knit and I'm slowly making my first scarf. The scarf isn't long enough, and I'm running out of blue wool. All the edges are curling.

Kids take over the dining room when it isn't mealtime. A dozen of us play the longest running Monopoly games. Tonight, it takes forever for me to get my turn. I knit another row, waiting for kids to land on my property. It's hard to demand rent, but the kids won't let me be shy, even though I hardly know them. Monopoly makes me feel smart. I often win because I buy every property and put houses and hotels on them as fast as I can.

Outside are two swings, a slide and one of those wooden carousels you can hop on and off of and it goes round and round. I sit on it forever, waiting to get my turn on the swings, even when nobody makes the carousel rotate. Aaron and I seesaw whenever it's free. I love it because my legs are longer than his, so I'm in control.

My brother and I do errands for the old people. They send us down the road to the dairy farmhouse to fill their tin jugs with fresh, warm milk. We sit by the well, watching cows being milked, while other cows quietly and slowly eat the fields of grass. They're smelly as the sewer on 90th Street. I watch pigs being fed, but most intensely relate with the restless, hungry chickens scurrying around to eat as much as possible. We carry back warm eggs and jugs of milk.

MY STREET

Mom's taking us out to pick blueberries. She carries our neighbor's big aluminum soup pot. Aaron insists on holding the pot as we fill it with the berries we don't eat. Our mouths are turning purple from eating so many berries. I spot birds singing in the trees and brush. I count yellow and white striped butterflies as they pause in their quest for nectar and wonder if I could catch such a fragile creature and keep it as my pet. Suddenly, Aaron lifts up his hands in panic and starts running. The pot turns over and berries scatter in the dirt. Mom runs after him, even more panicked. She shouts, "Help, Aaron's been bit by a snake," in her hysterical voice.

They both run in the opposite direction from the boarding house and I chase after them yelling, "Wrong way, wrong way!"

We finally find our way back, exhausted and empty-handed. Mom shows the ladies the spot on my brother's ankle that she thinks is a snake bite. It turns out to be a bee sting. The ladies think she's crazy.

I've started taking night walks. The full moon sits within a reddening circle of cloud and beckons me as I walk down the gravel path towards the vast darkness of the meadow at the edge of the woods. Something in the air adds silence as the temperature cools down. As I gaze up and out into the universe, a poem appears in my mind:

the night so still
only clouds move
faster than the world
the speed of their movement
stays within my body

I like thinking in poems for when you are concentrating within them, there is no beginning and no end.

Dad arrived this afternoon. Tomorrow is Sunday and he'll drive us home. We're all surprised when Mom decides to cook supper. At home, we don't eat together, maybe because our kitchen is so small and we only have two chairs. She knows how to cook two things: pork chops with sauerkraut and macaroni and cheese. We don't eat them together or at any regular mealtime, just whenever it's done and we're hungry. Today Mom cooks on the small stove assigned to our family -- pork chops and canned peas. We're all hungry. The chops and peas are done, but the potatoes aren't. We eat the tough meat and soggy canned peas. Then Dad takes my brother and me to sit on the steps outside in the cooling night and wait for the potatoes.

When Mom finally calls us back, Dad says, "Well, let's go in for the next shit--shift." This is the first time I remember us all eating together. The other women give us dirty looks and spit over their right shoulder to keep away evil because you're not supposed to cook pork in this kitchen.

After our dinner disaster, Dad opens up his fist and inside is a gold chain with a gold star. I can't believe it! I never thought I would get a present! One, two, three, four, five, six-points! In the star's center, a silver scroll represents the Ten Commandments. I feel my whole body go glad, even though I wish it had come wrapped in a box with red ribbons. I love it! I love my dad! I put it on and vow to never take it off. Now I don't need a charm bracelet because my Jewish star will keep me safe. This is my beginning of feeling Jewish. Being called 'Jew-baby' because I was afraid of squigglies doesn't count.

This vacation is first-rate fabulous! Now, finally, I can pretend we're a real family that eats together and gives presents. I feel I belong now, like other kids. On Sunday afternoon, before we leave, all us kids stage a talent show. I bravely sing my favorite songs: "Buttons and Bows" and "Mule Train." Then Dad yells out a request for "Home on the Range." Usually I just get his joking request for "Long Ago and Far Away."

My Mogen David became my only present from my father. It enabled me to have a public face, to pretend we were a real family with a religion. I still wear it and it carries the same aura, gold and silver with love, yet feeling the familiar punch of loss and piercing aloneness. Reality thru the prism of religion, but it depends on the lighting and how you turn the glass. Thanks to this two weeks in the Catskills, I see God in a ladybug, in an eagle whose eyes are as searching and intense as every unanswered question.

Funny how all of nature appears tranquil in spite of the changing weather and my realization that everything is fighting for survival. So am I. There is no impotence in nature. At night, sometimes I lie on the grass in the park. I reach out to my fellow travelers, the trees and shrubs old enough to have survived their daily onslaughts for so many years — what spiritual strength has reached them from the sky, air and water. The sky teases playfully. I feel the infinite space above me more than the ground I'm lying upon.

⋈⋈⋈⋈⋈⋈⋈⋈⋈⋈⋈⋈⋈⋈⋈

Birthdays and Holidays, September 1949

On our first day back at school, I'm picked to be a book monitor again. Monitors get to go to the book room and find the right editions to distribute to all the kids in our class. I love the excitement of new books. But in sixth grade, Miss Pendergast doesn't start that way. "Pick your four favorite holidays and end with your last birthday," she commands. "After you turn your paper in, you can go to the book room and get your books. The list is on the board."

I need to hurry before only the dog-eared ones with scribbles are left. Our family doesn't celebrate holidays and I think about making something up. Pretending comes easy for ten-year-olds. With a few white lies, faking it could be rewarded with an "O" for Outstanding. I wouldn't tell a real lie. My parochial school friends tried to help me understand the difference between venial and mortal sins. Not sure of the boundaries, I just have a shadowy afterimage. Should I risk candor? Mom always says, "Never tell our neighbors anything." Dad says, "People who love truth make dull companions." But I opt for it, with all its risks, even though we're not supposed to rat or reveal anything to our neighbors and friends.

Diana Ruth Krohn   *September 11, 1949*

     St. Patty's Day: the best parade. We sit on the curb on Hudson Boulevard as the parade passes -- clowns, policemen on horses, the monkey-man. Catholic schools have marching bands, but there aren't many Catholic schools, so sometimes it's a long wait. I feel the drums beating in my chest. No floats, but hundreds of people march, similar to Veterans Day. Politicians throw pennies to us and I collect eighteen cents.

     Easter: I know when it comes because I go to the Stations of the Cross with my friends. But I never get ashes on my forehead on Ash Wednesday. I'm afraid of the priest touching me and feeling that I'm Jewish. This year I got a spring coat that my cousin outgrew. I wore my Easter bonnet from last year and Dad took my picture with Maureen.

<u>Thanksgiving</u>: my favorite holiday. We don't have a feast, but Maureen and I wear our mother's clothes, with babushkas covering our hair and Lone Ranger masks to disguise our faces. We go from door to door, begging "Anything for Thanksgiving?" The elastic on my mask is broken, but I hold it in place. People give us canned food and treats. We fill our shopping bags and check to see who got the best and the most. People give me more because I'm littler than Maureen, except my feet and hands are bigger. We trade the foods we don't like with Victor and the Sinagra kids. It's not scary like Halloween. I hate Halloween when mean older kids roam around in gangs. I'm afraid of their tricks. They go through our pillowcases of candy and take the good stuff, the peepers, chocolate and licorice ropes.

Last Thanksgiving, we were invited to join Aunt Miriam's family. She's very proper, but special, and she makes me feel special too. While she tells us where to sit, I glance over at the side table loaded with foods. I'm always hungry, but also wary of new foods, especially when they may be cooked with garlic. Uncle Joe carves the turkey with drama and skill. Mom never made a turkey and I wonder if Dad could carve it.

It's strange to feel Dad take a back seat to Uncle Joe. Suddenly I realize our whole family is in the backseat. I become uncomfortable and quiet as I sense what we don't have. Then I notice Barbara Zaretsky leaving the classroom to get her books. Gotta finish.

Christmas: We celebrated Christmas once. It was Christmas Eve, already dark, the street lights on. Mom and I were heading home from Zarrett's Pharmacy. As we passed the Christmas tree lot, she turned back to look at the trees. She seemed to be considering a tree, but it cost too much. Finally, the man sold her a branch that had broken off for fifteen cents and we brought it home. She must have bought presents and hid them in the coat closet because from my parlor bed, I saw her take them out and place them under the branch. I realized there is no Santa Claus, so I wasn't surprised. In the morning I got a red metal hooker to make potholders and Aaron got a little metal toy car. I spent Christmas Day making silly potholders.

Birthdays: On my eighth birthday, our neighbor, Mrs. McClanahan, brought a chocolate cake, smaller than a bakery cake, with no writing or decorations. Four of us squeezed around our little kitchen table — Mom, Aaron, Mrs. McClanahan, and me. So far, it's my only birthday party and we didn't sing "Happy Birthday."

MY STREET

Not many post-war children had birthday parties, but their holidays were extravaganzas. Since my parents didn't celebrate holidays either, my wishes for celebrations were unfulfilled. My birthday took a backseat to Groundhog Day when Punxsutawney Phil came out of his burrow. If he saw his shadow, it portended six more weeks of winter weather. I couldn't wait to read the Journal on February 2nd.

Now my birthdays and my children's and grandchildren's birthdays are joyous events for me. Families share an intriguing symbiotic relationship; we give so much and we receive so much. My mother missed many meaningful times by not celebrating special events. If she felt things, they remained unexpressed.

My second birthday party, when I turned thirty, was a hilarious event with my friend Myra who shared the same birthday. My second cake, covered with white whipped cream, was presented to me on the middle of Myra's living room floor. I was directed to bend over, make a wish and blow out the candles. We had all costumed ourselves as dirty words; you can imagine the rest. Down on my knees, I realized the top was decorated with a giant whipped cream male organ! I should have worn my glasses.

For most of my life, I've chosen to hike alone on my special day, appreciating my existence, toasting my family in my thoughts and enjoying a cold beer back at the trailhead. I did have a surprise Medicare party and a big 7-0! Enough, I thought. They come too quickly now, but I realize I'm too old for empty birthdays. I can't pretend they're unimportant and I admit that birthday parties make me feel loved.

Rereading my words for Miss Pendergast's assignment, I mark these seemingly ordinary moments before they slide into obscurity. Nostalgia offers a holiday for your mind, rekindling old breaths with new perspective. Yet somewhere there's a clock quietly ticking away, moving us into the future. What will become of all these memory snapshots, too many and not enough? The fading photos freeze us in our youth, not even hinting of the effects of time on our faces and bodies. Decades from now, someone in our family may stumble upon these photographs and ask, "Who was that?"

◦◦◦◦◦◦◦◦◦◦◦◦◦◦◦◦◦

Aaron's Operation, October 1949

When the chill of fall arrives, so does our hunger. Aaron and I usually play a game at the kitchen table with a loaf of Wonder Bread, fresh from the store in its red, white and blue-circled wrapping. I add two phone books to Aaron's chair so he can reach our toaster that makes two slices -- light, the way we like it. The more we eat, the warmer we get. He officiously inserts the bread and pushes the lever down. We stare at the toaster, waiting for our slices to pop up. I butter the slices while Aaron inserts the next two. Our challenge is to eat them both before the next ones pop up. We chomp the whole loaf – "Building strong bodies eight ways."

Aaron gets excited about this game. He's usually quiet, like me, except for when he makes his crazy car noises. Vroom, eeek, vroom. Sometimes he makes noises and no one sees the little car he's holding in his pants pocket. However, for the last ten days, Aaron stopped getting excited about anything. He stopped eating -- even his favorites, cereal and bread. He doesn't want anything. He lies in his crib like when he fell off the neighbor's trike last spring and was in a coma. His pale face makes his brown eyes appear dark as his thick black hair. He used to look like he was too big for his crib. After all, he's five years old. Now he's become so skinny that the bones in his legs protrude.

I watch him sleep, trying to figure out how he does it. I hum softly, "hush-a-bye, don't you cry, go to sleep little

75

baby" and watch his quiet breath escape from his lips. His face seems soft and pasty as vanilla pudding. I watch his eyelids and they don't ever quiver, so I know he's really sleeping. I hardly ever sleep. At night, when I'm pretending to sleep, I worry that I don't pretend well and Mom might see *my* eyelids quiver when she checks me. If she thinks I'm not sleeping, she will try to keep me home from school.

After school today, I head to Aaron's crib to see if he's better. He's gone. The room feels cold, empty. I run to Dad, sitting in his chair. "Where's Aaron?"

"Aaron went to the hospital," Dad explains. "He'll be home before you know it."

"The hospital? What's wrong?"

"He needed an operation to remove a small tumor." Dad adds, "It's in his mouth."

I wait and wait for days, but Aaron isn't back in his crib. I ask, "How's he doing?"

Mom won't talk about it. She just makes her crinkly, faraway, Poor Eva face as she rubs sheets on the washboard in the kitchen sink.

I ask again, everyday. "When is Aaron coming home?"

She doesn't answer. Sometimes I suspect she's crying, but I'm not sure because it's her fall hay fever time. It's no fun to make toast alone, so I wait and wait, squeezing my hands and biting my fingernails.

A few days later, Dad arrives home and tells me, "Guess what, Baby Snooks? Aaron will be home tomorrow. He's all better."

Dad only calls me Baby Snooks when he's happy. His eyes aren't circled by dark shadows, so I know it's true. Relief sweeps over me because now Aaron can get back to being himself. The shadows fade from our parlor. I hear the radiator hissing steam and the traffic screeching on Hudson Boulevard. The world stretches out alive again, wrapping me with joy.

"Goody, Dad. Can I have fourteen cents to buy Wonder Bread?"

Aaron's had rough breaks in life. He was too young to be as influenced by our father as I was. We were both naive. In his teens, his handsome face became disfigured by cancer surgery. I've always believed that his cancer began when he fell from that trike.

They say a person needs just three things to be truly happy: someone to love, something to do and something to hope for. I pray for Aaron to find all three.

‹○›‹○›‹○›‹○›‹○›‹○›‹○›‹○›‹○›‹○›‹○›‹○›

The Fight, December 1949

One out. Gabriel has two balls and two strikes and I'm next up. My least favorite game is stickball. I'm terrible! Aaron and I don't even own a ball, even though we troll the sewers trying to find one. So we don't get much chance to practice. Nor do we get to feel powerful from ownership of anything. This winter is cold and colorless. Today, I was unable to avoid stickball because the kids were desperate for a player. Believe me, they don't ask me otherwise. Feels like standing within a freezing white cloud, as I wait to bat. Hardly aware of the game, I chew my fingernails till they ooze blood. I hate doing things that make me look bad.

Gabriel strikes out and I'm up. My fingers tense around the broomstick as I walk up to the plate. I miss the first toss from Carl, the greatest pitcher. No one expects me to connect. Carl patiently pitches a soft underhand girl one, thank goodness. I hit the second pitch, but it goes backwards, a foul. Rosemary misses it and the ball rolls into the sewer. When this happens, we all help get it out. We press wadded bubble gum to the end of Victor's yellow broomstick, then slowly lift the ball from the black stinky muck through the grate, hoping the gum holds and the ball doesn't fall back in.

We clean off the icky ball and stick with our spit and I'm back for another try. I hit the next pitch (*I hit it! I hit it!*), but I must have thrown the stick as I ran to first base. Victor's face reddened like his father's does when he gets really mad. It's his mother's broomstick and maybe he didn't tell her he was using it.

Hitting the ball gives me such a feeling of exhilaration that I'm not myself. The game seems so different from first base. But Victor's yelling bloody murder, threatening me with his pointing finger. His words blur together, lost in my confused head. His angry face barely sticks out of his hood. His eyes look like eyes I've never seen before. Victor's nose drips thick yellow snot that travels towards his mouth.

I didn't mean to crack his stick. I reach my arm up to explain, but suddenly feel so incensed, so frustrated, yet so liberated, that I hit his nose with my fist. The blow shoots back through my body, making me suddenly cold. I don't quite realize what happened. We're all shocked, Victor more than anyone. Girls don't hit boys and I never hit anyone in my life, not even my little brother. Blood runs from Victor's nose covering his snot. It looks like a gunshot wound. We stare at each other for a minute until I realize the best thing for me to do is run home really fast.

Sometimes our sense of play runs aground. No one said anything to me about it and no one on the street made me play stickball again. Victor's bloody nose had such a negative effect on my sporting life, I avoided any pursuit of softball, focusing on sports that came more naturally like basketball. I've regretted all my avoidances and wish I'd risen to the challenge.

As a teacher, I endured the humiliation of my students attempting to teach me to deal with a baseball bat so they wouldn't be embarrassed by my lack of proficiency in our annual school game. It was too late; I was still hopeless. Once I whacked the ball for a base hit, but then broke my wrist sliding into second base. The boys told me I didn't need to slide. I had room to spare.

Too many opportunities linger back there in places like the batting cage, never to be played. Some fears came from my own experience, or lack of experience, and others resulted from my mother's anxious warnings. Avoidance has such long-term consequences. I still read every label for the presence of garlic and am overly careful walking on ice. I've conquered many fears by taking up the gauntlet. I've learned to swim, hike the sides of steep mountains and even piloted a plane. Avoidance, the easy way out, has proved to be so limiting.

◇◇◇◇◇◇◇◇◇◇◇◇◇◇◇◇◇◇◇

Mom at School, spring 1950

"Don't swing too high. You'll fall off." "Don't go in the water. You'll drown." "Hide from the lightning." Mom always worries about my little brother and me. She's overly full of cautions.

I love the awesome sounds of the storms with the rain beating on our window, the trees and signs on Hudson Boulevard bending in the wind. The dark room brightens momentarily with each bolt, but our mom pulls us away from the rattling window and makes us hide in the closet to be safe.

Mom admonishes us with old wives' tales. "Don't walk under a ladder," "Don't go too close to the edge. You'll fall over," "Watch out so you don't fall down the stairs," and "Don't cross your eyes or they'll stay that way." There are No-Nos such as "No hands under the covers." "No hands near the stove."

Sometimes when I wake up, I only dream I wake up. I imagine going in my parent's bedroom to pick my clothes. Except they're great clothes, a circle skirt with a felt poodle. Until I feel convinced I'm actually dressed. But I'm not and now I'm late. Yet I'm still unsure, even as I safety pin my faded hand-me-down skirt, if I'm awake.

79

MY STREET

I remember how humiliated I was on the morning Mom came into my third-grade classroom, right up to Mrs. Rash as she's explaining our arithmetic problem. In front of all the kids, Mom tells her, "Di-ann didn't eat breakfast this morning." Everyone looked at me. I had no place to hide. That's when I realized I must resist her efforts to interfere in my life.

My first success was to keep her from walking me to school. She's afraid of me crossing streets alone. She's afraid I'll slip on the icy sidewalks. She's afraid I'll get lost. She's afraid I'll talk to strangers. By fourth grade, I was running out of the apartment, down the stairs and out the vestibule before she was ready. Without Mom, I'm much faster and start getting to school on time. If I worry that I won't remember the way, I talk myself through it, following familiar landmarks. I hum my favorite song, "Don't Fence Me In."

John Henkel is the morning crossing monitor. I'm fascinated by the way he stands at the corner and directs us. I like his neatly combed brown hair and the white crossing guard straps crisscrossing his shoulders and chest. He holds a whistle and sometimes he blows it at the cars. He seems so confident and yet friendly. He looks at me to indicate I can cross. He smiles at me, his right arm in the air, as I cross Hudson Boulevard. He's so cute, but I don't think he knows my name. I start watching for him in the hall. Guess he's my first crush. I'm sure he doesn't know because I never say one word to him. He's one grade ahead of me and the boys are in separate classrooms.

Eventually I catch up with other kids: Carl, whose mother is a teacher, Barbara Zaretsky, whose father owns Zarett's drug store--the popular kids who live in houses. We join together like birds migrating in a flock with no leader. We challenge each other with tongue twisters. We play twenty questions, typically about movie stars. We also play initials. You give a famous person's initials and the players get three guesses. I know the baseball jocks and their statistics. I love movies and movie stars, so I do well in spite of my shyness.

We often walk the entire two miles without stepping on a crack. I hate storeowners who don't shovel or throw down salt on their icy sidewalks. I'm afraid I'll slip. If anyone notices me slow down, I pretend to blow my nose or tie my shoelace, and I catch up again within a few minutes.

A constant rebellion starts over Mom making me stay home sick. I was absent forty-five days last term. Anything becomes an excuse for her to keep me home. So I take the thermometer out of my mouth when she isn't looking, never tell her about stomach aches or nausea, and wipe my snotty nose on the bed sheet so it won't be runny when she comes in the parlor where I sleep.

I still have a tough time with the weather. "No, Mom, it's not too cold." "No, Mom, I'm sure they have the sidewalks shoveled." She insists there can't be school when the weather is bad, so I pretend to call the school office to verify I can go. I never mind the weather, but wish I owned a warmer coat with a lining and a wool scarf instead of a thin kerchief. What I really long for is a fur muff like Barbara Zaretsky's!

It isn't as easy to stop Mom from picking me up. Sometimes she still shows up at the cafeteria to make sure I eat lunch. Kids that live in the houses near school go home for lunch. The popular girls live close in real houses. I live very far, so I have to eat in the cafeteria. There's round tables and chairs and a counter where you stand to order your food. I always have the same thing: a baked potato with butter and sour cream and a small carton of chocolate milk. Mom doesn't cook baked potatoes and I love the taste and warmth of this combination that Grandma Krohn made for me. The lady behind the counter always asks, "Is that all?" I quietly say, "Yes."

Once they had no potatoes, so I ordered nothing. I'm too timid to try anything new and unfamiliar. We have to stay in the cafeteria until the bell rings for us to go to the walled concrete recess yard. Unfortunately, that day Mom showed up and caught me sitting there without lunch. She yelled, "Di-ann, you have to eat. You'll get sick and die." But stubborn me still doesn't eat anything but potatoes from that cafeteria. And I don't die.

Now that I've reached the age of eleven, I thought Mom finally stopped coming, but today, even though I'm in sixth grade and it's 1950, Mom shows up in the cafeteria. By this time, I've probably eaten over 1,000 baked potatoes with butter and sour cream. She's the only mother in the cafeteria and she never takes her black cloth coat off. She waits as I eat my potato and then shows me what is in the paper bag she's carrying. A new dress! From a store! With price tags and labels! Mom actually bought it. I didn't get to go to the store and pick it out myself and I'm sure it came from a bargain table at the Five and Dime. But I love that dress anyway. It's summery, white with little red flowers, not too many, and the fabric is soft, sheer and flowing. I own it! It belongs to me! Even though I can't stop Mom from coming to school, I love my store-bought dress and I do love my Mom.

How can a girl write about her mother? A kluger farshteyt fun eyn vort tsvey. (A wise person hears one word and understands two.) My mother's umbilical cord reached all the way to Horace Mann School. I hated being attached, but didn't know how to cut it.

I was too young to understand why my mother was afraid and confused. Did her anxiety begin with her mother's sudden and early death and her family's subsequent uprooting? Displaced people lose their orientation. My mother's angst still leaves me with many unanswered questions. Her warnings reflected her fears. Most prohibitions I learned to ignore. Some I obeyed and thus fell heir to, but mostly I was just afraid of not being

*good enough. Fear keeps us dependent. I too have
experienced loss and the sense of not belonging, but it
hasn't helped me to understand or penetrate my mother's
mind.*

∞∞∞∞∞∞∞∞∞∞∞∞∞∞

Circles, a Potpourri, spring 1950

Miss Pendergast, my sixth-grade teacher, often
disciplines me for yawning. "Diana," she says, "people
don't want to see the insides of your mouth."

I try to be careful so I don't get sent to the principal to
get whacked with the wooden paddle that hangs silent over
our classroom door. So far, I've never been sent to the
principal. No one knows what happens when you're sent,
and even if they tell (which is forbidden), I might not
believe them. So my imagination rules. The doomed wait in
the worn wood slatted chair by his closed door. Imagine
anticipating meeting the anger of this tall skinny Dracula-
type principal with his smelly hair slicked back and his
broken tooth showing when he smiled, which he hardly
ever did. Waiting, thinking and resolving not to cry or care.
Fearing the consequences of getting caught with gum or
staying in the hall too long, throwing spit balls or erasers,
or even really bad stuff like cheating on a test or talking
back to Miss Pendergast.

When one of my classmates, Dorothy, fell asleep at her
desk, Miss Pendergast took down the paddle and sent her to
the principal's office with it. Dorothy told me it hurt bad. I
was glad it wasn't me. So far, so good. However, Miss
Pendergast often raps my knuckles with her long wooden
ruler when I don't pay attention.

This afternoon, Miss Pendergast calls some of us to the
blackboard to write out the arithmetic problems we did for
homework. Each girl gets a section of the blackboard,
between the cracks, to write out a problem and its proof. I

83

don't get called on much even though I love writing on the board and usually know the right answers. If I do get chosen, I try real hard to keep the chalk from screeching.

In the waiting time, I pick the pills off the black sweater my cousin Barbara gave me and get lost in an unending inner conversation. It starts...all mixed together. I wonder what it's like, before we're born. I wonder about my birth. Was there fear and blood in the sanitized hospital room? Was my dad there? What it was like in Mom's tummy, before being born? We don't know any more about that than we do about after we stop breathing. Then I contemplate my family owning a grocery with tasty food and many customers. Mom as more of a Molly Goldberg type. A house with real furniture. My parents with a real bed, not a mattress where rusty, metal springs broke through and Mom had to have a shot and stitches in her butt.

Mostly I daydream in ever-widening circles that match my expanding experiences.

Circle 1 was bounded by my crib and playpen within our apartment.

Circle 2 began when I met Maureen in the hall and she led me down to 90th Street with its box-like apartment buildings and houses laid in flat rows. Electrical lines were strung and at night, street lamps illuminated the dark scenes that extended beyond the height of our building. The street became my happy place, a good circle, like never-ending Palmer Method circles when we practice penmanship. Nothing, not even the changing seasons, affects the strong beat of our games. We spend our time playing in this lively circle, noisily popping pink bubble gum.

Yet, in drawing class, the art teacher draws lines on the board. We copy them e-x-a-c-t-l-y on art paper: brown for the trunk, green for the leaves and blue for the sky. All our trees look alike, but they don't look normal. My picture doesn't show what the street shows, that all things fight for survival. Life seems so uncertain. We should be allowed to draw real trees and streak our sky with the colors of the rainbow.

Other disturbing events pop up. I imagine the haunted house at the end of 90th Street, the one with the high wall where the old lady lives by herself, practicing black magic. Her eyes stare at nothing, like the flat eyes on the dead fish we find at the shore. I picture grotesque, scary souls hidden by the horrible lady's high bushes, creating a thicket of shadows, though I never even peek over the wall.

Monsters aren't part of my reveries. There's already too many frightening things in my life to create more. Some teachers are monsters. Dogs are like monsters. I never had any pets, even bugs or goldfish. Not many kids have them because our apartments are small and it takes money to feed pets. Dogs intimidate me. I fear the unknown and dogs are unknowns. Maybe they'll bite me. I don't like them sniffing at me. Sometimes I have to pass a dog and I try to avoid it. Dogs sniffing at my crotch are so embarrassing.

Circle 3 became the tavern across Hudson Boulevard, a separate darker circle our dads let us kids enter. The bar people let us sip the leftover bits of their drinks because we are so cute. Whatever we drink seems to move through me like heat spreading out to my toes and fingertips. The back of my neck tingles and grows numb. The men transform into characters and, in my dreamy mind, I uncover things they might want to hide: weird jobs, police records and big messes at home.

Circle 4, our school, is far away, but the territory in-between seems like a no-man's land, except for the deli pickle barrel and the malt shop. That circle becomes an escape and adventure into the smallest, most densely populated county in New Jersey. Some teachers are mean, but I'm going to be a first-rate teacher someday so I'll never stop going to school. However, I'll make sure my slip doesn't hang like Miss Pendergast's, two inches below her dress.

I perceive things differently, more clearly, in daydreams. Somewhat like when Miss Pendergast told Mom to get me glasses. Mom chose the most awful, cheapest ones with pink frames. I didn't want to wear them, but the optometrist in Journal Square said, "If you wear these glasses every day, you won't have to wear them after you are eighteen."

When I walked out of the eyeglass store, the world appeared different, sharpened up. I see the attractive eyeglass frames in the store window. I want to notice everything. All the cars and the people in Journal Square seem brighter, more colorful, more alive. I can now read street signs and numbers on the buses. Back in my classroom, I see the dusty formulas Miss Pendergast writes on the blackboard. The dresses my friends wear to school are amazing colors. Plaid, polka dots and flowers brighten our classroom with purples, tiger orange, sky blues, sunshine yellows and reds. Glasses, like daydreams, make the world appear more special.

I dream about superheroes. Captain Marvel and Flash Gordon remind me of Bobby and Wally. No kids are heroes except I know two girls with their own bedroom: the mean Joan and the smart Barbara, my rival for a first-row seat in class. I once stood in the doorway of Barbara's fluffy, colorful, cozy bedroom. I wanted to see what made it that way, but was too embarrassed to stare. My quick glance revealed her collection of dolls and stuffed animals across her pillows.

If I had my own bedroom, it would have daunting warning signs on the door: *KEEP OUT MOM, YOU'RE TOO CLOSE IF YOU CAN READ THIS* or *POISON.* Hopefully, the signs will terrorize Mom and Aaron from entering. The door will be locked. I'll keep a towel on the floor and tape on the knob to prevent peeking. Then Mom can't read my mail, go into my drawers and give my things away without asking.

Inside, I'll create a nest, a canopy bed with a soft thick

mattress and puffy comforter just like Barbara's. Fluffy feather pillows hug my cold skinny body all night. Green linens will match my eyes and accent the blue walls. I love colors that blend with the sky or stand out against the sky. No flowery stuff, but I want to see real flowers outside my window. Enough to hide the fire escape, but so I can still see the sun by day and the moon by night (when the sky is clear of crud). My closet will be filled with angora sweaters, crinolines, skirts that aren't plaid and brassieres for when I get my breasts to grow. I do "I must, I must, I must increase my bust" every night.

Circle 5 takes me past North Bergen. We don't use our car much, but there are buses and trains. Rich people travel on ocean liners and Pan American Airlines can fly you around the world. My knowledge of the world comes from geography lessons, historical novels and movies. I remember a scene from a movie at the Embassy Theatre, towards the end of the war. Nazi soldiers were assembled in a huge courtyard or square. A woman was dragged into the center and tied to a column with her hands behind her back. The commander was trying to get her to cooperate or confess, but she stayed silent. Finally, he grabbed her long hair with one hand and pulled her hair from her head. She crumpled to the ground. The soldiers marched off, leaving her lying there with blood flowing from her head. I was young, but I can't forget that scene. It still feels like the heat-blast when Mr. Fusco shovels more coal into the huge furnace in our basement. How can people be so horrible?

Circle 6, the unknown and beyond to ancient cultures and faraway lands. What would it be like to be there? What if there's another war? How can people fight and kill each other? How did the world become so broken? Does time exist, like tree rings, or is it merely a trick to keep everything from happening all at once, like my thoughts all mixing together again? I wonder, is what we remember more important than what we forget?

MY STREET

Would life seem less empty with religion? With a God to guide me and keep me safe? My family's religion is patriotism for the flag, President Truman and our country. G-O-D = U-S-A. I wonder what Jews in Europe, not killed in the ovens, believe in. I notice the browning daffodils dying on Miss Pendergast's desk and wonder about death and if your soul dies too. Maybe it will stay in the universe, rotating in a dark meadow like a star in the silence of the night sky saying, "Come here."

I softly hum a tune to myself and picture the words, 'when you walk through a storm, hold your head up high, and don't be afraid of the dark.' I hum the melody over and over, feeling the vibration on my teeth and in my throat. I remember when Bobby gave me that record sung by Frank Sinatra. He brought his beautiful new wife, Dorothy who smiled with her lips and blue-green eyes. He's twenty-four, she's twenty-two, and I'm almost eleven, but we like the same song. It makes me feel safe like humming soothing lullabies to my little brother.

Since I was little, when I miss my older brothers, I take out my paper doll heroines, pretending they're me. I dress them up for parties and grand balls ready to be escorted by Bobby and Wally. Cutting the clothes out of a new paper doll book is exciting. My fantasy is to be beautiful and popular. I wear incredible clothes instead of ones that are so big I don't think I'll ever outgrow them. I throw away my high tops and wear show-off shoes. Tinkly charm bracelets adorn my wrist. My proper purse holds my busy calendar and hides secret beauty products. The miracle girl I long to be is formed from fragments of Esther Williams, Deanna Durbin, Veronica Lake, and mostly, Katharine Hepburn. I wear pants that aren't droopy-drawers, put my long hair in a bun, and talk bravely like she does. I collect slick 8x10 personally autographed photos of these glamorous women by writing letters to their movie studios. I wait at the mailbox for the big brown envelopes from California, although waiting doesn't suit me.

My mind moves around like clouds marbled in the sky outside our classroom window. Drifting along, shifting shape, changing hues, casting long shadows in the afternoon. I love clouds and wait patiently for them to settle into recognizable shapes. I imagine them merging into a huge hollow terminal at the edge of the world where they collect at the end of the day. That way they never end, just re-form in the morning to roam the skies again. Nothing should be limited to only one form, when it can be free…like my daydreams.

My father teased me, saying I was always chasing rainbows, but I still love to fantasize, even though I grew up in an era when you didn't color out of the lines. Woolgathering and mind chatter may be my salvation. It's a pleasant way to leave where you are. My circles are much larger, freer. If I could, I would eat daydreams and sleep in the cocooning circles they create. I can look outside myself or inside myself and the world around me becomes silent, weightless as floating in a pool. Fun possibilities erupt like discordant music or like traveling matter and antimatter. I see moonlight on snow-covered trees, the lightness of a beginning snowfall, the mystery of a canyon at night, cuddling with a man… I hear and see things in slow motion, one sense supporting the other. The slow-motion bends space until time slows so much its shape ripples like oil dripping from a leaky pipe. Try it. In order to listen, you need silence. Close your eyes and the dreams are there.

With the increasing isolation of aging, I still put my eyeglasses on and today's world snaps into focus. Retrospection merges with vision and clarity, revealing new perceptions. But when life hurts, when the lake of pain ripples out in circles, Bobby's present to me still offers me the words I need: "…keep your chin up high…walk on with hope in your heart…you'll never walk alone."

MY STREET

The Bomb of the Twentieth Century, spring 1950

Waaah -- Waaah -- Waaah, the air raid signal pulses loud enough to drive us mad. We walk in line out to the hall. I concentrate on curling up my tall skinny body as close to the wall as possible. I study the progress of several crusty scabs on my knees. The good part is that it's May and school will be out for the summer in a month.

Government-ordered drills have always been part of school life, like lining up for lice checks. In Kindergarten when the air raid sirens sounded, our teacher stopped talking and led us, in straight lines, down the stairwell to the dank basement. Trays, already set up for recess, were stacked with Oreos and cartons of milk and a bucket to put the dime we brought from home. If the bomb fell, at least we'd all have our snack before the deadly atoms changed us and the sun darkened.

The drills continued after the war ended. We saw pictures of the mushroom clouds over Hiroshima and Nagasaki, but not the ones of people dying. Our town kept their equipment and men in place since Russia was testing atom bombs. By fourth grade, we couldn't all fit in the basement so we older kids simply crawled under our wooden desks and waited for the anticipated force of the dooming blast. This was supposed to save us from flying shards of glass. I remember hitting the protruding inkwell with my head and Miss Pendergast yelling at me for squirming and biting my nails.

Now, in sixth grade, the drill changed again. We still live in the nuclear bulls-eye, but our government rule makers decide proximity to windows isn't safe after all. So we move to the hall outside our classrooms and squat into our air raid drill position, head between our knees, leaning into the wall, with our arms over our head. Russia has the bomb and Miss Pendergast says we have stockpiled over two hundred. She says, "It seems to be a situation of the strong get stronger. Only countries that invest in developing a bomb become superpowers."

90

I'm glad we're a superpower! My friends and I talk about protons, electrons and neutrons the way we talk about sex, repeating the naughty words, but vague about their meaning. Words without mental pictures. We must not be too afraid, because our interest in sex words is definitely stronger. Do we always live ahead of our own understanding? Or is the information on the bomb too terrible to be believed? Many adults are afraid. For years, they've been waiting for the bomb to drop. Many knew or read about people in Europe bombed, gassed, buried alive. The Bible has trained them for Armageddon. If anything is wrong in the world -- a change in the weather, people having too many babies, committing too many crimes or acting crazy -- it must be due to the secret underground tests. The greater the scientific advance, the more primal the fear.

Waiting for the all-clear bell, I contemplate the shock of detonation, the breaking of windows, the violence of their upheaval from the bomb's power. I wait for the fire-cloud to mushroom and break our windows as our world upends. Maureen and I go to "sores and spores" movies about innocent people exposed to ionizing radiation. They graphically portray the horrors people experience before slow death takes their nuked bodies to wherever they go. They don't deserve hell and certainly heaven can't accept them. They are too far-gone to be made well again, but the flowers at their feet produce gargantuan blooms.

My classmates and I accept Miss Pendergast's conviction that, as long as the United States keeps the biggest pile of nuclear bombs in the Cold War, we are superior and safe. Especially now, since it looks like we may be fighting Communists in Korea. Being a believer, I'm not afraid. These drills are just something we do, like the fire drills we always hope will happen during a test or in the middle of an arithmetic word problem, the hard kind at the bottom of the page.

My contemplation is interrupted, not by the bell, but the tingle I feel on my ankle. I peek back through my legs and catch John Henkel's hand touching my foot as he monitors the hall! My crossing guard! I still have a silent crush on him. Instead of a nuclear shock, I sense the kind of shock felt when you know something has just happened, and yet it's happening for the first time -- sort of like 'so that's what it feels like.' His hand burns through the worn cotton threads of my sock. Then the bell rings and we rise from the dusty floor.

Saturday's newsreels at the Embassy featured dire glimpses of the larger world of cold war, complex cities going up in smoke, political takeovers, crime and propaganda. They planted images in my brain, but weren't part of my daily life. The history we learned at school wasn't localized. Geography consisted of memorizing places on a pull-down map of the forty-eight states and photographs of the Seven Wonders of the World in indistinguishable places. Learning focused on the 3 R's. The fading factories revealed no stories, the railroad tracks merely took me to my cousins, the churches belonged to my friends, not me. Even threats of nuclear bombs didn't reach our pattern of days and seasons.

Dad's First Heart Attack, June 1950

I walk in from school, hungry for a big slice of toasted pound cake. We had films today and no gymnastics. I received the highest test score in arithmetic finals. I like the way Miss Pendergast sounded my name when she announced the results, *Di-ann-a*. I put my books down by the radio and drop my pink cardigan on the chair. I realize Dad is yelling, "God, oh God" again and again. Mom must hear the hall door close because she yells out, "Di-ann, don't come in!" Her voice sounds high-pitched, like Mrs. Aldrich calling "Hen-ry," as she shakily adds, "Dr. Friedman is on his way."

I fall onto the low couch, shocked at hearing my father begging for help. "God, oh God" he continues to scream -- over and over. An awful sound that breaks the air and hurts me. I don't know what to do. This is not the time to make a mistake. I'm not there but a few minutes when Uncle Ted comes through our front door and rushes to the bedroom. I don't think he even sees me.

Cripes! Uncle Ted, my father's older brother who always wears a suit and overcoat! He's NEVER come to our apartment. Something is really wrong. I don't know what's happening in the bedroom. Is Dad getting medicine, a shot? Is Mom okay? I listen to every moan, every cry. Dad celebrated his 50th birthday last week at Aunt Jean's house, but kids weren't invited. Did something happen to make him sick?

I feel so scared, so scared. I want to do something. I decide to pray and this comes out of me, my first prayer ever, "God, please don't let my daddy die. God, please don't let my daddy die." I fall into the rhythm of his moans, and I don't know why, but this becomes my chant. I say it over and over. I can't stop. "God, please don't let my daddy die." The words pour out like they've been stored inside me and have to escape. I rub my Jewish star Dad gave me last summer. It's the best I can do and I really mean it. I pray it over and over, hoping it will make a difference. I don't think I'm loud, but Uncle Ted comes out of the bedroom, glares at me and shouts, "SHUT UP!"

I don't know what to do to stop the hurting. The space of quietness is so big and muffled. I bury myself in the blanket, creating a deep darkness all my own. My fingers rub the soft ripped binding. I peek out to the shadows drifting through the room, settling on the dusty table. Dr. Friedman arrives with his familiar black bag. He's in the bedroom a long time before Dad's yells, crying, begging

"Oh God," finally slow down. Then two beefy men in white uniforms arrive with a stretcher and take Dad away, carrying him past me. He screams again with pain. He's so close. I want to touch him but it all happens so fast. I feel like a bare tree in frozen ground. No one notices me. I'm too scared to say anything. Uncle Ted follows them. Mom stays in the bedroom. I'm afraid to go in there.

That disastrous June day, waiting on threadbare sheets, I felt a chasm form. Until then, my greatest fears had been of slipping on icy sidewalks, not getting picked on a team during recess or being pelted with squigglies from the trees by the kids on my street. This dreadful horror changed what I knew about the world. Time started moving faster. There is no reprise from time; another minute starts as the last one ends. I began to cry for my father…and for the childhood I was leaving behind. I felt myself walk into the stillness at the center of the dance.

<hr />

Out on a Limb, August 1950

Before this summer of 1950, I could only imagine what happened in the lot across the street from our apartment. I knew that's where kids smoked and did things you're not supposed to do. Only older kids were brave enough, or tough enough, to take on the challenge. There were hidden places in the lot where no one could see you, even from the rooftops of our tenements, even after the leaves had fallen.

But I'll be a seventh grader this fall and Dad's still in the hospital. I feel like a stitch out of place in the scarf I'm sitting and knitting. This sunny August morning I decide I'm old enough to play in the lot.

"C'mon Maureen, let's do it," I beg as we head downstairs.

"Nah, I have to take care of my sister today."

"No, you don't. It's now or never. Let's do it. Zip-a-dee-doo-dah!"

We enter slowly, acting like we're simply taking a walk up the tree-lined dirt path. Crows glide low over our heads. Pretending like we're not scared, we choose the wider of the two weedy parallel paths -- not the one along Hudson Boulevard, but the center one, unseen from the street.

As we walk uphill, at first we only notice the sky and each other, no streets, no apartments. I don't know why we waited so long. This secretive lot is a wonderland of clover and spaces that remind me of the smile of my little brother with his missing baby teeth. Trees, wildflowers and grasses spread out for a long distance. I don't know plant names, probably some genus of weeds.

Under a wide stand of trees, we find some kids playing *Truth, Dare, Consequences, Repeat or Hilltop*. We recognize Rosemary Sinagra with her new Toni perm. Last week she promised to give me one. She invites us to join them on the prickly grass, sheltered under trees that hide them from the road. "Pick one," someone says to me, to start the game.

She did it!

MY STREET

I have to be honest, accept a dare, pick a consequence, repeat loudly or take something off. I pick *Dare*. It feels the safest. "I dare you to carve your name on the tree." The game is getting harder, so I try to stick to *Dare*. Except the big boys dare us to lick burned flash bulbs and eat laundry starch, ants, their gum and spit. We get Indian burns when we fail. I get down to my slip in *Hilltop*, but I decide I'll never admit it, or that I liked it.

Then some sound, change in the air, a secret signal, a voice amidst the shouts of kids in the lot – reaches me -- makes me break away like Maureen did a while ago -- makes me say, *enuf*, and climb the massive tree near the path. Its bottom branches are easy, familiar as the steps leading to my apartment. I climb from branch to branch, reaching up as high as my courage will allow me, holding on to the bark. The cracking of dead branches scares me, so my ceiling stays quite low.

A few limbs up, the silence begins. Amazing that such quiet can exist so close to our noisy street. I'm alone in a new fantasy as my fingers touch old leaves in crevices and dead insects that once climbed on the tree as I do. Flitting birds perch momentarily as I lodge myself in a fork of the tree. The world feels exactly as beautiful as it can be. I hide on my temporary perch, feel the July heat rise, and observe the ants, spiders and unnamed tree critters as I pick bark. Sunshine warms the air and brightens the fragile green leaves. A slight wind muffles the sounds below – currents of air that seems to stir from nowhere, whisper to me, and then drift on. As the branches sway, I look up to the sky, painted so blue, through the leaves. Why isn't it golden from the influence of the sun's energy? No clouds or shadows, no darkness, no bottom.

The rough touch of tree bark and softness of leaves strongly confirms how earthy life can feel, like making mud pies after it rains. I see the transparent sky, kids playing cowboys and Indians, a cardinal landing in the branch below, squirrels gathering acorns. Such a beautiful world, in slow motion.

From that time on, Maureen and I set out for the innermost sections of the lot, away from the path. We played our mutable games under trees shaded by low hanging leaves or sitting on rocks that warmed our bodies. We practiced walking silently like Indians, without snapping a twig. We made a fort from piles of rocks and branches where steep mounds provided privacy. We started digging a hole to China, but gave up after a sweaty hour of hard soil. As summer ended, I sometimes went alone to search for four-leaf clovers while stringing flowers into long clover-chain necklaces. Amazing that wildflowers blossom in such stillness.

◌◌◌◌◌◌◌◌◌◌◌◌◌◌◌◌◌◌

Leaving Childhood Behind, October 1950

My Jewish star worked. Dad's finally home from his three-month stay in North Hudson Hospital. His nighttime groans soften so I can't make out his words. Dr. Kolodin says he's on the slow road to recovery from his heart attack. I look up 'heart attack' in the dictionary, but don't understand how Dad's heart got permanently damaged. I feel my heart beating in my chest, keeping me alive, and don't ever want it to stop.

Nothing is the same. I rarely play in the street or even go to the lot anymore. Since seventh grade started in September, I have a different daily pattern. After school, I sit with dad and listen to radio reports of General McArthur's landings in places like Inchon Harbor. I think about Aunt Miriam's visit last Sunday. She sat on my couch bed and said, softly, "This is your time with your dad. Think of it as stolen, and therefore more valuable."

I move closer to dad. When I look at him, I picture his enlarged heart taking up all the space in his chest. I imagine what's happening in his mind -- after hearing the doctor's pessimistic prognosis: "Irving, your heart is so big, I don't know what keeps you alive."

97

Dad speaks quietly now, but not gently, trying to get his breath. My stomach grows tight with the raspy sound. But even in his changed voice, he still tells me jokes until he falls asleep.

"Want some pound cake?" Mom quietly asks. She doesn't want to wake Dad. Of course I want some. Toasted pound cake is my favorite, especially slathered with butter. Mom's more confused since Dad got sick. I can tell she's scared because she's filled with warnings like, "Sing before breakfast and you'll cry before supper." "If you laugh too hard, you'll swallow your tongue." Does she think Dad's heart attack is her fault? I imagine her mind outlined, like the diagrams in the headache ads in the Sunday Journal. In the line drawing, her brain looks like a map filled with tunnels like the Lincoln and Holland tunnel we used to drive through when we had our car. Her thoughts seem stuck, like they're burrowed in those tunnels that look like they might have been created by worms. But I know no one ever sees anyone else's mind. We only peer in by interpreting actions. I think our mind ages like our body, stooping, thickening like grandparents before they die. Its million thoughts of past, present and future fuse like the mean Joan's kaleidoscope.

There are many things to worry about. I try to help by taking care of Aaron. I don't baby him like Mom does. If you baby someone, they'll never grow up. We quietly play the "Pick me" game with the latest Sears catalog. It has everything you could want. I know all the sections even though it's thicker than a phone book. My favorite is the beds. We each pick the best item on each page. Most of the items we choose are the same every time we play.

Risks are not taken when there is a base of insecurity. Funny how your mouth turns dry and your brain becomes vulnerable. I closed down for months, experiencing the weight of solitude until, slowly, my friends got used to my changed life. The same chill reoccurs with illnesses, deaths, divorce and moves — like a bag that's emptied suddenly and takes awhile to fill back up into a conscious life. It's hard not to drift back into the past when there's been so much of it. So many people already moved on and I still love them. Except now, my years of experiences, beliefs and values provide a spiritual vaccination. My adaptation to endings became more gradual, like dripping time syrup.

◁◁◁◁◁◁◁◁◁◁◁◁◁◁◁◁

Television, December 1950

It's freezing and it's only early December. The weak violet sky above our rooftop has a dingy glare. Mom and I are pinning sheets onto the clothesline pulleyed across our tar paper roof. They freeze, stiffening even as we hang them. I hand Mom my favorite clothespins first, the ones that look like tall stick people with long legs. Dad opens the heavy door to the roof and rasps, "Come and see what I bought. Hurry, the Sears & Roebuck man just delivered it." I'm so excited that one of those short springy clothespins snaps my middle finger hard. I hate that kind of clothespin.

The deliveryman unpacks our new mahogany Hallicrafters -- a 7" screen, the first television in our apartment building. Dad tells me to bring our two kitchen chairs into the parlor for the neighbors. Even Maureen comes. We sit as the screen warms up, until the black and white picture appears. Everyone except Mom. She stays in the kitchen. Dad adjusts the rabbit ears until they're almost on their side, reaching out into the room, with a chair back to brace them from falling over. Our first television program is a movie called "The Picture of Dorian Gray."

The whole idea of TV is so timely. Maureen and I have become so-o-o bored with our same old games. We never know what to play, so we make lists of 100 things to do and then eliminate them by doing "Eenie meenie."

eeny meenie miney mo
catch a tiger by the toe
if it hollers let it go
eeney meeny miney mo
my mother says to pick
this -- here -- one.

But we never want to play the game that remains.

When I was little, Dad took me to see *Alexander's Ragtime Band* -- "c'mon along, c'mon along"... Singing feels so good. Since I was ten last year, Mom's allowed me to take the bus to Loews Theater in Journal Square to see first-run movies with Maureen. Going around the corner seems far away, so going all the way to Journal Square becomes really special. We each give the driver a nickel and sit together for the crowded ride on Hudson Boulevard. We watch people in tailored coats and gloves entering or leaving the stores. Ladies wear hats instead of kerchiefs, in bright colors like red and orange. When I'm grown up and can buy clothes, they'll be blue and green. We try not to smell the bad air from the boys in the back of the bus.

We watch a double feature, plus cartoons and newsreels for a quarter. Roy Rogers, Doris Day, Judy Garland...and they give away a dish each week. Last month I won a set of dishes with painted flowers. It's the first thing I ever won. Mom loves them and I smile every time we use them.

I've never seen a movie like Dorian Gray, even at Journal Square. No singing, dancing or riding horses into the sunset. The main character is a good-looking but shadowy man. A fading portrait sits in his attic and at the end, you get to see that the portrait has aged and taken on the evilness of the man's ugly, horrible bad deeds. It makes me afraid to do any wrongs, even though no one can see into my mind, because I understand the sin in the painting. I don't want to be bad because once I'm bad, I'd have no reason to be good and then I'd become ugly like Dorian Gray.

Now that we have a TV, I want a bedroom like Barbara Zaretsky's more than ever. A room I don't have to share with everyone who's watching TV, a room with a closet and a bed and dresser. I'd even take a teeny room if it were all mine. Aaron and I used to wait for the radio to go off. Now we wait for the national anthem and snowflakes when the TV stations close for the night.

Mom never watches TV or reads or listens to music on the radio. She does chores and writes letters in handwriting that she's so proud of. Dad stays home more than ever, and he lets me use his Underwood. Pecking my name on the little round keys with letters in the middle becomes as exciting as anything I've done. I love to learn new things. Dad shows me how to keep the TV running by using the tube tester at the hardware store. If the tube doesn't light up, it's bad and you replace it with new ones shelved below the tube tester. I'm discovering I can do things myself and vow to help Dad every time the chance arises.

I'm still in a learning relationship with television, or I was until Charlie Rose was fired. But what are we learning? So much of TV and social media play with matches in a drought impoverished forest. The advertisers, marketers and opinionated programming manipulate us and trivialize our life by excessively promoting superficial and short-lived values. It was fun when it was new, but eventually, since I almost lived in front of the TV with my father, the enjoyment burned off quickly. Too many other directions to spread myself into, learn and enjoy.

My Autobiography, January 1951

When we return from Christmas break, Mrs. Farley assigns us to write the story of our lives. "Dad," I ask, "please tell me some facts about our family so I can get a good grade."

"I'll write it for you," he replies. Dad loves to write and I'm so glad he'll help me. His index fingers hunt and peck on his Underwood, beginning my first autobiography. He types, I watch. Dad makes our life look so easy on paper, like a put-together outfit instead of poorly thought out, random ill-fitting bits. He practices often, writing 'Dear Folks' letters to his brothers and sisters that are full of humor with a bit of bragging. As he types, I unquestioningly copy his words on lined school paper in my perfect Palmer Method handwriting.

Dad describes taking me to the 1939 World's Fair in Long Island during my first summer. We paste in a photo of me sitting on Mom's lap on a ride. He writes that I tasted my first candy and soda and cried for a hot dog. Dad likes to add humor. He says a chocolate bar was my reward for behaving nicely on the rides, but Mom ate most of it.

Now he types loudly. When the bell dings at the end of each line, he pauses before pulling the carriage lever across. Then my transcription brings a weak smile of shock. Dad had another wife before Mom...*Is this possible?* I want to stop him from typing any more, but don't. A year and a half after his first wife's death, he met Mom when she was visiting her stepsister's family in Bloomfield. They married in July 1937.

Dad continues typing words. He seems unaware of their effect on me. Of course I already knew that I was born on January 31, 1939 at Montclair Community Hospital. And Dad's already made too many jokes about how disappointed he was when I wasn't born on January 30th, Franklin Delano Roosevelt's birthday. FDR was his hero. Dad is a staunch Democrat, his secular faith, and he was hoping I'd "come out" on time!

As he keeps typing, more unknown information hits the paper. He states that he lost his awning and shade store due to competition and his illness. 'What kind of illness?' I think, but I don't interrupt him. He quickly taps keys that describe when he opted for a new start in Miami. The job he moved for didn't work out and I had rickets. He then writes about going to work for the government traveling over nine states over the next four years.

I continue to copy and probe Dad's writing, but my mind grows too busy. Was this story always there to see and know? He states his boys, Bob and Wally, were very kind to me when I was little. I remember them visiting and they were always fun. He adds that Bob told me to 'save a dime' to call him when I reached the age of eighteen. I don't remember this, but I do remember charging Maureen a dime to come into our apartment when my brother Wally visited after the war. He was 'movie-star quality' good-looking in his Navy whites.

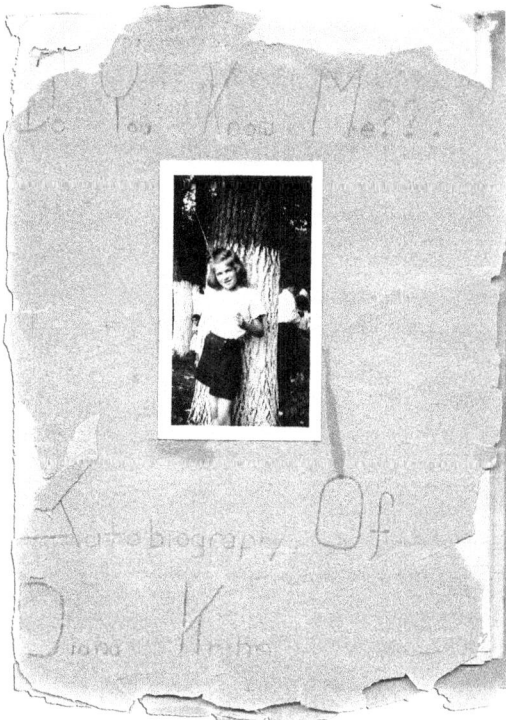

Now I smile as I read my father's sanitized view of our family that launched a collision of information without apparent connections. I still paste that same smile across my face when I learn something new until the pieces vaguely floating in my puzzled brain fit together.

With all the whys in my head, why didn't I ask 'Whys' about my own story? We notice the clues in hindsight, but miss them in the moment -- miss the look, the word choice, the shrug. As a child, I accepted my father's perspective. Now I'm painfully frustrated because it's all I have. Why didn't he tell me what was really happening? It wouldn't have changed anything. I loved my brothers, but felt a bit deceived and cheated by my father's withheld secrets. No matter how many whys and hows I continue to ask, I still haven't compiled 'the answer'. But I haven't given up.

Who was the Anon that said, "We do not see life as it is; we see it as we are." What a lesson from the past, the importance of veracity. There must be truth, otherwise there would not be a word for it. Some events in my stories are not pleasant, but I include them because otherwise they would not reflect my reality. Reflection has also taught me that truth is not easily discovered. My premature autobiography ended in 1950 and I got an 'E' for Excellent, but now my story continues into the snowy winter of 1951.

◦◦◦◦◦◦◦◦◦◦◦◦◦◦◦◦◦◦◦◦◦

Last, January 1951

I'm lucky enough to have Mrs. Farley as my seventh-grade teacher, even though she raps my knuckles with a ruler for yawning, just like Miss Pendergast. She always says, "Where are you, Diana? You're somewhere else."

Each year since first grade, we get similar books from the piles in the dusty book room. Dick and Jane style readers where nothing memorable happens, except a few new vocabulary words woven into predictable stories. New spellers in the same format since first grade. Arithmetic that mostly reviews last year's arithmetic. Some history, if we have time, focused on boring dates. Grammar that we parse in ever more complex diagrams.

But with Mrs. Farley, if we're good, we play baseball games for spelling and history. Mostly she focuses on 'correct language' using grammar rules as the questions that get us to first base. Much easier than trying to hit a real ball. She assigns homework in arithmetic. I've never had homework before. I call my new friend, Marlene Goldberg, to compare answers. Oh, the triumph and relief when my answers are right! Our phone hardly ever rang, except for those party line phantom rings, until Marlene and I became friends. She's my first school friend who's also my friend after school. It's good to have a Jewish friend. Sometimes I pick up the phone intending to dial Marlene, but quietly listen to the conversations on our four-party line.

I like word and arithmetic games and don't mind homework, but I hate standing in gym class not being picked, trying to stand up straight without looking uncomfortable. I feel embarrassed and anxious in my blue gym blouse and elasticized bloomers exposing the longest, skinniest legs in the class. Why would anyone pick me? Pink eye glasses slide down my nose. Freckles. Chocolate-brown, high-top baby shoes. I'm only good at games like jump rope, hopscotch and Russia.

Yuck! Now only three of us! I don't want to stand here, waiting. "Please pick me," I pray, a tight grimace taking over my face. I would love to be good at gym sports, but I'm not. I suffer as the happy ones get picked first and the usable ones fill in the team. Oh, the agony of being a leftover. Finally, the Jersey Sirens team picks me. At least the girls aren't mean to me, even though I'm terrible at most sports.

I don't hate when we line up for our desk assignments at the end of each semester. We take our books, pencils and bottle of ink out of our desk and stand along the blackboard wall like a silent geometry problem. Our teacher calls our names in order of our grades. The smartest girl gets to sit in the first seat of the first row, on the right-hand side by the door. Barbara Zaretsky usually gets it and Deanna's second. More names are called to fill up the six seats in the first row.

I've always been in the first row, but now in seventh grade, I prefer the first seat in the second row because it's closest to the classroom door that's kept open. You can scrutinize the boys exiled from their room. They stand out in the hall as punishment for chewing gum or whispering or not doing their homework. They parade up and down the hall on their way to the bathroom or whatever excuse enables a hall pass and momentary freedom. I prefer sitting behind Deanna's perfect pageboy which quietly flips when she moves her head. I hear the soft tinkling of Deanna's and Barbara's charm bracelets.

I sit securely in my prize seat, as the rest of the girls are assigned their place. There's a girl named Dorothy who's mostly last, like me in gym class. She's a girl you don't notice, nondescript with mousy hair, a chubby and colorless body, who quietly accepts her place. Maybe it's better than being left back. Sometimes girls disappear that way. Good thing gym scores don't count.

Will Dorothy always be last? I hope not.

We take on so many life-limiting thoughts and actions that sometimes it feels impossible to be true to ourselves and get the most out of our lives. We come into the world with enough innate potential to override most genetic predisposition. All we need to do is know ourselves and then guide ourselves through the mire of life's challenges. Seems simple enough, yet many of us are held back like Dorothy. We lose our way, accept a lesser modality or compromise away bits of our potential.

I still have moments when being alone, not by choice, implies no one wants to be with me. Alone feels like wasting

Diana Ruth Krohn

part of a day. Social isolation is weakening and difficult to bear. Sadness results in negative thinking, malfunctioning and an over-focus on past and current mistakes. I'm lucky to have many older role models who inspire me to quickly return to aliveness, gumption and confidence: Betty Rykoff, Verna Beard, Dorothy Kroloff, Leona Shapiro — even celebrities like Kathryn Hepburn, Lauren Bacall and Sandra Day O'Connor. I exist in a world where those who made me have ceased to exist. My hair is graying, like the white seeds of a dandelion that blow into the air. Now I'm the 'oldest' generation, enjoying my life in Arizona and the challenge of finding MY way.

The Lot in Winter, February 1951

The leaves have fallen and snow piles lure me outside. This morning, a few flakes still drift down in swirls and irregular bursts. I run across the street, to the lot where the naked branches of the trees have turned white. The cold snow muffles the traffic, eddies icy wet against my face. Silence…then blue sky injects a heavy stillness on the air. Gravity, settling in denser than usual as I search for animal tracks in the snow.

In winter, sledding prevails in our lot. We have a hill almost two hundred feet from the highest point down to 88th Street where the lot ends. The weak sun creates soft shadows across the powdery snow as I gaze down from my perch on the tree. Victor yells over, "Hey, Di, hop on and I'll give you a ride."

I'm afraid of going downhill, but try not to show it. I hope we don't go too fast or hit a tree or another sled. I hop on to the worn wooden slats, blinking up at the sun as I lean back. I sit in front in my hooded plaid jacket because, in every way, Victor's bigger than me. He feels solid and maybe that's why we don't get very far before we're stuck in a pile of snow.

107

Getting back up the hill is hard work. I trudge up sideways, following Victor who pulls the sled. This time I expect to get stuck again, so I'm not as scared. I love the feel of the sled, the ease of its gliding. The sled feels just as cold and hard, but I enjoy the soothing effect of Victor's arms wrapping around me and we sail down the hill, gaining speed on the icy segments. We don't need to talk. I listen to the sounds of the wind in the bare treetops and the runners of the sled on the snow. We're accelerating, going faster than the world, until we fly apart when we stop before we hit 88th Street. I feel bigness taking over, with a hint of adventurous days to come. I roll in the snow, cocooned. We laugh and relive the ride.

It lightens my heart to re-experience these pleasing sensations from my past. We spent the afternoon riding downhill on Victor's magical sled, because having fun reigns in a child's world. I suppose the past is never past. It lingers somewhere in our brain, directing us like an undercover traffic cop. Like a mountain storing an echo deep inside its core, we're left with a collective longing for the simpler life of childhood.

◠◠◠◠◠◠◠◠◠◠◠◠◠◠◠◠◠

Howdy Doody Time, March 1951

Mom's making me go with Aaron to "The Howdy Doody Show" with Buffalo Bob Smith. Yuck! I can't believe it. All the way on two buses to Rockefeller Center in Manhattan and on the elevator to NBC Studios in 3A, I try to tell her, "I'm way too old. I won't do it. No seventh grader goes to Howdy Doody!"

The usher leads me to the Peanut Gallery with my six-year-old brother. I feel like a doofus scrunching myself down on these little seats, hoping no one I know still watches Howdy Doody. My knees reach my chin. The usher tells us to sit still, smile at the camera and sing real loud when he signals.

Buffalo Bob Smith enters in his cowboy clothes and waves to us. "Say kids, what time is it?" Mr. Smith asks and I know the show has begun. His whiskey breath smells like the men's breath in our tavern on Hudson Boulevard.

"It's Howdy Doody time," we all have to yell.

Oh, pul-ease! Howdy reveals himself as a freckle-faced marionette operated by strings. I crunch down further, counting his freckles. He's supposed to have forty-eight, one for each state. Strings let his mouth fall down when he talks and sings. His big teeth show. It's better if you don't know what's going on and just watch it on TV at home.

I ignore Clarabelle Hornblow, the Clown, blowing his 'yes-no' horn instead of saying anything. He smiles for the camera, but not for us. What kind of grown man wants to run around in a clown's face honking his horn and squirting Mr. Smith with his bottle of seltzer water? Who would want him for a dad once they're past Kindergarten. What girl would want to marry a clown named Clarabelle. Not me, for sure.

The staging is so obvious and silly, like the elastic showing on the fake cotton beard on the red-faced Santa at Macys. I sit frowning, clutching my small chair tightly, hoping nobody sees me, waiting for the trickery and my discomfort to end.

I find it increasingly hard to find truths that remain constant. But if I believe my past memories to be factual, I need to include even this silly fragment. The illusion of Howdy Dorky made me skeptical of other television and radio shows, even though I still faithfully followed them with my father. I remember my disappointment when tricked by drunk Uncle Don on WOR. Years of rigged quiz shows took the fun out of trying to be the first to guess the answers. I gave up on most shows, except for 'Hit Parade.' Kind of like giving up on a friend when you learn they're not really your friend.

*While attending college during the Vietnam War, I was
sitting in my second period lit class when a man came into
our classroom to announce that a TV camera crew would
be on campus to film our protest at 11 a.m. He directed us
to leave our classes and participate in the protest. Of
course we all left, but I took the opportunity to head home
to be with my newest baby. I certainly wanted the war to
end, but the "TV is coming; let's protest mentality" has
been extremely disturbing to me ever since. Everyone
makes a different distortion but that kind of blatant
distortion creates its own changes to our lives.*

ⰔⰔⰔⰔⰔⰔⰔⰔⰔⰔⰔⰔⰔⰔⰔⰔ

Passover, April 1951

Uncle Ted and Aunt Ida invite us for Passover, my first
Seder. Aunt Miriam drives us to her house first. As we sit in
her parlor, she says, "Diana, would you like to borrow a
dress from Florence?"

My older cousin, Florence, always looks so beautiful. I
hate borrowed clothes because they don't fit me right, but I
don't say anything. I just follow her into Florence's room, a
bedroom with all the things I've dreamed a bedroom should
have. A dresser with a mirror, perfume bottles and
hairbrushes. Her closet has many clothes. Aunt Miriam
picks a deep lilac satin dress with large covered buttons and
a matching satin belt.

"You'll like this one," she says. "It's a shirtwaist so it
fits everybody. It will show off your star necklace." I take
off my plaid skirt and sweater. She finds me a slip in
Florence's drawer. The dress seems to come to me and put
its arms around me as I tuck my body into its cool luxury.
Aunt Miriam helps me with the buttons. Cloth buttons are
difficult to fit in the buttonholes. I feel like a princess.

"Look in the mirror at how grown up you look." It's
true. I'm twelve and stand tall. It's good, and it's me. I'm

110

ready and we leave for Uncle Ted's house in Verona.

Uncle Ted lives in the most elegant house with an ivy-covered hillside entrance. Everything feels like it's where it should be. The foyer with its grand staircase, the colorful paintings and rugs, Uncle Ted's inkwell collection and the shiny black grand piano in the front room. The adults gather in front of the fireplace as Aunt Esther plays the piano. I know everyone: Aunt Jean, Uncle Dan, Aunt Miriam, Uncle Joe, Aunt Esther, Uncle Ted and Aunt Ida. My cousins Florence, David, Daron, Marvin and I wander outside through the conservatory facing the garden. We walk across the backyard lawn, turning left and climbing the stones up a slope to the hidden yard behind the garage. I listen to them chat, feeling part of the group even though I don't say anything. When Aunt Ida calls, "Come in, children," we all walk inside to dinner.

Passover is more formal than Thanksgiving. Sitting around Aunt Ida's large dining room table, we take turns reading a book called the Haggadah, but Uncle Ted reads all the Hebrew. It's my first time to hear Hebrew. The resonating sounds fascinate my ears and mind. When it's Mom's turn, she won't read. She never reads. She says it's because she needs glasses, but I think she has no confidence because her stepmother took her out of school to go to work when she was twelve.

The readings take a long time, much longer than 'The Lord is my Shepherd' and the 'Pledge of Allegiance.' We listen to the story of leaving Egypt and following God's guidance to become free instead of slaves. Then we get to eat. Aunt Ida makes warm and tasty foods like Grandma Krohn's potatoes, but no bread. I love being here with everyone and wearing Florence's beautiful dress. I learn new ways to tell classy people. By the way one eats, and by one's shoes that are polished without leaving rubbings on your socks. Higher class people know where their next meal is coming from. They don't gulp it all down in a hurry, eat too much or pick things up with their hands. They don't talk with food in their mouth, make smacky noises or use a toothpick at the table. They have interesting, but polite, conversations.

After dinner, I dry dishes for Aunt Ida. We're alone in the kitchen. "What do you want to be when you grow up?" she asks in her pleasant voice.

I never seriously even think about it, but I remember when I was little and wanted to be a teacher. "A teacher," I respond.

Aunt Ida smiles, saying, "Very good. You'll make an excellent teacher." So I suppose that's it. My first Passover was perfect, except for having to return Florence's dress. I felt so connected wearing it, a different me.

Perhaps it was our story of Moses, a glimpse at testing behavior. More like a Cliff Notes version because my limited information didn't explain what the Passover story was all about. So how do I remember the reality from that evening at Aunt Ida's in a way that's helped me view my life? Every gathering has its moment; the spark between two people that goes beyond the small talk. A conversation with hinges. My future decided in a hesitant exchange within an economy of words.

Teaching was my job with the most love, creativity and learning. But unfortunately, financially limiting and leading to a deeply difficult decision. Not enough income to fund three college educations and assisting my mother and brother. With age, we are reminded of the things we intended to do, but didn't — and the things we shouldn't have done, but did.

Show Business, May 1951

This hard, straight-back wooden chair hurts. I'm sitting in this auditorium at Horace Mann School that has more seats than the Embassy Theater. My butt has sore places no matter how much I wiggle. Only a few of us sit. Most of my seventh-grade classmates act in this end-of-the-year school play. Mrs. Farley, my teacher, directs us. We've practiced all afternoon, every afternoon, for almost two weeks.

However, I don't practice. I only sit, my daydreams a pleasant distraction as I track the rehearsals. I'm an understudy for five parts. Most of us sitters are understudies. In my case, it's because I hardly ever talk. Shyness may be acceptable at six or seven, but I'm embarrassed to still be so shy at twelve. I hesitate before I speak and then, most often, don't speak because everyone teases me when the pink spots on my cheek turn crimson. Mrs. Farley would never take a chance on me.

Our play is a mystery about a family with problems to be solved. By the end of the play, the heroine (played by teeny Deanna with the shiny brown page boy) has solved the mysteries and her parents are tickled pink. I suspect all kids try to solve their parents' problems. I certainly try, but there's so many, too many.

Today's our last rehearsal and my butt bones are so glad. The performance begins at 5:30. I feel like I know all the parts by heart. It's fun and easy when I have nothing to do. But as the rehearsal ends, on our way back to our classrooms, Deanna falls down the stairs. I hear the thud before the girls begin screaming, "Don't touch her. Her leg is bent."

Ahead of me, I see the kids gathered around her and I join them. Deanna lies there crying. The nurse arrives and sends us back into our classroom. We sit quietly at our desks, not knowing what to do. We girls usually chatter all the time, but we keep remembering Deanna's twisted leg.

Mrs. Farley finally returns as the 'time to go home bell' rings. She announces, "Deanna's at the hospital with a broken femur. Diana, you will have to play her part tonight. Stay after school and we'll talk."

Mrs. Farley doesn't look happy, but she tries to sound reassuring. You know how adults think they can do that. She says, "Just read the play script. I circled your parts. Don't worry and speak as loud as you can."

I walk home, my head heavy with shock, wondering if I can do it. I don't want to. Maybe I can say I'm throwing up. I feel like it. But I imagine Deanna's beautiful hair on her hospital bed and put on my nicest skirt, the red plaid one my cousin Barbara gave me, and my tomato red sweater. I put new carbon paper cardboard to cover the holes in my soles, in case it rains, and head back to school. I hurry, but feel like I'm hurrying to my doom.

Mrs. Farley waits backstage, looking as gloomy as I feel. She walks through the opening in the curtain, announces the play and the substitution and here I go. I've never stood onstage. What an awesome feeling when the curtain opens and the kids and parents in the audience are dark! As the mom starts the play with her first lines, I stare into the dark indignantly. At my cue, I read my part in my loudest voice – loudest, shaky voice. But as we continue, I stop reading and just say the lines. I really do know the script. I sense the audience and their reaction. Holy Moley! How amazing! Their interest gives me energy. It's going okay. Mrs. Farley smiles.

Near the end of the play, I'm actually acting on a big stage. In my last big speech, I explain to everyone how I solved the family's mystery so we don't have to move. Rodney, who plays the dad, comes back onstage and my lines are done! Yeah! The play will end when he kisses my cheek.

But Rodney just looks at me. 'Kiss me,' I think, staring at him. He looks around, runs offstage and brings back a chair. I stand there like a total square waiting to be kissed, with nothing left to say. The audience starts shifting in their seats and talking. Mrs. Farley holds her forehead. Rodney climbs on the chair, so he can reach my cheek, and he carefully kisses me. As the audience howls with laughter, I realize I'm too tall for the part. I'm so ashamed. I ruined the play!

Life is like a chocolate souffle; sometimes it collapses like I did at the end of our play. Years of Toastmasters, Broadway Babies, choir performances, speeches and awards and I still hear that persistent whisper, 'you're an uncomfortable leggy dork.' What stories are concealed beneath appearance? Are there ever some who don't laugh?

ଔଔଔଔଔଔଔଔଔଔଔଔଔଔଔ

Cleveland, summer 1951

This summer, Dad's become a larger part of my life -- no more side jobs, no more jobs on the road. When he's not at Alcoa, the Buena Vista, or in the hospital, he hunches over his Underwood writing 'Dear Folks' letters to his five brothers and sisters. His fingers tap the keyboard hard in order to get through the thickness of the carbon copies. All those thoughts in his head click into words. His back crouches and a cigarette dangles from his lips. The smoke mixes with the steam that hangs over his coffee cup. He still wears his white shirt and tie with his long sleeves rolled up at the cuffs – K for Krohn on the handkerchief in his pocket.

Our phone's ringing. Maybe something's wrong? Probably a mistake, ringing for someone on our party line. Long Distance! That usually means bad news, but in this case, it's really good news. Bobby and Dorothy had their first baby. Dad's a grandfather to a boy named Michael.

He's so happy he doesn't even care if someone listens on our party line. He promises Bobby he'll visit Cleveland this summer to meet his grandson. As he hangs up the phone, he tells me that I'll have to come with him because Dr. Kolodin won't let him travel alone.

Holy smokes! I'm gonna go on a long train ride soon. I implant it in my head, chanting the jump rope rhyme:

Engine, engine Number 9...Going down Chicago Line...
See it sparkle, see it shine...Engine, engine Number 9...
If the train should jump the track...
Will I get my money back?
Yes? No? Maybe so...

I queue up in the line for tickets so Dad can sit and read the Daily News. Most of the passengers in our line wear magazine-style clothes and carry umbrellas, coats and large valises. The conductors wear dark uniforms and hats, exceedingly different from the uniforms of the soldiers or the Catholic schools. A very tall conductor points out which car to board.

Never before have I been on such a plush train. Very different from the Bloomfield train or Eighth Avenue subway. It starts raining right after we leave Grand Central Station. Even though the N.Y. Central train's splendid, the towns we pass have old, rotting buildings crumbling into termite dust along the track. Why don't the towns demolish them and turn the land back into parks? I stare at the people who live along the tracks, looking for clues about their lives on their clotheslines sagging with wet patched Levis, faded flannel shirts, one-piece long underwear and uniforms.

I get tummy cramps. The bathroom's already dirty, smelly and running out of toilet paper. Back in my seat, Dad is having the kind of chest pains that cause him to take his Nitroglycerin pills. I don't want to leave him, so I don't get to explore the rest of the cars. I hope his pain goes away.

At Buffalo, we leave the train, carrying our valise across the platform for a side trip to Niagara Falls. We ride that shorter train through the most terrifying thunderstorm like riding through the dark, scary part of a fairy tale. It's not very far and I'm glad to get off at the small concrete station and move my legs. This old town's streets are lined with souvenir shops and shabby hotels offering honeymoon specials. Dad buys me a rabbit's foot key chain stamped with a picture of the Falls.

We look around for a place to have lunch. It's already after two o'clock. "Let's eat at the Greeks," Dad says. "That's usually the tastiest food."

We each take a stool at the counter. Dad starts telling the man behind the counter one of his St. Peter's Gate jokes. I don't know what to order. The overpowering smell of garlic takes away my appetite. The menu feels greasy and it's hard to read the worn, blurred words. Maybe tuna fish... maybe a hot dog.

"Well," Dad says, laughing at his joke, "Tell the man what you want."

"Maybe a tuna sandwich," I reply hesitantly.

"Why don't you get the grilled cheese with French fries," Dad suggests.

I gratefully mumble, "Okay."

When the man goes away to cook, Dad whispers, "Don't ever order anything that cooks can mix with their hands." I immediately imagine the cook glopping his dirty hands, kneading tuna salad in a bowl, squeezing grayed mayonnaise through his fingers.

Our trip gets better after our late lunch. As we approach Niagara Falls, the roar reaches out to us, removing the damper from my day. I go right to the tippy edge; my hand tightens cautiously on the cyclone fence in the slippery drizzle. Mom would be yelling warnings here for sure. I look down, hoping to see someone going over in a barrel. I wouldn't be afraid to try as long as the barrel is closed. I imagine the fun, but no one enters the water as it just pours over the rocky edge, sending up spray, dropping, dropping. You can pick a drop and follow it with your eyes till it gets too far down, lost in the mist. I shout down, "Hey," listening to the sound hang there until my voice washes away into the heavy, moist air.

"We need to hurry to catch the Five twenty-five," Dad says. I really want to stay, breathing in the steadiness of the falling river.

It's dark as our train arrives in Cleveland. We're both tired. Bobby waves and smiles as we walk through the dimly lit station. We drive to where he lives in the upstairs of somebody else's house. They are having trouble with mice and I grimace at the turds all over, even in the empty playpen. Bobby and Dorothy let me sleep on their comfortable couch even though it isn't wrapped in plastic. With all those turds, I'm glad not to sleep on the floor like we do at Aunt Estelle's.

In the morning, my new nephew, Mike, bops and bops the Shmoo I brought him. However, even though he's cute and smart, he cries a lot and drips sour smelling stuff on his bib. We have breakfast, but Dorothy calls it brunch. Scrambled eggs and cinnamon buns that she baked. We spend the afternoon talking, laughing and looking at photographs of baby Mike. Then Dorothy cooks her special chop suey, for what she calls 'dinner' instead of supper. She lets me help with the chopping.

After dinner, we drive to visit Mrs. Gedeon, Dorothy's mother. We sit on her big open porch during a really long, thrilling thunderstorm. Dad makes us laugh with his jokes. He tells one of my favorites, about the lightning hitting the outhouse. I listen to every word they speak. Bobby quietly holds his son. I'm happy we're all together, like people in old, grainy photographs taken by a slow camera that reminds me of an accordion.

Mrs. Gedeon makes floats by mixing root beer soda with vanilla ice cream. It's one of the best tasting treats I've ever had. When I'm noisily slurping the bottom through my straw, she offers me seconds. "Yes, thank you!" I say happily, thinking she's really perfect and so is this trip after all. I love traveling with Dad, having him all to myself and enjoying our adventures.

Days later, we arrive back at Newark's Central Station and find the bus to North Bergen. Once home, you'd think Dad would be tired, but he's already typing another 'Dear Folks' letter onto a thick mass of onionskin and carbons stuffed around the carriage. All his words are about Mike's cuteness and brilliant gurgles. He stops and smokes for a few seconds and I study the map of his hand through the smoke. I realize that his words do not reflect my experience, and that they can also be frustratingly limiting when I'm trying to explain something truly wonderful, like being an aunt and traveling to Cleveland.

My obsession with trains grew, plus I benefitted from my peek into Bobby's family life. We learn so much when we escape from our norms. Bobby made great choices! The closeness I observed in his marriage contained the passion of life. It added a higher understanding, as many life experiences do, but still was far from a reality I didn't totally comprehend.

We never know reality; we're always interpreting it. Nobody's life seems easy when you get up close. Everyone jumps around within their continuum. But people like Bobby and Dorothy, who knew themselves and expressed themselves, gain the most comfort from closeness. The art of life is love and the inspired moments existent within deep affection, at times preceding understanding, attained brushstroke by brushstroke.

<hr/>

Bradley Beach, summer 1951

Another warm summer day. Another train trip, this time to Bradley Beach, but without Dad. We board the crowded, hot car packed with too many people. I have to sit by myself in the prickly wicker seat several rows away from Mom and Aaron. Towns appear and disappear as the train streaks south. Alongside the track, fields of August corn and tomatoes extend to the crowded towns. Roads, bridges, children, the world is so much the same.

Trains are a bridge between cities, between familiar and faraway places, connected by wires and tracks, in our case between Jersey City and Bradley Beach. From the stations, you see 'Main Street' in every town we pass. You'd never believe we're near the ocean, except for the names on the station signs: Elizabethport... Perth Amboy... Red Bank... Long Branch... Allenhurst... Asbury Park... and finally, Bradley Beach. Paint chips off the old hotels. A few are converted to boarding houses and one has become an old people's home. The sidewalks are full of cracks and spit. We pass a jeweler, a typewriter store, a small grocery, a pharmacy as we slowly enter our station.

We walk the few blocks to the apartment where Mom's aunt lives, over a dry cleaners, on Main Street. From her window you can see the train station across the tracks. Mom and her aunt don't look related. Maybe she's related to Mom's stepmother, who disappeared from our lives when Grandpa died. Mom's aunt looks short and thin with a salt and pepper bun and a brownish dress with no pattern. She wears brown high tops, like mine, and she double knots her laces. She appears spinsterish, but must have had a husband once because she has a daughter I never met. Maybe her daughter escaped, leaving her mother behind. No extra room in the small apartment, so Aaron and I sleep on her parlor floor.

I love mornings at the shore. The cool smell of salty air, ledges with dead plants in pots, women sitting on porches playing Canasta and Mah Jong. We set our blanket on the sand, alongside my aunts and cousins who rented cottages for a week. Mom loves the sun, but I know I'll be peeling her back within a few days. I'm good at meeting the challenge of keeping her peeled skin intact as I scrape it off her burnt body.

I feel the sun's heat spread down my neck and back. The sand burns my feet. I love being here, even though I'm afraid of the big chilly waves that knock me down. You can hold onto thick, strong ropes, so you don't get hurt by the waves as they smash against the shore at high tide. Fat ladies in black bathing suits stand in the yellow foam, holding onto the ropes. It's more dangerous to stand between them than getting caught in unseen currents.

Aunt Estelle's son David joins Aaron and me. We walk along the beach, between blankets, around hawkers. Occasional waves wash the coarse sand off our feet. We find two dead fish under a pier and decide to sell them. It certainly livens up and adds purpose to our walk, but no one responds to our 'fish for sale,' so we toss those smelly staring creatures into a garbage can and head back to our family on their blankets.

MY STREET

Now that I'm twelve, Mom makes me babysit my seven-year old brother. After our very late lunch, she sends us outside so she can talk to her aunt. "Take Aaron where he can see the choo-choo trains, but don't go anywhere near the tracks. Be back before dark," she orders as she sits, lighting her cigarette, in the small kitchen.

To keep Aaron happy, we head right to the train station. We walk past businesses, each with their distinct smells: talcum powder from the barber shop, vanilla from the ice cream store, and harsh chemicals from the dry cleaners. In the long silence between trains, the station offers quiet sanctuary. We sit together, on the wooden bench, waiting for a rumbling engine to round the bend. We must seem a bit of a spectacle. Skinny children in hand-me-down clothes, unnoticed by the passing people, their footsteps echoing in the emptiness of the platform between trains. People walk around us with smiling politeness and impenetrable faces. Maybe they smell the dead fish we carried.

I hum, 'Choo-choo train, chug-chuggin at the station…' Since my train trip this summer, I love songs about trains. They're filled with magic words and sounds of power. I wait on the wooden bench with my brother. Behind us are posters with two green Coca Cola bottles simply saying 'Drink Coke', a cowboy amongst blue skies that reads 'I'd Walk a Mile for a Camel', and penguins standing on an ice floe saying, 'Smoke Kool.' Men stand around, smoking and spitting. I suspect they need something to fiddle with, like boys who fiddle with the knobs on the radio. They spit as they walk. They spit when they declare something. They smell of Old Spice aftershave and sweat.

A slow black engine approaches, hissing as its cars stop. People get off and on. The porter leans on the platform Dutch door. "All 'board!" As the train wheels chug-a-chug leaving the station, it picks up speed. Aaron calmly focuses on the engine, spellbound by its steamy magnificence. The cars are differing shades from black to silvery-gray. Even the windows are a mottled gray ash that makes the world seem colorless. I still feel the engine's vibration after it leaves.

My thoughts wind this way and that on their own track. Another engine pulls into the station. Its wheels, whirring strongly, are at our eye-level. Everything works, whether the train moves slower or faster, the same movement, only faster, sure and strong. Even freight trains loaded with coal move in their connected way. The engines have names and the cars have numbers. Aaron and I count the boxcars, all 102 of them. They creak gingerly through the station, gasping out their smoky steam of damp nothingness. The tracks have many switches so we can never be sure where the train will stop. The engine whistle wails as the wheel flanges shriek.

Sometimes I see things, not important things, but they play over and over in my imagination. I'm beginning to worry about my brother. He sits too intently focused as trains leave the station. He doesn't seem to notice anything else. In the fading light of dusk, it could be anytime. We watch until there's nothing left but the caboose and we smile because cabooses make us smile. I walk Aaron back to the apartment, thinking that things in your head always change at the end of a train journey.

Time to step out of the story as scattered day-blind stars unbutton their life. Nobody can tell me when Aaron first got lost: as a coddled child eating cereal and playing with toy cars, a teen cancer patient, his Haight Ashbury experiences and intensely growing into the man he is today. Can a boy growing up without a man become a man? Was his flight into living alone caused by passion, rage, fear, confusion or some old instinct? We survive until one day a major or minor event causes us to fall through the fault line. What we resist persists. I pray that he's happy with his choices.

◇◇◇◇◇◇◇◇◇◇◇◇◇◇◇◇◇◇

The End, summer 1951

It's the not-quite dark of an August evening. I head home from jumping rope on Fifth Avenue, hoping there's still chocolate milk in our ice box. Our apartment door pushes open easily. Can this be our apartment? All the furniture's gone. Mom sweeps dirt, dust balls and crunchy cockroaches into the middle of the bare floor. Funny how they hide during their lives and are so visible in death. Mom's barefoot. Her corns must be bothering her.

"Don't step in my pile," she yells, meaning leave me alone.

Bare windows, closed, expose our empty parlor, expose my shock, and make our apartment appear bigger. Mom pulls down our yellowed shades. The dimmed space suggests pale shadows from our past years. Nothing remains hidden anymore. I wander through all four rooms. My parent's bedroom is empty. The bared kitchen shows its wear and tear.

"I can't believe this." I say. "No one told me we're leaving. Where are we going?"

Mom doesn't answer. Aaron races his toy car along the worn wood floor, ignoring me. Mom just looks down at her dirt pile. "Hurry and go to the bathroom," she finally says. "Uncle Dan is on his way."

My face looks bloated in our bathroom mirror. The

124

tarnished glass reflects the spotted walls and empty towel bars. I feel blemished like the rusting tub. Mom forgot to pack the rubber stopper and the toilet pump. What if the toilet runs over in our next apartment. I wonder if she packed my doll, my potholder maker and my paper dolls. What about my bag full of afghan squares?

"Nobody's ever left 90th Street since we moved here," I try to tell Mom. "How come we have to leave?"

Silence. No explanation. Do I need one? Dad's in the hospital again. But no one told me we were moving. Does it matter? Mrs. Farley always said, "Innocence is not an excuse." I feel like shouting, "Got me!"

"We have a new apartment," Mom finally answers. "In Edgewater." Then, again, silence. No neighbors say goodbye as we walk down the stairs. The traffic even seems to have stopped. There's nothing to say. Will anything of me remain in this building where I have lived for ten years?

Uncle Dan walks through our lobby quickly, smiling like a carefree boy. "Let's go. We have to beat the moving truck to Edgewater."

"But," I run up to explain to him, "but I didn't know about any move. Where is Edgewater?"

He just looks at Mom, so it's no use. The disapproval of a child must have unsettled him. Then he answers, "Edgewater is closer to your dad's job. And your new apartment doesn't have five flights of stairs for him to climb."

I feel tired. No second chance. So this is the end, the last chapter. I beg Mom, "I need to say goodbye to Maureen and my friends. I need to check my peach pit tree. Please."

"No time. You'll do it later," she tells me. "We'll come back." But I know we never will.

Last times live in our minds in a worn box labeled THE PAST. Some lie anchored at the bottom because we chose not to return to them. The people who became too mean, the places that changed so much it hurts to remember them.

Higher in the pile are the last times too awkward to recall. Goodbyes when you leave a job you love. Teas and dinners given for you when you move around the country, vowing to stay in touch. But staying in touch isn't the same as doing things together and the easy friendships become more difficult to maintain. Visits replaced by letters, then phone calls, e-mails. Finally, only e-mail jokes and a spattering of greeting cards.

The haunting last times at the top of the box happened when I didn't realize they were last times: sleighing down a hillside that became a gas station, the last car trip before my father's heart attack, moving from North Bergen.

Diana Ruth Krohn

PART 2. Transplanted Without Roots
Edgewater/Bloomfield/Edgewater
June 1951 to January 1955

And you, my father, there on the sad height,
Curse, bless, me now with your fierce tears, I pray.
Do not go gentle into that good night.
Rage, rage against the dying of the light.
                    Dylan Thomas

Changed Rhythms, August 1951

When I pass the wooden bus stop shed on our corner on this muggy day in Edgewater, I realize I won't be able to walk to school with Maureen...

Dear Maureen,   *August 24, 1951*

We're in Edgewater now, closer to my dad's job at Alcoa Aluminum. Sorry I didn't get to say good-bye. We moved into a new garden apartment that sits above the level of a gray concrete wall separating our building from the road. From this elevation, we look past the Buena Vista Tavern to the Hudson River and Manhattan.

Remember that poem we read in Mrs. Farley's class. "Life is like a Garden." This garden apartment makes me feel like a transplanted flower without roots. Aaron and I don't know any kids yet. We spent this afternoon walking through our small town. We're only two miles from the George Washington Bridge.

No one was on the street, no street games, no one outside. We looked hard at the windows on the houses, hoping to satisfy our curiosity. A few houses have wild gardens with tall bushy stands of flowers and bird feeders. Others are barren, effortless, stranded dirt and rocks. Along the river, we see small barges with clotheslines of men's dungarees and undershirts.

127

MY STREET

Part way to the bridge, we passed a small grocery. Aaron wanted a package of Wrigley's bubble gum. Inside, the store was dim and dingy. While Aaron paid the man, I noticed several older boys sitting around a table in the back room. Their feet were raised onto the table and their arms dangled with indifference. They burped, then laughed and farted when they looked at us. We left quickly to get away from the smell. But I turned and caught one tall, lanky boy watching me. I liked the way he looks.

Feeling trashed after that awful store, we walked in silence until we were under the bridge on the weedy banks of the Hudson. We heard the loud hum from traffic on the busiest bridge in the world, a suspension bridge made of cables and steel beams. Barges and ships passed underneath. A sign stated "George Washington Crossed Here," documents this narrow part of the river. I tried to imagine George Washington in his boat, but couldn't.

We hung around for a while, then walked back, past our apartment, past Alcoa where Dad works as a timekeeper, past the Spry factory. We stopped at a padlocked cyclone fence with decayed signs from the 125th Street Ferry that closed down before we moved here. A small group of kids poked sticks in a trash heap by the river. Inside the fence, the empty lot had become littered with cigarette butts, shards from beer bottles, old newspapers, wads of dried gum and other unmentionable stuff.

Edgewater has no town center, no movie theater. A few street corners have small stores and taverns. The narrow town only has two main streets. Undercliff Avenue runs below the Palisades and River Road parallels the Hudson. Walking home, we watched the river flow past. You'd love the barges and the New York skyscrapers.

Our building isn't finished. Just a few neighbors and no other kids live here yet. Mrs. McMahon, our upstairs neighbor, plays her Spinet piano. She's short, like Mrs. McNaught, with frizzy-permed mousy hair. She always smiles and invites us to visit her anytime. Mrs. McMahon has no children. I don't know why not. Her husband Joe builds skyscrapers in New York. As we approached our hall entrance, we heard her piano. We went upstairs and were surprised to find Mom visiting. Mrs. McMahon's chubby fingers played songs she called "ragtime."

"C'mon," she insists as she grabbed our hands. "Let's go to the window to check out the river. Edgewater people are called river rats," she explained. "Most people in our town are poor, with many living in rotting barges or makeshift houses along the slime of the polluted Hudson. But we have these beautiful garden apartments."

We watched the #10 River Road bus head toward the bridge, speeding past the thriving lilac trees flourishing near the tavern courtyard. Mrs. McMahon told us, "Lilacs grow wild in the Hudson River Valley from West Point almost all the way to the Atlantic Ocean." You can tell Mrs. McMahon used to be a teacher.

Well, I'd hoped we'd at least have a two-bedroom apartment, but Aaron and I still sleep in the parlor. However, the toilet and shades work. We have fewer things here in Edgewater than in North Bergen. Our apartment seems smaller, simple. There's no eating space in the kitchen, but Aunt Miriam gave us her old mahogany table for the parlor. Not much insulation either, so the smells and sounds come through. We know when someone enters our hallway. In addition to Mrs. McMahon's piano, we hear her TV and flushing toilet. At night, when cars enter the parking lot, their headlights play on our walls and windows.

MY STREET

Our parlor has a picture window, just like Mrs. McMahon's. It makes our small room seem bigger. I gaze at the Hudson, active with loaded barges, tug boats, ferries and little motorboats. This week's rain cleaned the mud-colored water to streaks of deep blue and light green. Yesterday we had the most exciting thunderstorm. Mom hid in the closet yelling, "Careful, Di-annn, you'll get hit by lightning. Get in the closet with me and Aaron."

I remember putting my pen down and staring out at the river, thinking, "Careful!" Careful, to mom, turned into another word for fear. I wanted to live beyond the careful place. I wanted to live in that instant of connecting eyes when I peeked at the boy. I love the exact place where the gray of the water merges with the gray of the sky, when lightning hits the river with its teasing jolts of light and thunderous sounds not far behind. I imagine it stirs up all the life within, its messages absorbed my body and brain. I'd rather spend my life with the clouds, wind and electricity that prevail. The current moves at its own quick pace, not slowed down by the activity along the miles of its riverbank. It passes by skyscrapers looking down at their long shadows below the surface and by boys taking the dare and jumping from the trash heaps along its banks. I watched its quickening movement as, unafraid, it wildly sought the ocean. But wonder if, when it finds it, does it cease to be?

Funny how we turn our past into anecdotes. My mother's "NO's" so terrified me of water that I could never become a fish. In my freshman year of college, it was mandatory to pass swimming. I was so scared, it took me a semester just to get my other foot off the bottom. I had developed a stroke that fooled everyone but my instructor, so I didn't pass the five-minute deep water test. But after a year of me, any sane instructor would look the other way.

Somehow, on my own, I finally lost my uptightness.

130

Now when I arrive home, my pool awaits, filled with shimmering reflections of late afternoon sun. My clothes peel off and the music goes on. Exhilarating, the water just feels too good. My first strokes in my pool are exploratory, searching for bugs, leaves, grass and other solid intruders. My limbs loosen up for my lap workout, my arms grow longer and longer. I have a visual image of a layer of fat at the bottom of the pool, years of fat that might otherwise have remained on my body.

In the middle of a hot Arizona night, I wander outside to twinkling stars, moving clouds or a knowing moon that watches me. I play Esther Williams or an Indian in silence. Remember the old movies where Indians soundlessly swim across the water. I love to swim slowly, feeling the water more than the movement. I glide to meet the challenge of trying to be soundless. Not a stir of the water. You never know when you might need this stroke; I've been practicing for years.

George Washington School, 1951

Dear Maureen,   *November 13, 1951*

There's BOYS in our class, but even boys can't stop the severe boredom. I watch Miss Stutz, my old maid eighth grade teacher, rolling down maps of indistinguishable countries in Africa, Asia and South America. She tests us, using her pointer, squeaking chalk on the cloudy blackboard. No one seems to care or know the answers. Her elastic stockings flop down from her bony white knees. She's hopelessly out-of-date, with gray-streaked brown hair piled in dandruffy rolls on top of her head and long white hairs hanging from her chin.

George Washington School is a two-story brick building rooted in patches of crabgrass bordered by old sycamore trees.

George Washington supposedly also crossed the Hudson at this site during the Revolutionary War. Dad jokes about the places Washington traveled and the beds he slept in, but spending my day in this classroom isn't a joke.

Miss Stutz asks lots of questions. Which is the longest river...the largest continent...the capital of Montana...the largest number? No one answers. They just stare or leaf through their books. I learned the responses at Horace Mann. But just like the map quizzes, I don't speak unless Miss Stutz calls on me.

Sometimes Miss Stutz excuses a few of us to look up words in the big dictionary on a marble stand in the hall. Our two most looked-up are the "p...." and the "f.." ones. Guess Mrs. McMahon was right when she commented to dad, "Edgewater IQ's are noticeably lower than the temperature of the water in the Hudson."

That humongous leather-bound dictionary contains so many words. Their sounds and tastes spin around us. We grab them and they survive. I want to use really powerful words. At home, I use my <u>Readers Digest Ten Words a Day Workbook</u> my cousin Barbara gave me, even though they are often obtuse (my new favorite word) and brainless. I'm lucky she never wrote in it, so I'm working my way through the book, but only on rainy days.

The Edgewater kids must think I'm lucky cause they say things like, "Oh, you live in the garden apartments," as if they're impressed. But I'd rather be in North Bergen.

Pablo Neruda wrote, "Everything exists in the word... An idea goes through a complete change because one word shifted its place, or because another settled down like a spoiled little thing inside a phrase that was not expecting her but obeys her...They have shadow, transparence, weight, feathers, hair and everything they gathered from so much rolling down the river, from so much wandering from country to country, from being roots so long."

Words contain many layers of possible meaning. Solitude implies longing or fear. Forgiveness suggests people erring and needing mercy. Mercy vs Merci (thanks). Space might mean sitting and reading a book, noticing the moving leaves and the squirrels robbing the bird feeders. Rage vs Peace may mean not caring that birds are eating the birdseed. Peace — are peace and solitude the same? Order, does it bring peace or cause compulsion?

Is life ever understood? Why does mine seem like confusion? Guess it's more interesting that way. Certainly many options. All the 'yeses' add up to understanding and adventure. In a group with three new people and five old ones with comfortable faces, I want to hug them all, help them and experience their thinking.

Writing is rarely small talk. It's so large it can't be held in. Unbound by grammar, spelling, arthritis and technology, and the pail of things learned in classes— they're only good when they light a fire inside me. Whatever I have and feel, I can't question, since it reflects my trying. Poetry accentuates a metaphorical lens of truth with its conciseness. Prose becomes more rewarding when it borders on prose poetry. We seek results which, to me, means certainty.

By the time we turn seventy, we've collected pieces of our life as we need them. I peruse the walls in the home of my childhood, sounds from the radio, the very long walk to school, the ball connecting with the broomstick, watch my daughter emerge from my body in a hand mirror, feel love every time I gaze at my lovers. Sometimes I wonder what's left. Will it now just be left-overs? Seems like the more you know and have experienced, the less often you still notice a budding flower. Where is the new, the untried, the stimulation from fresh insight? Where do you have to dig to stir up the new buds? Or do you just sit and wait for them to show up?

This morning I awoke from a dream where I lived in a future to come. Feeling the strength of dark churning water, yet making headway. Traveling empty-handed, with time to stop and pick up what I need, feeling myself connecting to another place. That was a 'new bud' dream—no fishing around in my past. No known boundaries. Makes you wonder what's next. No wonder I'm addicted to radar on the weather channel.

◇◇◇◇◇◇◇◇◇◇◇◇◇◇◇◇◇◇

Trouble, November 1951

New town, new school, and I still daydream. But Miss Stutz doesn't yell or rap my knuckles. Our small class contains several older boys waiting to drop out of school on the day they're sixteen. The two Richie's, Richie Vincent and Richie Cohen, are in eighth grade for the third year. They can't pass. They never study or pay attention. All they talk about is getting a job and buying a car. Joe White, the most handsome boy, combs his shiny black hair just like Ricky Nelson. I could never like a boy with a crew cut!

The girls are okay, not mean. I have no friends yet, no one to hang out with after school. I'm very quiet so no one knows me. There are days I feel like a blushing stranger on this earth. Kay walks home in my direction, to a real house with a porch and a garden. Her mother seems snobby. "Mom says I can't play with you," she tells me apologetically. Not sure whether it's because we're poor or Jewish.

I can't play anyway. After school I wait at the bus stop for dad. We walk home together and watch TV. Boxing on Wednesday night. All the Yankees, Giants and Dodgers baseball games. I have our nightly lineups memorized. We both love quiz shows and try to beat each other to the answers. With very few clues, I beat the clock, naming the song titles and word quizzes.

In class, it's frustrating for the other kids when I know the answers and they don't. So Miss Stutz assigns me to be the office assistant for two hours every morning. Mr. Wall, our principal, asks me to file papers and answer the telephone with two lines. I don't mind running the ditto machine or recording attendance, but office work offers nothing special.

...until this morning. Usually Mr. Wall arrives late, removes his old brown slouchy hat and combs his hair, plastering it down trying to cover his bald spot. He's a big man, much bigger than Dad, even before Dad's sickness. Mr. Wall wears wrinkly trousers, not neatly pressed like Dad's. I'll bet he's mean and paddles to hurt. Oh well, only a half-hour left.

Three boys from my class, Richie, Vinnie and John, slouch through the door, slowly. I can tell they've been bad. "We need to see Mr. Wall," John mutters, a note in his hand.

"What did you do?" I ask sympathetically. I would hate getting caught.

"Aw, nuthin," they mumble. They are mad. Richie's cheeks and ears are beyond blushing red. John's face is full of sweat dribbles that look like zits. Their hair, slicked back into DAs, are messed up and their tees aren't tucked. They smell of unwashed hair, vinegary.

"Mr. Wall's in the safe," I tell them. All eyes, even mine, move down to the open metal door of the walk-in safe. We look intently into the gap. It's totally quiet in there. Mr. Wall's probably taking a nap. I wonder how long the boys will wait. I don't know what to do, so I just wait with them.

Then Vinnie gets up, with a smile on his face that looks like a stifled giggle. As he walks towards the safe, Richie and John join him. They close the safe door. The vibration frightens me. So does the quiet. *Ooooh, Mr. Wall is locked inside!*

I look at the guys and they look at me. We giggle, really giggle. Then they walk out down the hall. I don't know what to do except bite my nails, but it's exactly eleven o'clock. Time to return to the classroom. I feel a knot in my throat, but it's a small knot. I remember the sharp click and picture Mr. Wall at that single instant, surrounded by dark. I hope Mr. Wall doesn't breathe too much stale air.

After lunch, Miss Stutz announces, "Diana, please report to the office immediately." I'm careful not to look at anyone as I walk out.

"No, I didn't see anyone. I didn't know you were locked in," I tell Mr. Wall and the two Edgewater police officers. I figure facts can be altered, it is in newspaper columns every day. I call mine "healthy truth." They ask several more questions, but I stick to my story. I learned not to rat in North Bergen.

Was there more truth when I was younger than there is now? I still dwell on that word until it's become an implacable, painful obsession. When actuality catches me by surprise, it hurts to see a part of me I don't want to see but need to see. The outtakes of life's disappointments inevitably get re-imagined or softened with filters or telepathy.

Presenting opinion as fact is presumptuous. We forget the observation and live with the interpretation now masquerading as fact. How can we speak in such absolute terms when nothing is absolute? The pseudo-calm of ancient superstitions and stubborn resistance of arrogant thinking conspire to conceal truth behind biased eyes and closed minds. Evil is a mask for those who never find the truth—perhaps resulting from stupidity or lack of love. Casualties, especially in war, make truth obvious.

There are many ways to glimpse truth. Even when it can be brightening, I still question how much is bright and how much is self-deception? Avoidance may keep me busy and having fun, but not comfortable. We need strength to sift through ideas and refine abstract concepts until, inevitably, the magic unknowns reveal themselves. Not sure how much brightness I'm ready to let in. Truths are not for everyone; even small ones can be dangerous. Once seen clearly, each expression rarely permits itself to lie hidden again. Its greatest ally is time, evoking its own peace.

<hr />

Loneliness, 1951

Dear Maureen,   December 17, 1951

It's already mid-December. In case you wondered, no one found out who locked Mr. Wall in the safe. But my classmates are really nice to me. The boys ask me to carry their knives and cigarettes on school trips. They beg me to write their excuse notes once they realize I can spell and imitate their parents' handwriting with my new ball point pen. After school, Dorothy Raba invites me to join the girls at her house. We play 45-rpm records like "Shrimp Boats" with "Jambalaya" on the other side. It's first-rate to giggle with new friends before I run home to pick up dad.

I've decided to NEVER cut my barbered hair again. I can't wait till I have a ponytail even though it will take hours for my hair to dry. I want to read True Confessions and Hit Parade magazine just like my friends. You should buy Hit Parade magazine. It has all the lyrics to the popular songs so you can sing along.

I was chosen to narrate the Christmas pageant, the only speaking part. My family didn't come, but I'm proud anyway, even though I still hear the quiet voice inside murmuring, "You don't belong." Strange, isn't it, when a year quietly comes to its *end. Who knows what's hidden in the stillness. I hope bearded old father time chooses to erase our dishonorable deeds before he wanders off. I hope the bouncing baby boy waiting to replace him knows nothing about who locked Mr. Wall in the safe and never finds out. Maybe 1952 will be better.*

Now I sense, with a peculiar discomforting clarity, what was missing in Edgewater: the street. The stimulating security of all those games! Jump rope with rhythms that strengthened my body and rhymes that led to my love for language. I couldn't share my memories because I didn't want to dilute them and nobody cared. My father's heart attack, then Edgewater. Hours, days, mostly nights when loneliness settled in. Nights when it felt like not getting picked for the team. I still led with my left foot in dancing, got stepped on for it and confused by it. Narrating the Christmas Pageant or carrying boys' knives didn't count. They were inconsequential. I longed for the kind of strength that results from connection. My mother must have longed for connection too.

I've moved more than twenty times, far from my roots. I know how it feels to be an outsider. Loneliness brings a desperation to crawl out, survive, attempt to belong again, like people in a singles' bar where laughter hides the fear of feeling unconnected. Desperation warps perception and brings the risk of bad choices, mistakes and wasting time. Thanks to reviving my childhood years, I recall the strength that feeling connected brings. Better to keep seeking the happiness I felt on 90th Street.

River Views, February 1952

The waters of the river have gone silent. Ice thickens along its surface hiding the flow underneath. Where, in this hidden movement, does New Jersey stop and New York start? No boys or men are fishing. Business on the river stops, no barges, no boats. The ice grows dirty and dangerous. People living along the river grow grim and silent, waiting, locked in like trash frozen in the ice.

I stand alone at the narrow window facing River Road, down the hall from our eighth-grade classroom, scratching the scab on my elbow, breathing steam on the glass, puzzling over what I want to be when I grow up. Definitely not like Mom. She's always losing her keys, her handbag, her shoes. She doesn't know how to fix stuff and broken things alarm her. She's afraid the oven will explode when she lights it with a match to bake macaroni and cheese. Dad isn't afraid of anything, even his enlarged heart that I picture filling his chest. I'd rather be like Dad, except I keep forgetting parts of the plot in his jokes and the critical bit of the punch line.

It feels good to see the big city across the river and be part of the world, but I wonder when the human race will become extinct. It doesn't seem likely since so many children are born, but we make so many mistakes, the first of course, being The Bomb. I read that in ancient Rome, wealthy people took baths in public pools. Water came through lead pipes, slowly poisoning rich Romans without their knowing the cause. We're probably being poisoned today and don't know it. Maybe there will be another Ice Age and we'll become frozen fossils with all the things we've ever learned invisibly stored in our brain like ice cubes.

We think hatred is invisible, but it's not. It isn't even deeply buried. When will we believe that war is a hopeless cause? There's so much killing, yet we seem to ignore it. Korean war killings on both sides of the 38th Parallel, gang wars, assassinations, the Holocaust, even death from poverty and starvation. We don't seem to fix hatred with human rights statements and politicians' handshakes. Was the jail put on the monopoly board to teach us kids a lesson? Is jail a warning against greed, or was it placed there in acceptance of human nature?

Yet I know so many good people. Dave McGarry, one of the boys in my class, is sickly. I don't know what's wrong and am too shy to ask. He's skinnier than me, gaunt and quiet. He wears T-shirts and dungarees and has a slicked back haircut like the other guys. The boys like him, include him in their stuff and sit with him in the schoolyard. How does he not feel sad to be so sick?

Through the window, I notice a barge slowly attempting to haul its lumber down the middle of the river. The first sign that the rapid thaw of spring may be underway. I can't wait to walk home from school watching everything start again.

When we're young, life moves so much slower, minimizing the awareness of time passing. As I age, the pace changes. Instead of slowing down, it speeds up. Each day goes so fast, like the swollen Hudson in springtime, rushing to the Atlantic Ocean. We can learn so much from water, always moving, yet always there. A similar liquidity exists throughout life as we gain more depth. They say we design our own finales. As I continue to exert some impact on the world, life becomes more beautiful. That's why sunsets are so glorious.

◦◦◦◦◦◦◦◦◦◦◦◦◦◦◦◦◦◦◦◦◦

Conversation with Bobby, March 1952

"Hey, let's go outside and cool off," my brother Bobby says as he touches my shoulder and leads the way. We walk around our apartment building in the late afternoon. I look up at the smile beneath his hat and perch myself on the swing.

"We don't get to see each other often enough. You're getting as tall as me; almost fourteen already. Are you wondering what you'll do when you grow up?"

I hesitate, not having any idea – not even feeling like I'm growing up. "Aunt Ida asked me the same question when Aunt Miriam brought us for Passover," I answer in my quiet voice. "A teacher,' I told her and when she nodded, it felt comfortable. I'd like to keep learning forever."

He pushes my swing higher and higher, "I didn't mean what you want to be, just what interests you? "

My eyes notice the sky, the colors of sunset blending with the blues as I think and think. "Truth, but I don't know how to find it. I keep thinking I know it and then find out I don't."

He stops swinging me, which is good because I was way too high. We sit on the bench facing the play area. "There are as many truths as people," he says as he winds his wrist watch. "What kind are you looking for?"

I think about that and notice the stubborn patches of grass in the sidewalk. "See those patches," I point. "Those weeds are trying their best to have a good life. Why doesn't God help them? Why do men build sidewalks with cracks?"

"Wow! You're talking about religion. Tough questions to answer." Bobby got quiet for a long time; then said, "God is inside my head. If you grow up to take after me, your religion may form inside your head too. It's easier there, without the archaic trappings."

Hmmm, I think about going to church with my friends in North Bergen -- kneeling and not knowing what to do. "You're right," I say. "I remember the Jewish mumbles at Grandpa Steinberg's funeral, not understanding anything."

Maybe he's right. However, I'm not sure if Jewish mumbles are archaic trappings and I hesitate to ask. An old black Pontiac enters the parking lot that borders the play area and stops in front of us. Even as I watch the driver get out and walk around towards the front of our building, I still think about what Bobby's telling me. I hope when religion forms in my head, I'll know truth too. I want to tell

Bobby about my feeling the sounds of Hebrew, but he interrupts.

"You'll certainly understand more by asking questions, like you're doing now. Keep it up." He pauses, scratching his head, then continues, "One of the most real things about life is that we're here for a finite period. Now. That's why I asked you. What do you want to accomplish for yourself? How do you plan to help the world become better?"

I don't know what to say. I just want Dad to get better so we can move back to 90th Street where the world was better. Instead I ask him, "When did you start thinking about what you want? ...In the war...or the camp?" Dad said never to mention this to him, but I need to know.

"I watch people," he responds in an almost inaudible whisper. "War had rules and rank that often took precedence over common sense. Peace is possible only if your neighbors share your sense of right and wrong.

"But what about bravery? Audie Murphy, Tab Hunter and Burt Lancaster make movies about brave people that win. I know it's only movies, but some are real stories."

"Courage is situational and so is war and peace. We'll talk about this again," he says, raising his hands behind his head. "But I'd really like to know some things you want to do in your life."

I raise my hands above my head too and as he laughs, I answer with a question again. "What about you, Bobby? What do you want to do?"

"Wish I could have a baby. Imagine having a new life growing inside you. I was with Dorothy when our son Mike was born. Now she's taking a nap 'cause she's pregnant again." He leans back and pats his tummy. "Someday you'll realize how lucky you are to be a woman."

"I can't imagine you're saying that. Maureen and I used to laugh when a man pushed a baby carriage on Hudson Boulevard." I become dejected when I remember Maureen. I miss her so much.

"Diana, choose your passion. Don't be stymied by what other people think." He rubs my neck as I listen. "Just try what seems interesting to you and decide what you want. There's so much to do; you'll need to try everything."

"But I get confused about what's right."

"That understanding will come. Just carefully use that smartness inside yourself. Listen to what your head and heart tells you. Then you won't hurt yourself or others."

I love talking to my brother. No matter how long he's away, he still seems like Bobby. The shadows grow longer and I notice the soil holding that grass in the cracks. I start to comprehend what he's telling me.

"Don't be one of those people who just sit it out – talking about weather, what kind of car they want and what they like to eat. They think about what's on TV or how to make money," Bobby slowly continues with his mouth turning into a frown. "Anything but their purpose for existing...or their wish for immortality."

"But Bobby, we're not immortal. Sometimes, when I'm in a group of people, I have freaky thoughts. I think, 'All these people are going to die.' It takes a while to put those thoughts back into hiding."

We sit together and listen to the night sounds. Traffic rumbling on River Road, the Kotter's dog barking, leaves whispering in the breeze, voices from other windows, unconnected sounds hovering like shadows densing into shapes of my fears, fading around corners, moving like clocks.

"Don't be afraid," he says, hugging me. "You're not a child anymore, but you're still not an adult. Someday you'll understand; possibly not till you're seventy years old. All I know now is that I don't want to turn seventy and realize I missed something and then it will be too late."

And Bobby takes my hand. As we walk back inside into our small apartment. I think, 'I wish I could know exactly everything Bobby knows.' But I do not tell him.

MY STREET

Bobby didn't make it to seventy. But he was right, passion fuels accomplishment. He died at forty-five, the day he had his heart attack. He took all those answers with him. Now he's remembered and loved by a dwindling number of people who understood how deeply he lived. We die slowly as the people who remember us die, until we too are unknown, gone, united with the earth where forgotten bones sleep.

∘⟨∘⟩∘⟨∘⟩∘⟨∘⟩∘⟨∘⟩∘⟨∘⟩∘⟨∘⟩∘

Trading, April, 1952

Dear Maureen,   April 2, 1952

The neatest thing happened. Mr. Wall launched an experiment this spring term. Girls get to take Shop and boys have to take Home Ec. I'm so glad because I hated the taste of the foods we made, especially ones with garlic. Our only fun was when the teacher left us alone in the kitchen with its three sinks. We grabbed those faucet hoses and got into water spraying fights.

I love everything about Shop. We learn to hammer nails with our thumb over the handle to balance and control where the nail goes. We choose what we want to make. I picked a footstool for my dad. The top is filled with foam and covered with fabric which is nailed on. When you lift the top, you can store magazines or anything you want inside.

We trace our design on the wood to make cuts. Then we line up to use the saw, but the teacher helps us. My footstool requires a curvy shape, but the teacher said I'm very patient and diligent. I love sanding and staining the mahogany finish. We only get one hour a week, but when I finally brought Dad my finished footstool, I was proud. It's our first new piece of furniture and I made it.

Meanwhile, the boys were cooking, ignoring the teacher, just *like they ignore Miss Stutz. You should have been in our class the day they brought back their still hot chocolate chip cookies. Vinnie was supposed to add 1/2 cup of chopped nuts, but he added 1/2 cup nutmeg. Our mouths burned from the snippy taste. The best food they made was baked potatoes. They were perfect. Which reminds me, Dad went to Macys in Manhattan and bought a waffle iron. It was on sale now that Fair Trade is being challenged. I learned to make waffles and they're perfect too.*

Mom says I can visit you this summer before I start ninth grade. I can't wait.

Maureen wrote me letters too. Even though she moved to Teaneck, she still wrote about Carl and boys from the Sinagra family in Italy starting their life in America — on the street I had loved. I read them over and over, collecting them in a shoebox -- until Mom threw them away in one of her confused cleaning frenzies.

∞∞∞∞∞∞∞∞∞∞∞∞∞∞

What Counts, April 1952

Most people have cars. There's no one else on our bus to the bridge as Mom, Aaron and I head to the Bronx to visit Aunt Estelle. Dad is in the hospital again. Surrounded by empty seats, we feel the reverberation of the bus' efforts to gain traction on the inclined road.

Not thinking about much, I notice a few boys from my eighth-grade class sitting on the wall by our school. Dave, the two Richies and someone I don't know. After we drive past, in my mind I still see Dave. His image becomes a still life, staying in my head, giving my thoughts an opportunity to shift. The school bricks become a deep red. The grass becomes a taller and greener backdrop to the boys quietly perched.

Dave comes into focus. The gaunt skinny boy who sits in the back row of Miss Stutz' class and never talks. His Adam's apple protrudes. We all know he's sick, but I'm new and don't know what's wrong. Maybe these boys know what horrible thing happened to him and that's why they're drawn to care for him. Suddenly I realize these boys are kindhearted. So what if they fart sometimes and won't graduate. Feels like I'm gaining traction too.

Flying home from Wally's funeral, I realized I was the oldest sibling. No more spoiling, comforting phone calls or chances to understand the world through Bobby's and Wally's perspectives. But I comprehend, as my brothers did, that life is a promise with consequences. Perhaps Dave and his friends understood that also.

What counts is time for reflection. Time to walk a trail, get out of the crowd. The rocks, perhaps produced in minutes, like our creative moments, briefly dominate our lives. Tell me clouds are doing something to the moon they never did before. Sometimes my girls teach me lessons. Long nights of sparked conversations with men, friends or an intriguing stranger. What causes this— the things you never notice till you notice. Like shadows moving across a rocky hillside as my day ends… We all want more time.

◇◇◇◇◇◇◇◇◇◇◇◇◇◇◇◇◇◇◇

West Point, May 1952

Dad signed my permission slip. I'm going on a real field trip, my first ever. Dad gave me a fifty-cent piece to buy lunch. I tucked it through the hole in my jacket pocket, safely buried near the hem. We're on our way to West Point Military Academy for our class graduation trip. I sit near the front of the school bus, my zits covered in Clearasil. Adolescent pimples are stifling, puss-filled things that require hours of attention with zit-poppers and witch hazel.

146

It's still cold this morning. I prefer cold even though it's fun to see the trees greening. Warmth feels stifling, enervating like Richie's knife tucked into my sock, so I can't cross my legs.

Last year I saw the movie "West Point" with Gordon McRay and Doris Day. Modern Romance magazine said that Doris Day gets rubbed every night with Vaseline. She sleeps that way so she will stay young. Yuck! The movie wasn't great, but it was my first movie since I moved to Edgewater. You need a car to get to the movie theater in Fort Lee and we don't have one.

The grounds at West Point are large, acres and acres. We visit a library filled with books about wars and information about weapons. Next, we stop in the museum to look at the old guns and rifles in glass cases. We stop for lunch and I buy a Milky Way and ice cream sandwich.

After lunch, Miss Stutz takes us to the parade grounds where we sit on benches. The cadets march and do their drills for us. The closely cropped plebes contrast with my classmates who walk around smoothing their ducktails. Peg and I whisper about which cadet we want to kiss us on the Kissing Walk, but Miss Stutz gives us one of her "Be Quiet" looks, so we listen to the speeches. Even though truce talks are going on, our soldiers are still fighting. A man whose chest is covered with ribbons reads names of Army soldiers killed last month. I don't understand war. Next time my brother Bobby visits, I'll ask him even though Dad forbids me to talk to him about the war and his imprisonment in the POW camp.

We've wasted all this time on speeches. Now it's already time to go back to Edgewater. Someday I will return and stay until I've seen everything and been kissed. And I'll bring money to buy souvenirs at the gift shop.

Never made it back to West Point, but for years I cheered for their football team when the Army-Navy game was on the radio. Although Army was my favorite, I learned to respect all our military. I'm proud of my work on the Army's Apache helicopter line. This aircraft saved many lives, but I wish they weren't needed anymore. Until then, "First to fight for the right and to build the nation's might, and the Army goes rolling alone."

⧓⧓⧓⧓⧓⧓⧓⧓⧓⧓⧓⧓⧓⧓⧓

Eighth Grade Graduation, June 1952

Thirteen of us are graduating from my eighth-grade class. Since I'm the tallest, I have to stand in the middle. I'm 5'9" and still under 100 pounds, all arms and legs, a skinny oddity. The tall boys already quit school when they turned sixteen. Several other boys didn't pass.

Mom bought me White Rain shampoo so my hair could smell like the countryside. I'm trying to grow my hair long enough to braid like Carol Lawson. I watched Richie dip her braid into the inkwell, but she tugged it back. Miss Stutz didn't see them, just like she never sees us shoot spitballs and throw erasers. Dad says you only tease people you love. Does Richie love Carol?

Mom bought me a pink dress with a crinoline slip which I starched over and over in sugar water. Yuck, Miss Stutz is wearing a pink dress too and she fixed her hair in banana curls. What a nutcase!

At our graduation party at Dorothy's house, we play records and drink beer. Then Joe White yells, "Time for Spin the Bottle." I'm scared and worried about getting kissed, but hoping it's Joe. Everyone seems to laugh and enjoy their turn. The bottle comes to me, but I don't spin it hard enough. It doesn't point at anyone. "Spin it again," everyone yells. I grit my teeth and twist it as hard as I can. It ends up in front of Jimmy. My first kiss is ruined by a wet smooch from a stupid boy. I decide not to count it as a first kiss.

But there is a boy I'm ready for a reunion with. He was a sailor -- a cousin of my upstairs neighbor, Patty. She was one of those strong girls with short blond hair who could play sports. Patty and I had nothing in common except for being neighbors. I knew her from waiting at the school bus stop, but everyone in the building knew us because my father cried out in pain every night. Just like everyone in the building knew Mrs. McMahon who played the piano.

It was the summer of 1956, after my graduation from high school. Patty's cousin was a quiet sailor: young, pleasant features, tall. He merely wanted to 'go out' while he was on leave. I never learned anything about him. Was he heading back to Korea? Neither one of us said much. How can a young boy, who's too shy to talk, fight in a war? How can he be brave when he doesn't know anything yet?

I tried to copy everything Patty did cause my only other date had been in 9th grade. I don't remember where we went or who Patty was with. I just remember driving home down River Road in the back seat next to this blond sailor in his navies. He kissed me slowly — a real kiss -- not like the boys tried to do when we played "Spin the Bottle" at parties. His lips touched me softly, gently, naturally. I still remember the surprisingly pleasant taste.

Dearest Diane   June 25th 195

Many moments I sit and think
Just wishing you the best of everything
I was proud of you on this day June 25
My sincere wishes for your future Happine
Mother

June 19th 1952

Diana dear —
Each of us — a quarried stone in which lies imprisoned a god or a goddess — has the duty to chisel and allow ourselves to be carved — to please the utmost potentialities in ourselves. May the sculpture of your life be beautiful and true!
Every blessing upon you
Your uncle Buddy

To my darling niece, Diana,

As important as being well educated, is the talent of getting along well with people, and taking each situation as it comes, with wisdom and good humor. I wish you the best of everything, always.
love, Aunt Esther

6/18/52

Dear Diana —
Your sweet disposition — your consideration for others and your earnest desire for a full life — may you be blessed with all of these — and may it be my pleasure to help you hold on to the qualities you now possess —
— Aunt Mirian

June 23, 1952

To Diana —
Keep your face always towards the sunshine, and the shadows will fall behind you!
Florence & Joe McMahon

June 1952

Dear Diane:
May Life always go smoothly for you, as a sweet girl like you deserves the best of everything
Love Aunt Estelle
Uncle Arthur

June 23, 1952

When you get old
and out of shape
remember girdles are
only $2.98.

Your Classmate
Patty Geiler

June 20, 1952

In Chinese they say
" Zing Zay, Soo"
In American it means
" Good luck to you.

your friend
Joan Socoloff

June 20, 1952

Dear Diane,

California girls are pretty,
New York girls are smart,
But it takes a New
Jersey girl to win a
mans heart.
All the luck in
the years to come
Your old neighbor
Carmella Sinagra

6/19/52

Dear Diane,
You may fall
from a window,
you may fall from
above, But the best
way to fall, is to fall
in love.

2 young
2 go
4 boys

your friend,
Betty Maier

June 23, 1952

Dear Diana,

Girls in Ridgefield are pretty,
Girls in Englewood are smart,
But it took a girl from
Edgewater, To win "Billies"
heart.

your friend,
Dorothy Rabin.
"Denny"

6/19/52

to Diana

Don't kiss at the garden gate
love is blind but the neigbors
ain't

your friend
Cleo

6/23/52

To Diana:

You can take a local
You can take an express
But don't get off untill
you reach success.

Yours till
Bear Mountain
dresses
Pinky Roe

1952

To Diana,

Remember Grant,
Remember Lee,
The heck with them,
Remember me,

Patricia Sanders

Dear Diana,

There's a meter in the cellar
there's a meter in the park
But the best place to meet
her is to meet her in the
dark.

Marianne Petti

June 19, 1952

Diana,

A box of powder
a can of paint
Will make a girl
just what she ain't

2 good
2 be
4 gotten.

With love
Mary Vincent

152

6/23/52

The best of luck

from the handroom
Richard Cohen
52

To Diana

Good Luck

Dave Mc Garry

June 29, 1952

Dear Diana,
Roses are red violets
are blue, you have a
puss like a B-22

David Blosvern
Darling

June 23, 1952

Diana
two little boys
siting on a fence
one married Diana
and the other had
sence.

Max Schmidhamer

June 23, 1952

Good Luck
Diana

Joseph White

MY STREET

Pressure Cooker, summer 1952

Mom's banging pots out of our kitchen cabinet when I arrive home from my walk. I'm planning to fix bread and Swiss cheese, but our kitchen's as narrow as a railroad car aisle. One bustling, heavy-handed person fills it. While I wait, I steal a sip of Mom's instant Nescafe, still warm on the table in the parlor. Her cigarette is burning the corner of her ashtray. I stub out her butt and give up on her coffee. She adds canned Carnation milk and too much sugar.

I smell tomato sauce. The pressure cooker is starting to steam and whistle. I stand in the kitchen doorway, watching Mom chop iceberg lettuce on the kitchen drain. I'm curious, but not enough to ask. Mom hardly ever cooks. She uses the kitchen to wash clothes. Are we having company?

"What's up Mom?" I finally ask, not expecting an answer. At first, I don't get one. Then, "Bob and Dorothy have a new baby girl, Pattie. We'll have a special dinner to celebrate."

It seems to me that the pressure cooker is on much too high a flame. It's rocking on our chipped two-burner gas stovetop. Mom is distracted by the mayo/ketchup mixture she's stirring in a cup. I decide it's time to read <u>Little Women</u> once again. I'm trying to focus on Jo's exploits when the kitchen explodes. I run into a real mess. The pressure cooker has burst, as promised by its horrific noises. Chicken cacciatore, all over the ceiling, walls, kitchen counter, floor and Mom.

"Are you okay?" I yell.

At that moment, Dad opens our apartment door. Oops, I forgot to pick him up at the bus stop. He runs into the kitchen and grabs the pressure cooker off the stove. We stare at the mess. He looks at me and walks out the door.

I help Mom clean the floor, scrubbing away the onion bits and greasy sauce, red all over, like blotched blood. By the time I wash the floor the second time, Dad returns. He unwraps a T-bone steak and starts to fry it on the cleaned-up stove. I've never seen a T-bone before except on TV. He cuts me a small piece, well done, the way he likes meat. We take it to the table and sit down together to eat. It's not a pleasant moment. I can tell by my dad's face that he's in pain. I sense the discomfort in his chest and realize Mom doesn't help him. She keeps scouring the kitchen and Aaron eats his cereal. Suddenly I realize I'm going to have to help Dad -- much more than just picking him up at the bus. I jump up to bring him his nitroglycerin pills and sit with him so he won't be alone with his pain.

Every child begins to realize that adults don't have it so easy. Parents know things they don't tell us kids. I didn't know what was bugging my parents, but observing them created doubts about what was ahead for me. I hoped when I was grown up and free, I'd have a better life than my parents. Such childhood egotism makes me smile for we are an extension of our ancestors. Yet, in our youth, each generation wants to dissociate with the learning of their previous generation. Then something happens that reminds us who we are, what is the right thing to do. I first realized this when climbing my favorite gnarly tree in our North Bergen lot. Both difficult and fruitful years caused that tree to droop and bend, yet still continue to grow... so do we.

◇◇◇◇◇◇◇◇◇◇◇◇◇◇◇◇◇◇

The Breakdown, August 1952

Climbing the wooden stairs to the almost-empty elevated train platform scares me. I'm afraid of stairs with see-through spaces. Mom and I are the only ones waiting so far. Bloomfield station is so bright in the glare of the early August afternoon, before any shadows appear. The short train approaches, whooshing and clacking, a maze of colors. We climb into an empty car. The ripped rattan seats are not reversed, as if the conductor saved himself some work.

Mom is very quiet, very inaudible. She looks straight ahead like she's thinking. We do not talk. Riding the train without Dad is new to her. She worries about the route and bus connections. We don't have our car anymore, plus we live in a new town. I know Mom is upset. We just left Aunt Jean's house after Uncle Dan took Mom to visit Dad in the hospital. He's had a relapse, a second heart attack, one year after his first.

I look out the window and try to learn the names of the towns on my right as we stop at the stations: *Bloomfield, Watsessing Avenue...* A man gets off and two people get on. When I peek at Mom at each station stop, she is puckering her face and twisting her hands around the skirt of her black flowered dress, the good one with the white shawl collar and the carved buttons. I notice because my Uncle Arthur is a button salesman.

Newark, Jersey City, Hoboken... People stare at us as we board our bus that takes us past Palisades Park to Fort Lee. Mom's hat has fallen onto the floor. She must have lost her hatpin. Her hair is falling out of her rolls. Her feet, in squeaky Dr. Scholl's open-toed shoes, are starting to swell. Mom has big feet and perpetual corns. But she's still beautiful in spite of her big, distended stomach that prompts my friends to ask me if I'm going to have a new brother or sister.

Jersey City, West New York... Mom starts to murmur, "I've been poisoned. I'm going to die. Those Krohns poisoned me. They never liked me." She starts to yell, "Aaron, my baby, where are you? Watch out!" She turns and sees me sitting next to her in the empty car, "Di-ann, watch out, watch out, they'll poison you too. You'll see. They gave me poison. It was in my food. I'm going to die!"

*Cliffside Park...*I slouch down in my seat, thinking about what being poisoned means. I wonder if she ate arsenic like in the movies, or if they gave her something bad to drink. When she first told me, I thought she would get over it quick, but she doesn't. She repeats herself over and over, too softly to be understood, but faster and faster, with growing distress while warning me again to be careful. Finally, we get off by the George Washington Bridge in Ft. Lee.

People stare as we wait to board the bus to Edgewater. But Mom sits in silence on the two-mile ride along the Hudson, polluted with old car tires and beer cans. We get off at our stop. The murky river water, like the poison mom's afraid of, is lapping silently toward us. She's still silent for the half-block walk to our apartment, but it seems like a long journey.

Entering our parlor, instead of sensing safety in the warm summer twilight, Mom starts raging again. She lies on her back in her bed, crying out, her fear rippling out in circles to fill the room. I don't know how to help.

"I've been poisoned," she keeps explaining. Then her head goes someplace else. She shouts for Aaron to watch out, to be careful. She moans. She sobs.

"Aaron's with Aunt Estelle in the Bronx," I keep trying to tell her, but she still worries about my brother.

I don't know how to help. I don't want anyone to see her like this. Everyone already makes fun of her. She screams, again and again. I realize I have to do something. I bring her a glass of water from the kitchen to help the poison move through her body. She sees the glass and panics. She looks terrified, like the people Peg and I saw in science fiction movies when they find an "X" marked on their neck and know their bodies have been taken over by evil aliens.

Mom's become an alien, singing on one note. She spits at me as I watch her. I don't know how to make her stop. She continues spitting at me. Why does she treat me like this? Suddenly her spitting shifts me into a different place. Now I begin to wonder if maybe she isn't poisoned. I register the understanding that she needs help quick. Her mind seems powerless and soiled like the cities we passed through on the train and bus, where people live too close together.

I run into the bathroom and hide my face in the brown towel. I'm not sure what to do. Who can help her? None of her sisters. I can't call Dad. I don't even know which hospital he's in and sometimes he hits Mom. I can't let the neighbors hear her because Mom's afraid to let neighbors know about our family.

Then I do the unforgivable. I pick up our black telephone with its long-coiled cord and take it into the bathroom so Mom can't hear. I hide my face in the towel to muffle the sound, dial the operator and ask for Aunt Miriam's number. She's the one who's invited us for Thanksgiving, with everything done at the same time and everything tasting perfect. I also know she's my dad's sister, therefore she might be the enemy. But Mom is suffering. If she isn't poisoned, something is wrong--some horrible thing that makes her spit at me.

"Aunt Miriam," I whisper quietly into the mouthpiece. "Please help me. Mom is sick and she says she's going to die from poison." Such hard words to say.

Somehow I feel that Aunt Miriam understands me over the phone. She knows what to do. She tells me, "Stay with her. Talk softly to her and tell her you'll make her better. Listen for the door. I'm sending the doctor now."

I don't look in the bathroom mirror. I don't want to see myself. I'm still not sure I did the right thing. I feel broken. I listen till the dial tone clicks to its end. I listen till the doctor comes with his black bag. Then a police officer arrives and I answer his questions. Mom really screams when they go into the bedroom, then she just feebly moans and cries. The doctor uses our telephone and I overhear him talking about a place called Bellevue for evaluation. They wait for Aunt Miriam. It is very confusing. Nobody seems to notice me.

Many breakdowns during her remaining years. All those hospitals and half-way homes until the final eight years with congestive heart failure and dementia. Plenty of good memories in-between, especially her times with Judy, Margot and Valerie, her granddaughters. They brightened her face and her life and even got her to quit smoking.

◇◇◇◇◇◇◇◇◇◇◇◇◇◇◇◇◇◇◇

Bloomfield, September 1952

A few weeks ago, my life totally changed. Dad was home from the hospital after his second heart attack, but now Mom was far away in a different hospital. It felt like two bombs had now exploded, damaging my family beyond repair. I wasn't sure what to do. I lay on my stomach on my parent's bed, trying to pressure away my tummy ache. I should have been taking care of my dad and brother. I should have ordered food from the grocery, but Dad didn't leave any money. I should have been cooking dinner. But I felt dragged down, spiritless, guilty.

Dad arrived home from work and caught me lying on the bed. He didn't say anything. He took our phone into the bathroom. I put my ear to the door, but wasn't able to make out any words. I went into the kitchen and broke some eggs into a bowl. Then Dad joined me and declared, "Tonight you and Aaron are going to live with Aunt Jean and Uncle Danny for a while."

"Dad, I'll be good," I objected. "I like to help." He didn't say anything. He just packed our clothes in paper bags as I transformed Wonder bread into French toast.

We arrive late in this chilled September night. I rub my eyes to wake up. Aunt Jean opens the door, smiling, as we walk up the porch steps. She takes us into a hallway leading to gobs of rooms and a flight of stairs. "Shhhh as we go upstairs," she whispers. "Your cousins are already asleep because they have school tomorrow."

Aaron gets to sleep with Marvin in the bigger bedroom. I share my cousin Daron's room. I fall asleep on

159

the narrow folding army cot, but keep waking up during the dark night. No sounds of traffic, no clinks from the radiator, no snores from my parents. I lie there remembering my dream more than where I am and why. Mom was being taken away by two men. They don't notice me, but for a moment I lock eyes with Mom. She stares in panic, ready to scream or run. But I know she won't get the chance to run. I wake up realizing I'm in Daron's room and Mom is in the Asylum for the Insane in Morris Plains. It takes me a few moments to become aware of where I am when I'm in a place I've never been. I bury my head in the feather pillow and close my eyes hoping my dream will float away.

Inside my head, behind my eyes, is my secret plan. Dad will take us home and this time I will be a good girl. No more cramping tummy aches or lying in bed trying to make them go away. I know that's why we're at Aunt Jean's. I was a bad girl. I didn't take care of my dad and brother. I failed, just like Mom. But guilt over my inadequacies takes up too much room in my mind. I replay that evening in the fantasizing part of my brain, except I have supper ready, the house clean and everything under control. This is how dreams happen. Our heart beats faster and our imagination fires up with all the possible ways to fix things. Although I wish for a happy ending, I feel the strange dark desolation, the tightness of Daron's small bedroom. The ache of morning begins.

My dreams remain on the long walk to my new school at the other end of Bloomfield, my head under Aunt Jean's umbrella. The calm is eerie, even in the monotonous drumming rain. The whole world seems gray in the downpour. My brother and cousins are still in elementary. I must be the only junior high kid on this section of Washington Street since we live only a few blocks from Cedar Grove, the next town.

I was a new girl in eighth-grade last year. Now I'm the new girl again, in ninth grade. My thoughts keep me company through the confusion of changed classrooms, teachers and rules. After Miss Stutz' small eighth grade, I feel lost among hundreds of strangers who don't talk to me. They started school last week and know what to do.

I take a few wrong turns and arrive home late. All the lamps are lit. Aunt Jean greets me with, "You don't have to go to school for the next two days. It's a Jewish holiday."

Turns out it's the night before Yom Kippur. Aunt Jean and her sister Maxine are hurrying to finish making jumper dresses for Daron and her cousin Sharon. I watch them stitch boxes onto the corduroy with its puffy lining underneath. Seams, waistbands, underarm and neckline stitches hidden on the underside, and finally hems. They keep calling Daron and Sharon over to check for fitting. The dresses fit perfect, a vibrant blue, soft corduroy.

The temple is already crowded when we arrive early the next morning. It's a sweltering Indian summer day, but the Rabbi is soothingly interesting. He tells first-rate stories and pronounces witty comments to keep us praying and singing. When we don't sing loud enough, he pleads, "Sing, you sinners," and we smile.

Many kids leave to play outside in the courtyard. If I had a new blue corduroy jumper dress to show off, I'd probably go into the courtyard too. I'm wearing my plaid skirt with safety pins in the waist and my baggy white blouse. Anyway, I don't mind staying in the temple. I love the feel of infinity in existence, surrounded by people praying. It's comforting to be hidden in their depths.

Good thing I didn't have proper clothes because I experienced being in a temple for the first time. Playing outside in my safety-pinned hand-me-downs might not have left me with the same fond memories. Besides, I was the 'good girl'.

'Good-bad' dominated my 50's value system. When something bad happened, I'd feel vulnerable in a way I rarely experienced, a tiny hairline crack appears in my

self-image. I always tried to be a good. As the environment influenced my thinking, I refined my system to 'better-best'. Good-bad was easy. Better-best created a perfectionist monster. Raising my family meant being the first one up in the morning, preparing a nutritious breakfast with 100% of the USDA vitamins and minerals. Getting the kids off to school, the business suit, attending meetings and conferences assertively and efficiently. With homework in my attaché case, I rushed home to prepare a 30-minute gourmet dinner. Then the important time of day with the kids till their bedtime. Finally, the quiet time of companionship with my husband and hours of you-know-what.

Does this marketing of super people make us counterproductive? You try harder to get rid of guilt. But no matter how hard you try, there's always that seed of discontent with yourself for not achieving perfection. Even courses on relaxation leave me trying to attain the ultimate in relaxation. Now I realize the answer is within ourselves. There's another level of refinement in our decisions. When I lived with Uncle Buddy in 1957, he once cautioned me to recognize my big appetite and develop a sense of taste.

◇◇◇◇◇◇◇◇◇◇◇◇◇◇◇◇◇◇◇

Teenage Hunger, November, 1952

All the way home from school, I'm starving. I'm always hungry. Daron, Marvin and my brother and I stay in school clothes and do homework. No one plays in the street. I set the table for dinner: plates, forks, knives and teaspoons if we're getting ice cream for dessert. The plates don't match. Aunt Jean's rule is that chipped ones don't get thrown away until they crack completely. I set out jelly glasses for our sodas.

Sometimes I'm so hungry after school, I sneak Oreos from the pantry. When the dwindling supply is noticed by

Aunt Jean, she yells, "Who ate all the cookies? That's it! I'm never buying cookies again!" I act uninvolved, innocent, never admitting anything.

When I grow up, I plan to make supper every night just like Aunt Jean. Everyone will gather around my table enjoying good food. I will reign over my house, even if my kitchen floor is uneven and sagging just like Aunt Jean's, and the table, with its added leaves, is too close to the Formica counters, sink and stove.

Imagine my hungry anticipation, walking into the wash of warm light of the kitchen heated by steam from the pots on the stove, the smells of dinner cooking, ready to be served right from the pot. The tasty food fills some ancient longing in my body. Spaghetti with chop meat sauce, liver and onions (my favorite), hot dogs with beans, fish sticks, hamburgers and fried chicken with mashed potatoes. Kids get drumsticks, thighs and necks. I like the neck. On Friday night there's boxed cod for the kids and boxed breaded shrimp for Uncle Dan and Aunt Jean. Occasionally we get to taste a crunchy, chewy shrimp. Sounds of conversation fill me with comfort, even though I don't listen.

Everyone helps except Uncle Dan who sits like a guest of honor. Susie, the dog, gets the scraps, but I never leave

any. The mess is left for the kids to clean up. As the oldest, I usually wash the dishes, unless Aunt Jean is mad at someone and punishing them with dishwashing. I love everything about our dinners, but am too shy to tell Aunt Jean that I think she's super.

Loneliness and hunger have interesting similarities. Both are invisible under-layers that emerge when certain conditions erode. My marriage breaks into pieces like a cracker. Those who made us cease to exist. Traditional roles change. Jobs take our daily energy. Besides these more obvious triggers, underneath the surface a vast array of wounds and conditioning cause metaphorical cracks in our foundations. We hunger for food or diversions to shore up these cracks in the fault line to a certain degree. But, as Nietzsche observed, "The only way out is through."

Sometimes we learn when we're not aware that we're learning until we're in a situation where we need to use what we learned. Dinners at Aunt Jean's yielded more than nutritious foods. At her table, Aaron and I were part of a supportive family unit. Her example led to me keeping my kitchen stocked with predominately healthy foods, hot cups of tea prevalent, and holidays offering the overabundance of Jewish mother syndrome. Although the real cure comes from within, these reminiscences amplify the antidote to loneliness and hunger. As I write, in the sullen calm before sleep, memory becomes the passion with which I feed myself today.

∞∞∞∞∞∞∞∞∞∞∞∞∞∞

My First Date, spring 1953

Aunt Jean belts out "Though April showers may come your way..." Mom sang too, but Aunt Jean's melodies are cheerful. I wonder if Mom still sings and if there's anyone to listen. But she's locked away in a mental hospital and we're stuck living here. We aren't treated the same as our cousins. "You're the oldest," Aunt Jean always explains, "so you can do more."

I wash dinner dishes while the other three dry, each trying to do the silverware and avoid the pots. I pick up branches when Uncle Dan trims the tall bushes bordering the yard, but I don't mind. Every week I clean the bathroom, sweep out Aunt Jean's bedroom and ours. I sweep the dirt down each step and pick it up at the bottom. I only mind when Aunt Jean sits downstairs in her lounge chair, reading her romance novel, saying, "You missed some dust, Diana. Sweep the stairs again."

Aunt Jean lets me play with anyone. She doesn't ask what their father does. Since she's strict with Daron, I feel that what happens to me doesn't matter. Until a few days after Easter when Maurice Fox calls. "Diana, the phone's for you," Daron yells.

"Hi! Uh, this is Maurice from English class. Uh...I was wondering if you'd like to go to the movies with me this Friday night."

Sounds like he's reading from a script. Unfair, because I need more time to think about what's happening. I hardly know Maurice, although he's in my English class. Maybe it's just a joke. But after all, it's a chance for a real date. "Yes," I stammer into the holes in the black mouthpiece, praying not to hear laughter at the other end.

"Great! I'll pick you up at a quarter after six. I have to be at work by 6:30. I usher at the Center Theater and I'm allowed to bring a guest. See you soon."

I love the attention I get from Aunt Jean after his phone call.

"Which movie?"

"I don't know."

"How are you getting there?"

"I don't know."

"What do you know about him?"

"I don't know."

"Is he Jewish?"

"I don't know."

"I'm going to call your cousin David to see if he knows the family."

Maybe she cares about me after all. I assume Aunt Jean's satisfied with the answers because next thing I know it's Friday. Aunt Miriam loaned me another of Florence's dresses. I look real nice, but I feel strange. The wool doesn't feel right touching my skin in this spring weather. But it's too late to change and I have nothing special to change into.

I hear Maurice knocking at the front door. Oh no! Aunt Jean answers the door. Daron, Marvin and Aaron stand around watching Maurice walk in, smelling of talcum powder and aftershave lotion. I hardly recognize him away from school, here in Aunt Jean's entry hall wearing a black Philip Morris-type uniform. I wait while Aunt Jean says a bunch of stuff until Maurice interrupts, "My dad's waiting in the car. We better go."

I hadn't anticipated what a date would be like or what I should do. So I'm just my quiet self, even though I'm surprised when I get into the back seat of a black Lincoln, with Maurice holding the door. An older man and woman sit in the front seat.

"Mom and Dad, this is my friend Diana. Diana, this is my mom and dad."

Wow, he did it perfect, just like Mrs. Farley taught us to do introductions in seventh grade. I'd have been nervous as to who came first. I just said, "Nice to meet you."

"They're dropping us off at the theatre," Maurice explained, without looking at me. Then there was no more talking. I'd never met such polite people. I wonder if they're going to be our chaperones all evening.

"We'll pick you up when the movie's over," they said to Maurice as he helped me out of their car.

"I've got to usher during the movie," Maurice says as we walk into the lobby without paying. I must be wearing my perpetual frown because Maurice quickly adds, "You can have any candy you like. I get it free." I pick Good & Plenty, Tootsie Rolls, Licorice Nibs, Hershey's chocolate with almonds, Milky Way and spice drops. He escorts me to my seat and walks up and down the aisle keeping order.

I'm not a Doris Day fan, especially now that I know about her Vaseline addiction. *West Point* was a much better movie. Dad says she sings trite Tin Pan Alley songs. This movie, *By the Light of the Silvery Moon,* is exactly that kind of overdone cliché. Yet, I'd like to believe those silly but sweet words as I munch on my goodies. I even smile at Maurice as he passes me, winking, even tipping his Philip Morris hat.

After the movie, I scratch my itchy skin until Maurice comes to pick me up. I worry that he might try to kiss me. Yuck! But we don't say much because his parents are waiting outside to drive me home. They don't talk either. Possibly they're shy, like me.

"Thanks, Maurice. I had a great evening," I politely offer the conventional white lie, hoping my eyes don't change or vibrate. Life sure isn't like the movies. Your wishes don't come true. '*Que sera sera.*' It was a very boring date. Think I won't count it.

Everything has an expiration date. Aaron and I moved back to Edgewater in June and I never saw Maurice or my other Bloomfield friends again. They say we start over every day, but I didn't date again until my high school graduation party. That boy counted; he was the valedictorian.

◟◞◟◞◟◞◟◞◟◞◟◞◟◞◟◞◟◞◟◞◟◞

The Curse, May, 1953

Every year there must be tens of thousands of girls beginning to menstruate. Most of them are between eleven and thirteen, just like me. Hildegarde Schmidtheimer in Edgewater claimed to have gotten the curse when she was in fifth grade, but I also heard toilet paper crackling inside her bra, so I tended to not believe her. What will happen to my body is still a mystery. I'm the tallest and least curvy girl in my class.

Here's how I learn what I know. I listen to the girls as we walk down Franklin Street to school. They aren't my real friends, but we walk the same route. No short cuts. By the time we finish the trek to Bloomfield Junior High there's about a dozen of us.

Imagine us joining up every morning. We barely say *Hi* before someone has a complaint about their period. I pay attention, drinking in every word.

"I'm back in the saddle again," Kate moans.

"The curse is back," Marla complains another day.

Cindy tends to ask, "Can you smell it?" She does smell a bit foul in the heat, but that's Jersey for you.

"I took six Midol, lay down on six books, and I'm still dying from cramps," Amy whines every month. She also exaggerates about kissing boys. I'm usually silent, too shy to assert myself, but in this case I truly have nothing to say, which doesn't mean I don't care. I don't know what they're experiencing. I just don't know what they know.

On the route home, it's worse. No one thinks they're going to make it.

"I feel the blood pouring out. Is it showing?" Marla asks me, panicking. "I'm wearing Jumbos." Blood showing is much worse than your slip showing.

"I don't see any," I reply, really not wanting to look. What a horrible curse! We check her skirt constantly, looking for the telltale bloodstains. Girls that get blood on their skirt during class are mortified. Washing it in the girls' room doesn't help, it just makes a wet blood spot. All you can do is maneuver your skirt around so it looks like you ran into something from the side or front. Amy got a big blood spot last week in fourth period English class. At lunch, she cried and called her mom to come to school and get her. Then she didn't show up for days, claiming, "My period was sooo bad." But I'll bet it just took a few days to get over her embarrassment.

Every time our science teacher pulls down the Chart of the Periodic Table, we have to put our heads down to stifle our giggles. If we see any boys, our humiliation is worse. The boys in my class try to act tough and grown up. They say things to each other that we can't quite hear, and laugh. When they see us walking home, they raise their middle finger, the "f--k" hand signal. But they have more acne than facial hair. I have no interest in any boy.

I want to be like the other girls, but I hardly even have zits anymore. Sometimes I feel like gravity is settling into my stomach, but no real cramps. I scrutinize my chest in the bathroom mirror every morning. Nothing's growing.

Last week, Aunt Jean's mother, Mrs. Zwerling, took my second cousin, Toni (she's in ninth grade too), to buy a bra. We went to the lingerie store on Bloomfield Avenue, with hundreds of undies to choose from. The saleslady, a woman older and more wrinkled than Mrs. Zwerling, brought us into a small dressing room. When Toni removed her blouse and slip, I couldn't believe her boobs. They were perfect, rounded, the same color as the rest of her chest, but soft and new looking. Not like my Mom's which were the only other ones I've seen. Wow! When will this happen to me?

I was wearing my plaid dress, the one with gathers that almost makes me bulge a little. Mrs. Zwerling and the saleslady told me to take off my dress. I didn't want to, but I silently obeyed. They looked at my miserably flat chest and said, "No, you don't need a brassiere." "Not even ready for a trainer." Words with the power to shatter my face.

Then finally this afternoon, when I'm going to the bathroom, I wipe blood. I'm shocked, scared. As usual at Aunt Jean's house, there's a line outside the bathroom door, with everyone saying, "Hurry up!" I don't know what to do. I keep wiping, but I'm still bleeding. I stuff my panties with toilet paper. I sit on the edge of my cot in Daron's room, afraid to move, waiting to go back into the bathroom. Suddenly I realize this messy deal is "it". Neat!

I knock on the door to Aunt Jean's bedroom. She's taking her afternoon nap. Walking up to her bed, I notice how her legs taper abruptly at her ankles. I whisper softly, telling her what's happening. "Don't tell anyone," she says.

"You're the oldest. I don't want the younger kids to know anything." She shows me her hiding place for Kotex sanitary napkins, which we all knew about already. She hands me an elastic belt and shows me how to clip on the pad. Then she adds, "Careful not to get any blood on my sheets." That's it, like *Don't bother me*!

Hardly any cramps--nothing like the terrible ache each morning when I wish I could be home in Edgewater again instead of having to live in Bloomfield. I wish I could tell Mom, but she's in the hospital in Morris Plains. She'd have warnings and questions, but at least she'd care. I wouldn't tell Dad, but it would be nice to see him anyway. Sometimes on Sunday afternoon, he stops by on his way home from visiting Mom. I make myself leave that thought before tears start and force myself to think, *I can take care of myself.*

I decide not to tell anyone because I question what the girls tell me--things like when I'm in heat I can get pregnant or you shouldn't wash your hair when you're on the rag because it won't curl. I've heard you shouldn't take baths or touch flowers.

I pile up several school books, big ones so I won't have to use too many, and lie face down with them under my tummy. The corners dig into my ribs. It seems silly. Taking Midol and worrying about bloody drips seems silly.

We're always waiting for something: for supper or school to be out, for our grades or a sign that there is a God. In my case, I'm waiting for Mom to get out of the hospital. But the sad fact is that I wasted so much time over the past months, filling my mind with a hundred petty worries about getting my period. All those details that loomed so large add up to nothing special. Everything is finally happening like it's supposed to. They are small moments after all.

The dreaded curse became the beginning of the next part of my life. Such ridiculous worries: getting the curse, menopause, old age. Worrying can become a consuming preoccupation. My cure for my worry in high school was expanding perspectives: boys!

Some worry can be reassuring because it preempts what is, in actuality, an unknown future. But too much of my life was consumed by worrying. Money, relationships, children... Whether they're three, thirty or almost sixty, a child is always a child in the eyes of a parent. Can't forget health, the economy, even weather. Worrying about weather is a national pastime. Look at the number of TV hours and apps given over to weather. Would it add up to five years, ten years... Whatever the answer, the price of worry is too high and leads into remorse, like shadows crossing spaces that should remain free.

<hr>

Faces With No Names, May 1953

In New Jersey, one of the familiar put-down jokes used against someone is, "You're crazy. You belong in Bellevue or Morris Plains." It's easy to envision the inside of such a place because of the crazy-house scenes in movies. Mad zombie people in their bleak caged-in environments getting electric shock treatments and talking to psychiatrists who usually have foreign accents. I picture murderers, forgotten people, witches and evil men. Most lunatic asylums are on the outskirts of towns. The guards and nurses are depicted as cruel people, for who else would want to work in such a place.

This morning, Aunt Jean told Aaron and me to dress in good clothes. She announced, "Your dad is taking you to visit your mom at her psychiatric hospital." Then she softly added, "Your mom's about ready to go home. It's been almost a year and she's asked to see you."

Dad, Aaron and I exit the Morris & Essex train at Morris Plains. The sun is barely able to penetrate the cloudy May sky. We take a cab to a huge brownstone building surrounded by a brown lawn. Greystone Park State Lunatic Asylum is so much wider and taller than I expected, much bigger than our apartment building in North Bergen. I feel rain tapping at me until we walk inside towards a wrinkly ancient woman at the lobby desk. I'm not sure if she is one of the crazy ones. She talks to herself, ignoring us. "We're here to see Eva Krohn in Ward Twelve," Dad tells her. She still ignores him. Dad doesn't seem annoyed. He acts used to this place. He whispers to us about the building's secret underground tunnel system.

I assume the woman rang a bell or something to summon a guard, because a big, but short, man in a dirty white shirt and pants shows up and says, "Mr. Krohn, let's go in now."

We follow him through several chilly hallways with high ceilings like a church. The man unlocks doors and locks them again from the inside as we enter another corridor. He carries dozens of keys jingling on a keychain, more than our superintendent, Mr. Fuscoe, used to carry. He takes really long steps for a such a short man. I try to take longer steps too. I'll never find my way out if I get left behind.

We enter a big room full of people sitting around in lounge chairs and wheelchairs facing a small television set. "Wait here in this day room," the man tells Aaron and me.

He takes Dad through another door out of the room. Aaron and I look at each other. I take Aaron's hand. "We won't have to wait long," I tell him, hoping it's true.

The dispiriting smell is awful, the smell of urine and farts, cigarette smoke and Clorox and B. O. *Beeeee-oh* is one of our jokes at school. It's what you say to someone you don't like. The calendar on the wall is stuck on November 1951 even though it's 1953. Everyone stares at us. They talk to themselves as they talk to each other. They look broken in some way in the timid light filtering through those thick institutional windows. They don't smile right. There's a lurking look in their eyes. One old lady in a wheelchair is peeing. You can see the yellow puddle spread across her nightie. One of the men unzips his pants and quietly beckons, "Little girl, come over here."

The lady who peed starts crying. One of the men yells, "Change the channel," but there is no channel, just black and white blips across the screen with a buzzing sound.

We don't move. I can't even imagine making my body move. Some of the people try to move too, but they can't seem to. I realize they are just as afraid as we are. I wonder what kind of families they've left behind. I look at those people and try to see their young faces. I wonder what happened to them. One of the crippled men without teeth begs us to get him a cigarette, but we don't know where to get one. I think when they talk to us, they hope their loneliness will go away.

A woman with long streaky hair is trying to get up. "Help me," she moans and Aaron and I go over. Then I notice that her arms are all black and blue, so I'm afraid to touch her.

The guard returns. He doesn't say anything, just leads us through large double doors with two locks. When we see Dad's head sticking out of one of the doorways, we run into the small room. Mom is sitting on a contraption that must be her bed. It's held high by steel framing. Gray belts are attached to the frame. Mom doesn't look like my mother. Her black hair has whitened and she moves slowly. She sits on the edge of her bed and looks at us. Our real mom seems gone, stripped away. Dad says, "Give her a hug," but I'm afraid to go closer. She starts to quietly sob.

She glances up at Aaron. Her face looks crumpled and scared, like it's freezing into a bad mask. She yells, "Aaron, watch out. Watch out. They're going to get you! They're going to take you away!" Her finger points at Dad and me. She doesn't stop screaming. The guard comes and walks us to the lobby to wait for Dad. The old lady is gone from her desk. We are alone.

No one says anything as the cab starts down the wide street taking us to the station. Silence fills the air on the train ride back to Aunt Jean's house. After we climb down the steps, I stop and turn to watch the train leave the station, realizing it still goes on, day and night, just like those people, faces with no names, at the hospital. But they don't get to leave.

Dad sits at Aunt Jean's kitchen table, his face lit by a sliver of weak afternoon sunlight. He slumps like he's tired. His face breaks up into wrinkles. He starts to sob. I know he hurts, but I still can't cry. I still blame myself for Mom being in the hospital, that day I lay in bed instead of taking care of Dad and Aaron. I ruined everything. Now my dad's alone. He sits and cries because of me. I wish I could do it over. I slump down in my chair, miserable. After Dad leaves, I go to Daron's room and lie on my cot. I fabricate a better scene where Mom throws up the poison, gets better and we're still in Edgewater.

June, school's over. Dad's bringing us home this Sunday. Aunt Jean's house has become so familiar as we sit together in her family room after dinner. I've become aware of how much I like living here. Fantastic food and a bed in a bedroom, even if it's just an Army cot. Until this year in Bloomfield, Aaron and I lived without most of the things my cousins and friends take for granted. I glance around, remembering when Aunt Jean and Uncle Dan wallpapered the hunt scene. Uncle Dan and their dog, Susie, lie on the carpet in front of the brick fireplace, watching the flames shift in the air.

Families evolve like webs. We can't understand them without a sense of the whole structure. Our family's web was loosely woven before my father's heart attack. Afterwards, its core threads were strengthened by the support of his brothers and sisters.

When it was my turn to be wife and mother, I often felt like I walked in Aunt Jean's footsteps. She served as my role-model for putting family first. I never thanked her enough for that year of learning. Yet, when I wrote her letters, she didn't respond. I learned to accept that time moves on, clouds shift shape, days end and start once again. Nothing stays the same.

‿‿‿‿‿‿‿‿‿‿‿‿‿‿‿‿

Visiting Aunt Esther, July 1953

Back in Edgewater -- waiting. Not sure for what. It feels like writing, with cross-outs and restarts. Nothing happens till I'm walking Dad home.

"Aunt Esther is inviting you to visit," Dad rasps as he unbuttons his raincoat to take a soggy letter out of his pocket. He stops to rest, out-of-breath from the humid July heat and the walk up the hill from the bus stop. My head fills with thoughts. Dad's sister, Esther, lives someplace near Baltimore so she doesn't usually come to family events. I've never been there. When she does come to Jersey, Uncle Larry stays home with her adopted daughter, Dorothy. Our family knows Uncle Buddy arranged the adoption, even though it's a secret. At Horace Mann, being adopted is sort of an unkind joke. "You must be adopted," the mean kids say when they want to insult someone. But what would it be like to be left for adoption?

"Do you want to go? I can buy a train ticket for Friday morning."

I look up at Dad, although my head is exploding with questions about adoption. "Sure. Okay, I guess…" is all I manage.

I've never been there. *Why now?* I wonder. It's only a month since Aaron and I moved back from Aunt Jean's. Is Aunt Esther trying to adopt me? I don't want to leave Mom even though she embarrasses me. Who would take care of Dad and walk him home when he gets off the bus?

The Newark station is whoppingly big and dim, full of people. Dad and I watch the high board click its platform numbers until we see 'BALTIMORE TRK 14.' We hurry down the stairs, through a tunnel to where the train is waiting with its dim interior lights on. Dad sits me in a window seat and puts my shopping bag at my feet. "Don't talk to anyone," he warns as he leaves. As if I would!

I hope nobody sits next to me because I don't know where I'm going or why or even how long. But any trip on a train is a great start for an adventure. Here I come, woo-oo-woo-oo...

"Mind if we stop for corn on the way home?" Aunt Esther asks as we walk to her Buick. 'No', I think. I'm not sure if I'm thinking that or if I answer. It's quiet after the noisy train. The road soon becomes empty, surrounded by grassy meadows of yellow flowers and patchwork fields of vegetables. Aunt Esther chats about Dorothy: "She's not an easy girl...last week she fell off her bike...her face has stitches...she's away at camp for two weeks...we never thought a girl would be so active..."

Her phrases go on as I think, 'I better not act like Dorothy. I better not fall because I'm always getting bloody knees and elbows.' She talks until we stop at a farm. Aunt Esther chooses ears of corn from the stack. Mom would love this. She fills her bag with lettuce and peppers. "Sixty cents," the farmer's wife informs us.

Then we're back in her car. "Almost home," Aunt Esther promises. "I could have bought those delightful red tomatoes," she adds. "But wait till you see the ones in our garden."

I watch Aunt Esther start dinner. Good smells of frying chicken and fresh vegetables steaming. Then she tells me to go to the parlor and read my book until Uncle Larry arrives home. As I sit with Little Women, I keep glancing up at their pleasant house, not as fancy as Uncle Ted's, but neater than Aunt Jean's. Aunt Esther joins me and starts playing her piano, a grand piano that sits like a leading character in her parlor. Her music's soft, but full of sound. Melody blends with melody and I'm compelled to watch her hands move across the keys.

"Looks like you enjoy Liszt," she says. "I'll play Chopin next. They both lived in France a long time ago." I'm thinking, 'Someday I will own a house with a piano…this music is enchanting…Aunt Esther is beautiful when she plays piano…'

"Has my dad ever heard you play piano?" I ask as she turns the pages of her book, looking for another piece.

"Not very often. Not since we were little kids."

"He would love it. It would take his pain away," I confide to her as she sighs.

"I have eight piano students, but they don't return until September. On Sunday mornings, I play the organ at a church, the one with stone walls and stained-glass windows that we passed down the street."

"How can you play in a church when you are Jewish?" I ask. "I used to go to church with my friends, but felt guilty and a bit afraid. Besides, I didn't know what anything meant."

I already love talking to Aunt Esther. Her voice is so quiet. "Well," she tells me, "I wrote Uncle Buddy and asked him if it was all right." He wrote back, "Good deeds bring people closer together."

"Dad always says Uncle Buddy is larger than life, like FDR and Babe Ruth. Dad's always right, even though I'm taller than him. I love Uncle Buddy too. When he visits us in New Jersey, I feel his presence change the room, like breathing the air of a new place. Maybe someday I'll get to visit him."

"I hope you're enjoying your visit," Aunt Esther says as I notice her tearing eyes are exactly the same color as mine.

"Of course. I think I'll add a piano to my wish list of things I want."

"What else is on it?"

"A red wagon, a bike, a sled and a doll house," and 'I don't ever want to be adopted,' I think to myself.

'NO NIGGERS, DOGS or JEWS', the large black letters on the billboard read, as Aunt Esther and I walk along the fenced walkway leading to the Chesapeake swimming area. Tears leak down my face as I question Aunt Esther, "The sign says we're not allowed to swim here."

"Just be quiet and the man will let us in," she whispers.

"What if we get caught?

"Don't worry. We'll cool off and have so much fun."

Don't worry? Another white lie? And I do worry. I've seen the photos of the atrocities in this century and the frequent stories in our daily newspapers. Is there a human who is not prejudiced? How come Jews are listed after dogs? Negroes and dogs can be recognized, but how does the man know whether we're Jews? I won't know how to answer him if he questions us. I think I'm a Jew whether I practice my religion or not. Luckily, the water cools us and so does the double ice cream cone with chocolate sprinkles, so I finally stop wondering. I'm really just myself, no matter what anyone tries to label me.

It's been six days since I arrived. Each morning has opened with sunlight and good breakfast food from the garden. "Fill up this morning," Aunt Esther declares. "The town of Glen Burnie holds its yearly carnival starting today." Aunt Esther and her friends work as volunteers. I'm going to help them sell cakes. Next to her booth, a long-haired man runs a 'Guess Your Weight and Age Booth.' A huge poster explains how it works. If the man doesn't get the right answer, people win a prize. He calls me over and studies my skinny body. Finally he pronounces, "Sixty-nine inches, one hundred two pounds."

He's amazing! "How do you do it?" I ask.

"I'll teach you. Call me Barney," he answers.

So instead of selling cake, I help Barney. I learn to observe people: the thickness of their thighs, their muscles, the size of their shoes and the thickness of their wrists. Barney listens to my initial estimates and explains anything I miss. Then I start making guesses that count for prizes and do amazingly well. But I can't do one thing Barney does -- touch people wearing baggy clothes. I'm too shy. But it's astounding that I'm mostly right and it's fun to win.

"Come back next year," Barney says. "You've been a great help."

Too quickly, it's time for my train to Newark. "Goodbye, Aunt Esther," I softly say, boarding the coach car with my paper shopping bag. As the train releases its torrent of steam, I think about my week and how glad I am that I didn't get adopted.

After I married, the second piece of furniture we bought for our first home was a baby grand piano. I couldn't play it, but I could hear it playing in my head. It gave my home an identity, even while I still worked on my own identity at twenty-one. It kept Aunt Esther from becoming a forgotten vignette. Since then, it's added character and music to nine more homes.

Take Me Out to the Ballgame, August 1953

Yellow haze persists on this hot August day, not letting the summer of 1953 end. Dad and I walk up the long ramp, one slow step at a time, his left arm against his chest. Crowds of people pass us as I hold Dad's other arm to guide him. We keep stopping to rest and then continue, all the way to our seats in Seventh Heaven. "Yankee Stadium, the best stadium in the world," Dad brags as he takes his seat.

I'd been to Yankee Stadium once, before Dad was sick, when I was a younger girl. Mom, Aaron and I sat with Dad in the hot bleachers. I remember how hot it was then, also. Not a cloud in the sky. Old men wore their pocket handkerchiefs, corners tied in knots, on their heads.

"Hot dogs!" the vendors had yelled. "Peanuts...Cokes...Get your Ballantine beer here!

The hot dogs smelled so good as we passed them to people down our row. I tried not to spill their beers.

"Daddy, can we get hot dogs?" I pleaded.

I imagined that first bite, yum. But then Mom reached into the brown paper bag she had brought and passed down peanut butter and jelly sandwiches. I didn't really care if I was seen eating a homemade sandwich. I liked peanut butter and realized we didn't have extra money for hot dogs. Dad turned away from us in embarrassment and made an angry face. He muttered, "Eva, I'm never taking you again."

So today it's just Dad and me. We watch the crowds of fans and the preparations on the field. People are excited because President Eisenhower signed a Peace Treaty at Panmunjom. Our soldiers are starting to come home and the Yankees have a great team again this year: Mickey Mantle, Yogi Bera, Johnny Mize. Dad and I listen to their games on the radio and watch them on TV.

Vic Raschi gets another RBI as I'm busy passing beer down the row without spilling any. Dad yells, "Casey, you got a good one."

Dad buys us a bag of peanuts and hot dogs and he lets me sip his beer. He tells the man next to him, how well "The Old Perfessor knows his game."

The man is younger than Dad. He tips the brim of his Yankee's baseball cap in agreement and adds, "He's old. The only gray-haired man in uniform, but he made the Big Three this year."

Dad yells with excitement as the Yankees win over the St. Louis Browns, 11-3. "What a game we picked, Diana. Just remember that Number Seventeen got seven RBIs and you watched it. We're ready for playoffs and the World Series."

I never tell Dad, but my favorite team isn't the Yankees. It's the New York Giants: SayHey Willie, Alvin Dark, Hank Thompson. Unfortunately, they play too near where Mom's sisters live so Dad won't go there.

I loved traveling to Yankee Stadium with Dad via Port Authority and the subway. New York with its competing accents, faces from all races and ages, garbage, sour smells, homeless people sleeping on heating vents, smoke from cigarettes and fumes from buses, ads everywhere in this city of cosmopolitan soup.

◦◦◦◦◦◦◦◦◦◦◦◦◦◦◦◦◦◦

My Self-Imposed Immersion Into Judaism, fall 1953

Indian summer is gone. The clouds roll in, gray as the aluminum prototypes Dad brings home from Alcoa. I contemplate the clouds approaching the river, bringing rain from a bygone time. Maybe as far away as God. Since Yom Kippur in Bloomfield last year, no one's brought me back to temple. I'm still a spiritual knucklehead. I don't go to Hebrew School like Barbara, Deanna and Marlene in North Bergen.

Yesterday I found a Jewish book on that high shelf in the hall closet where Mom hides stuff she's afraid of -- the secret Mason book, Wally's New Testament from his grandma, the war picture of Bobby when he was found. Now, with this book, I decide to stay home from school and read for Rosh Hashanah, the New Year.

I put on my Jewish Star necklace, crunch onto my couch bed and hold the worn pages. These ancient words don't feel worn. They have a sheen like the Sinagra's crucifixes. They have guided generations of wandering ancestors subjected to limitations by governments and their neighbors. As I turn the pages, my mind replays the images of piles of bodies and emaciated survivors in newsreels at the Embassy Theater. I wish I could tell them that I'm reading their prayers.

The Rabbi in Bloomfield skipped some prayers, but I don't know which ones to skip. "It is good to give thanks..."

Besides, the thoughts feel special. "Take up the melody and sound the timbrel..."

They are not ordinary. "Blow the shofar at the new moon..."

The Biblical language feels pleasant on my tongue and stays in my mind, even after the sounds of them have stopped. "May the words of my mouth and the meditation of my heart be acceptable..."

Before I found this sacred book, my prayers had been silent ones. Real ones are an absolute gift. I hope God knows I'm reading these prayers even though I hardly understand them. Even the dictionary doesn't explain enough. What is my soul? Will it survive to meet up with Grandma Krohn or Pop, or are the thoughts running through my head all that remain of my grandparents? I still pray, feeling connected even without all the information. It doesn't matter. I know there's far more wisdom in Judaism than meets the eye. I'm learning how things hang together with our history. The mythological stories in the Bible breathe Jewish energy. I want the Jewish soul in me to grow as I grow, until I understand the Bible's mysteries and my heritage takes its natural place in my life.

In our family, it's always been something. Rickets, heart attacks, nervous breakdowns, rheumatic fever and jobs that kept Dad on the road. These events knit together like fractured bones that don't completely heal. We learn to make it look good on the surface, for the neighbors. My parents could use some religion, some prayers to still their sense of foreboding. I don't think there's a chance. They don't even eat Jewish foods or have Jewish friends. I wonder if they've ever been in a temple or if they think about religion. Are they afraid to be Jewish because of the millions murdered in Europe? If they saw the "No Niggers, Dogs or Jews allowed" billboard near Aunt Esther's house, would they be afraid to go inside the gates.

So many unanswered questions. Today, solitude is my temple. I sit, reading about centuries of human struggle, and pray for silence in my head. The clouds are wafting away so quickly, revealing bursts of brilliant sunlight pulsing with energy. I just need to thank God.

Sitting at my desk, I glance up at my bookcase full of Jewish poetry, fiction and texts on Pirkei Avot, Kabbalah, Zohar, Hassidism, Mussar and other enlightening themes building my expansive view of God. I have favorite authors—Weisel, Frankel, Steinsaltz, Sachs and Matt—who help me understand human reaction and human interaction. Why do I have so many books? My family, friends and I have varying degrees of faith or trust. Even secular Jews feel the energy of the Jew. But the more knowledge we have, whether accepted literally or metaphorically, the better decisions we can make. Whether comfortable or not, those decisions build our character and keep our soul from becoming dehydrated, empty or impoverished.

I'm lucky to have been personally influenced by four Rabbis—Krohn, Secher, Koppell and Allouche. Although I believe Judaic values take precedence over rules, I revel in the structure, dimensions, emotion and sense of belonging in religion, both modern practices as well as past mystical teachings.

The White Lie Syndrome, September 1953

What words should I use to tell someone why I was gone for a whole school year? We didn't move. I wasn't pregnant. I don't have an easy answer, so my only recourse is a white lie. I've pondered this syndrome for a long time. When does a cover-up become a white lie? When is it a real lie? At what point do they become sins? Every time I say, "Whoops, that wasn't quite true," I follow a rambling defining process that leads into conscience. What if I forget the cover-ups I've told people? Still, it's easier to live a white lie than to tell the truth.

People go about their ordinary business while events occur all the time. Even though people say, "Mind your own business," they still like to know all your secrets. Maybe if we shared our secrets, we could get closer. Even so, I don't share mine. It isn't just that Mom has been in a crazy house. It's also the way she acts now. It's like not all of her came back. She returned flat, as though an important part of her personality had been surgically removed. Her expression is faraway, distant, as if she's trying to keep her mind wound together like the threads she keeps to crochet doilies.

Mom doesn't speak of her year at the hospital. It's as if she buried time and sealed it away. The men that produced and dropped the bombs over Nagasaki and Hiroshima must have done the same. Even though I imagine her horrors, I don't think Mom will ever talk about that bad experience. Her pills don't remove the agitation crouching behind her eyes. Her face appears less defined and her body heavyset. She looks inches shorter, the weight of her distended stomach seems to pull her down. She hides her sadness in her clenched fists. I try to cheer her up, but she just stares out the window. My stomach tightens. I hate when she doesn't get dressed or comb her hair and when she won't speak to me.

Diana Ruth Krohn

Past our kitchen window, people walk on the sidewalk, peering in from outside with myopic camera eyes. From my parlor bed, I watch active shadows cross the kitchen wall -- across our pictures of a red Mexican boy and dull, muted fruit looking ready to mold. No joy in them or the dusty rays, mysterious shapes, dim features unseen by my mother. They steal past, move across the wall, dissipate into the night's obscurity. The long, spikey shadows retreat as morning light takes over the world I live in.

Mom always cautions, "Never tell the neighbors," so I never want people to know my home life. I long to say, "If you want secrets, read the *N.Y. Daily News*." Reading the personal tragedies of others is voyeurism. The *News* is full of exaggerated lawsuits, crimes and controversies about actors and politicians. I shake with the reminder of just how close to the edge we are in life. Miss Stutz taught us that the world started with a bang, but it appears to me like it's going to end with the whimper mom makes when she's startled. Sometimes I feel as if I'm growing old faster than everything around me.

I'm a bit of a zombie too. Tenth grade means nothing to me. Now that I've returned to Edgewater, Dwight Morrow High is just a place I go because I'm supposed to. Just so I don't get caught chewing gum or puffing cigarettes in the girls' bathrooms. Miss Mears, my guidance counselor, enrolled me in the vocational track. I take mind-numbing classes: typing, business writing and bookkeeping. In my business methods class, we learn to file alphabetically, order supplies, take minutes of meetings and create graphs for speeches.

My teachers usually arrive late, like they don't want to teach us, so the other kids and I kick back and tell jokes. I practice telling Dad's jokes, but most of the kids are Negroes and they know even better jokes than Dad. Englewood has a large Negro section; its most famous resident is Willie Mays. I don't understand how these smart Negro kids got placed in such no-brainer classes.

185

Gregg shorthand has become my secret code. I write everything in Gregg. I listen to the radio and write the lyrics to the pop songs on "Hit Parade" in shorthand. I enjoy the challenge of knowing the words to all the songs, reading them to decipher what I heard that slurred together or went too fast. I notate the news even though the announcer speaks really fast: Stalin's rise to power, Queen Elizabeth II's inauguration, the Rosenbergs' trial. Even headlines of unseasonably warm weather elicit controversy and alarm. I try to catch every word, no matter how fast the newscasters speak. Then I transcribe them on my Underwood portable typewriter.

In frustration, I visited Miss Mears this afternoon to request academic classes. I tried to tell her how squashed I feel in my vocational classes. After listening for only a minute, she interrupted, "Your Aunt Miriam informed me of your dad's illness." Looking down at her desk, she added, "You can't prepare for college since you'll have to support your mother and brother."

Another rejection. I'm being denied the opportunity to pursue the academic track and thus, college. I wonder if it's also because I'm from Edgewater. I wish Edgewater had its own high school. Miss Mears frowned as I pleaded, "I want to study ancient history, Shakespeare, physics and geometry.

"No academic classes are allowed on the vocational track."

"Miss Mears, if I can't study them, I'll be like the dropouts, living my life with only a half-filled brain. Instead of triangles and pyramids, I learn coding in shorthand."

I could tell Miss Mears was becoming sympathetic, so my complaint might have positive results.

"How'd you like to tutor boys in arithmetic? You could take the late school bus home?"

"Sure," I replied, not sure.

"You'll help a few of the football players," she added.

"If they fail arithmetic, they can't play. I'll tell you what else we'll try, Diana," Miss Mears went on. "Since your IQ test score is so high and you're on the Honor Roll, I'll try talking the administration into letting you take the academic history class in eleventh grade. I know you can do it and studying human affairs from the past may help you when you become a secretary. Maybe you can get into Katherine Gibbs Secretarial School after you graduate.

"Thanks Miss Mears."

"Just make an 'A' for me."

I remember thinking, 'Maybe her promises are just words, white lies.' I didn't believe her. I headed downstairs to my locker, tears washing my face of hope. For the rest of the school year, I tutored arithmetic two afternoons a week, mostly to football players, until the school bus arrived with its headlights on in the dim afternoon. It felt important to ride the almost empty late bus home.

Years later there's still that vacancy in my most vital chamber, my heart. Even though I received an award and check for being named "Most Progressive, Most Likely to Succeed" at my graduation from Dwight Morrow High School (523 seniors), I continue to long for that elusive academic education like I yearn for everything I didn't have or don't have anymore. With age, we are reminded of the things we intended to do, but didn't -- and the things we shouldn't have done, but did. Yet we're often guided by factors we couldn't change. Change comes with a price. After all that shorthand practice, I never had the money to apply at Katherine Gibbs. How much of what we put in our mind do we access? How much withers away over time? Metamorphosis seems inevitable -- separation from those we love, and in a different way, from ourselves as we were in the past.

And Mom stayed alone in the kitchen, fallen into the depths of her secret world, her unrevealed thoughts. She silently gripped the washboard with reddened hands, rough as a lizard perched in the bright sun. She braced the board against her stomach, wearing out sheets, underwear, socks in our narrow kitchen, its walls washed gray as the sky on a sunless day.

Abrasive kitchen sounds rub back through time. Pressure cooker steam, wet cloth pushing, pushing against that foggy glass board, ash trays clinking in dishwater, smells of toast, laundry bluing and Clorox. Her grim wrinkled face bore impressions of frowns, hushed passion and lost events. She looked like she was in pain. Yet, she was a loving mom. Perhaps some of her loving hid what she really was, a lonely frightened woman.

◇◇◇◇◇◇◇◇◇◇◇◇◇◇◇◇◇◇

Choices, November 1953

Still a few hours left before I meet Dad at the bus stop and I'm not going to sit in this boring parlor twiddling my thumbs when the sun is shining. Maybe time for a walk, just to get out of this apartment. As I step outside, the crisp air feels expansive as I move through it. The yellow and red leaves have fallen, leaving skeletal, bleak branches, revealing a strongly blue sky, as if it's been dyed with paint. I head up the hill toward Palisades Avenue, wanting to avoid people after my rowdy ride home from Englewood on our school bus.

Sam Schultz from eleventh grade quit school today. I walk the empty street thinking about kids who've dropped out of school. My world is shrinking too, like theirs in a way, limited by my parents' illnesses. Everyone's gossiping about Patricia, one of the juniors with hips and a waist and a bust that guaranteed her a ticket to the Prom. She got pregnant and had to drop out of school instead. Our principal thinks sex and marriage are synonymous.

I'd like to quit school too. Typing and shorthand aren't challenging, although Miss Mears promised me a history

188

class and an internship in the school office next year. Getting pregnant isn't the way out, I think, as I head south on Undercliff Avenue. I decide to walk up the road towards Palisades Amusement Park and then circle back down to River Road to meet Dad's bus.

I don't walk further than Palisades Park anymore, ever since my friend Dorothy and I saw the bloody dead bodies on the street in Cliffside Park. What a town! Mobsters, bookmakers and cops on the take. Before that day, we used to walk really far, gossiping about the horrible popular kids. When we stopped giggling, we'd make up stories about the people on the street. Munching on cherries, we'd spit the pits to see whose could land the farthest. Except one of the pits hit a man who screamed at us, "Bitches, Brats, get out of my neighborhood." Running and giggling, we finally sat down on the curb to keep from peeing in our pants.

Singing songs from "Hit Parade" magazine, I'd end up walking Dorothy home and then she'd walk me home till it got too silly and tiring. Until the day we saw those bloody bodies with staring eyes lying in the street. Bystanders were quickly walking away as police cars arrived. It was our first time to see dead people not safely in their coffins. We ran home crying with panic, the blood stains still in our vision. We neither told our parents nor went back to Cliffside Park.

As I reach the fenced amusement park, I relax. How great it is to live so close to this sand-lined grand swimming pool whose tidal salty water is pumped from the Hudson River. I lean on the iron gate on Palisades Avenue for a few minutes trying to catch a glimpse of my favorite places. The Ferris wheel's dinky, but the roller coaster is second only to the Cyclone at Coney Island. I hear the rumble and remember its quick descent before the ride ended and we calmly walked through the mazes of the adjacent fun house whose mirrors brought grotesque changes to my body.

Maximillian Schmidheimer's probably inside the park

right now. He quit eighth grade to work on the bumper car ride. Such a simple job. He just leans on the rusting yellow fence, focused on watching the girls. Wish there was more time to see if he's working today. He let me ride his bumper cars for free and he didn't yell when I bumped everybody. He brought me fluffy cotton candy from the Midway concessions when he returned from his breaks.

I usually take myself to the free-act stage, getting there early to get a good seat on the wooden benches. The cars aren't nearly as intriguing as when the human cannonball climbs down into the barrel of the cannon, into the tube's darkness, waiting for the catapulting shot into the safety net. Each time, as I wait in the growing twilight shadows, the risk seems to grow. I hold my breath, standing tall to see better. Boom! Out pops the human cannonball across the stage. Then the rock 'n' roll band starts playing at the free stage, making the air bouncy as he jumps out of his cocoon. Fun to remember, but it's time to turn back toward home as the lights start to reveal the grand iridescent skyline of Manhattan across the Hudson.

Some days I act happily poised to grab the brass ring, but this isn't one of those days. I'm not really happy and I'm scared to reach for the ring. I feel myself desperately begging for attention, but nobody notices. There used to be a spark when I chatted with Maximillian, but no Edgewater boy seems right for me. Even Joe White, my still unacknowledged crush, only plans to stay in school till he's old enough to join the Marines. I don't need to wear their rings around my neck. I'm not sure if I'm in slow start or false start or won't start. Boys are nasty. I remember how they spit in the bucket when it was the girls' turn to bob for apples on Halloween. As I head downhill along the stony cliffs of the Palisades, guys make dirty threats with their fingers as they drive by. I ignore them by looking up at the house I'm passing on Undercliff Road.

In the window is a polio machine, an iron lung, a coffin-like waxen missile, rocking...rocking... I've heard there's a girl inside, just a few years older than me. Slowly rocking, side to side. The movement keeps her alive, forcing air in and out of her lungs. I can't see her, but I imagine her staring out the window at the bare winter branches from her restricted view of the world.

Somedays, like today, I feel in a rut like a chicken stuck in our freezer with its legs tied up. However, being enclosed in the narrowness of Edgewater can't compare to lying in an iron lung. High school and my life with ill parents and my eight-year-old brother who eats only cereal and noisily plays with toy cars is difficult. Dropping out of school would be even more binding. Then I'd really be missing the boat. Betty Meier's cousin, Lili, dropped out of school and joined the navy. Then Betty told me she was released on a Section Eight and is becoming a nun.

By the time I reach the bus stop, I realize you only fail if you quit. Graduating high school is better in the long run. So I talk to myself, an emotive monologue. 'Diana, you're fourteen. Old enough to avoid crippling, imprisoning restrictions. Develop resistance to life's yo-yos. Stop feeling sad when people don't share the values you think are meaningful. If you don't fit in Edgewater, you can leave someday. You're not a tree. Even if you were, you couldn't be rooted in Edgewater.' Mmmmm. Maybe, I could be a tree in a national park, alongside a rushing brook, sheltered and admired.

Small steps may be all a girl like me needs to start out on a new path. I want to live with passion about everything and love for everyone in my life. I never want to feel like I'm just existing. I'll accept my privileged student key next fall and work in the high school office. With the money I earn, I'll start a Christmas Club account to save for Katherine Gibbs.

It's exactly 6:37. The long shadows of sundown have merged into deepening dusk. I see the headlights of Dad's approaching bus, right on time. I support his arm as he steps down. It's not hard. He's shrunken into a very slender

191

version of his body, down to bones. As we slowly walk up the hill, he complains, "They were supposed to build a staircase where this wall is. Then I wouldn't have to walk uphill. They didn't keep their promise." For the first time, I realize the move to Edgewater two years ago had been planned way ahead of my finding out. I wonder why no one told me. Trying to second-guess my family is like spitting into the wind. We slowly trudge up the hill to our apartment.

Life in our garden apartment was full of undercurrents I didn't understand. Unwritten struggles, unspoken pain and untold dreams, like discordant music without a beat or melody. Goal-setting models itself similar to a spider spinning a web. Do I weave a huge web, getting very hungry while attempting to direct my attention to its intricacies, or do I weave a small one and catch small flies? Reminds me of a Yiddish expression Uncle Buddy once told me, "Keyn breyre iz oykh a breyre. — A person who does not make a choice makes a choice."

Choices reflect different truths. Sometimes I'm most truly punished for the lies I tell myself. Sometimes I live in illusion when it's too painful to move towards understanding and acceptance. Sometimes I bow to the inevitable, the choice we make under pressure. Life seems less stifling if I don't look beyond the moment. After all, who seeks complexity? Do we want to see what's lurking in the wings? On the other hand, we have a dangerous capacity for self-delusion. When things are bad, looking ahead gives us hope. Which choices do we make? Hmmm... Self-improvement vs self-imprisonment?

Yet, these emotional moments became seared into memory, stop my breathing. They stack up in my mind until new insights burst through, life changes, new choices emerge. Although unpredictable, I welcome those altered moments when I notice the grass shiver in the breeze or become mesmerized by the changing light. We think we become who we are through our choices, but maybe we're who we are to start with and choice is only an illusion. I attempt to live for what counts, but maybe fate renders all our choices irrelevant in the end.

<hr>

Undaunted by Darts, February 1954

Tenth Grade equals 'Sewing' in the girls' vocational track. It's only February, but we've started making summer skirts with waistbands and zippers. Selvage, darts and basting meld into my vocabulary. We line up for our teacher to measure our waistlines with a cloth tape to determine the right size Simplicity pattern. When she says, "Twenty inches. Boy, are you skinny!" It's embarrassing. Most girls wear cinch belts and even then, their waist doesn't get to twenty inches.

We take a class field trip to the fabric store in Englewood to buy a pattern made with lines on tissue paper. Rows of bolts of fabric and drawers full of patterns offer amazing choices. They're expensive, eighty cents, but we get a school discount. Mom gave me her red pin cushion, shaped like a tomato, so I wouldn't have to buy one.

The cutting process is very slow, like the slow thaw of the Hudson. We stand in line to get the teacher's approval on each step: lay out the pattern with chalk, pin the pattern to the fabric, cut the fabric, pin our seams, baste our seams, rip out our mistakes with a seam ripper. You get the idea, most of sewing is not sewing.

Finally we're approved to take turns on one of the three sewing machines. The teacher raises her voice over the clickety-clacking noise. First we learn to thread the machine, fill up the bobbin, make straight seams on paper and then on practice fabric. Whirring sounds indicate the needle moving up and down to join with the bobbin thread. One of the girls in our class, Jeannie, sewed her finger. The needle went right into her pointer finger and she was taken to the nurse. She dropped the class.

The zipper requires a complicated attachment, but learning new things is exciting. Soon I'll be able to wear a skirt without safety pins to hold it up. It won't be an uninspired plaid. I'll make more skirts with bold flowers and wild prints. Clothes that fit, like Aunt Jean made for my cousin Daron.

I spend hours searching for the right buttons, touching pearlescent ones and big, bold, fun ones. Flowers, people, music notes, letters that can spell anything. You can't use tacky ones on your clothes. Choices are only limited by the size of your buttonhole. Children's fingers weren't made to fasten buttons, especially the cloth covered ones you remove for washing. Ironing around buttons without ironing wrinkles into the buttonholes was a challenge equal to not creating those brown burn spots.

Buttonholes are created with a complex attachment, accompanied by prayers and, often, cussing. They must be exactly the same size and evenly spaced. Men's buttonholes are on different sides of garments than women's buttonholes. You can sew corner stitches to make your buttonholes smaller, but never bigger. One of life's lessons.

Since I'm undaunted by darts, Dad says if I get an "A," he'll buy me a used Singer treadle machine. I'll design clothes like my paper dolls wore. When my cousins give me their hand-me-downs, I'll just pass them on to the really poor people in their rotting houseboats on the Hudson. I'll only wear beautiful clothes I sew for myself.

I began making most of my clothes. The most challenging was the two-piece suit in a pale green linen tweed for Aaron's bar mitzvah before I left New Jersey. That whole event made me proud since I had talked Aaron into having a bar mitzvah and found a Rabbi who gave him a tape to memorize for six months. I walked him to and from his practice sessions in Fort Lee, took him to the Lower East Side to buy a suit, tallit, yarmulke and new shoes (and pickles from the open barrels on the sidewalks). I invited all the family and a few friends. My second time in a temple! I gave him a small party in our garden apartment and paid for everything from my NYU salary. All went well— until Aunt Miriam called me over and quietly told me I had sewn one of my suit jacket sleeves on backwards! Live and learn!

On my 70th birthday, my daughters gave me a huge party. They created a slide show from our photo albums. Fun to remember the clothes I'd made for myself and my girls, even their little two-piece bathing suits. Embellishment became another key to fun.

∞∞∞∞∞∞∞∞∞∞∞∞∞∞

Emerging, March 1954

Miss Mears loaned me a book about Diana, the Goddess of the Hunt. The cover displays her picture, camouflaged in the earth tones of a lioness winning her prey. I learn that her mythical name also conjures up the distant moon, powerfully affecting our earth. All this focus on MY name!

"Mom, I'm named after a goddess."

"Actually, you're named after my mother, Badana. Diana is an Americanized version," Mom tells me. She pulls a photograph from her bottom drawer -- a portrait of a sturdy, proud woman arriving in America in 1911. Her thick black hair upswept in a bun, she's turned towards the camera with her two daughters, being photographed for posterity. Mom looks like she might topple without her mother's hand. I hold that photograph, realizing Badana didn't get to grow older. We never got to see her change. Her face never wrinkled. Her back never grew stooped. Although courageous enough to leave Europe with her husband, she wasn't strong enough to survive the influenza epidemic of 1919.

I cringe inside when I hear my name abused. Few people pronounce my name correctly. I'm not *Die*, as I'm called by my school friends. I'm not *Di-ann*, my mother's version. Her accent on *Di*, the elongated syllabification, the nasal quality and loudness of her yell leave me hugely embarrassed in front of my friends. I answer quickly so she'll shut up. She does this in stores, like no one else matters or exists. She has no inhibitions when she gets anxious and needs to feel my brother and me around her. The only one who gets it right is Paul Anka!

My name doesn't matter. I've passively adjusted to whatever it is. Now that I've grown tall, Diana fits me. My breasts have finally grown. My awareness of myself and my surroundings is different. My inner voice and conscience combines Badana's and the Goddess of the Hunt. I feel their power, but don't know what to do with it or what it means. Thank goodness for hormones, or I would still be passive little 'Di-ann'.

I love to be alone inside myself, staring out windows, mulling over what my teachers say or the lyrics of songs on the radio. Although I'm still shy, my silence outside does not lead to silence inside. My thoughts take up the empty space in my life. In my utopian reveries, I'm as poised as Cinderella with Prince Charming.

I'm not the only girl who fantasizes a romantic courtship, marriage and raising six adorable children in a grand home. The hopes of most teens reflect the top forty songs and popular romance novels, a combination that produces a cliched view of love. I'm not sure we should believe these dreams, hoping boys, houses and marriage will improve our lives. Maybe our optimism isn't realistic. I'll bet that's true for boys too. Searching for the perfect girl, they probably seek Doris Day or June Allyson, ready for love and marriage. Or perhaps a bit naughty like Kim Novak or Elizabeth Taylor. Maybe we were closer to the right track when we twisted those apple stems as ten-year-olds on 90th Street.

How can I find a real boyfriend? I think about signing up for a pen pal, but I'm too shy to start the letter. But I imagine writing letters until, by a long-awaited arrangement, we meet. A Norwegian blond, clean, grateful and uniformed. I love uniforms like my brothers wore in the war or John Henkel wore as our crossing guard at Horace Mann. Girls getting off our school bus at St. Cecelia's wear uniforms, plaid skirts and ironed white blouses. Uniforms could make us kids all the same and are certainly preferable to years of hand-me-downs held together with safety pins. I'm a somewhat structured girl, seeking guidelines like Arthur Murray's box footsteps. However, my only uniform is my maroon gym shorts with elastic around the bottom that makes my butt balloon out from my stick legs.

My tenth-grade reverie adorns me in an angora sweater going to fall football games with my BMOC boyfriend. He picks me up in a convertible, his loud radio playing rock 'n' roll. This yearning turned me into a football fanatic. I listen to games on the radio, fantasizing myself cheering for Army in fifty-yard line seats. After we win, I'm the life of the party, dancing the Jersey Bounce till dawn.

My daydreams are my secrets. I hug them to me with pleasure. But what if the reality never matches or even comes close to my yearnings? I'm somewhat sure this happened to mom and dad. I wonder if they still have dreams.

I no longer see my past selves as I gaze in my full-length mirror, but certainly they're in my brain. I remember how my growing pony tail flowed with restless energy. Did it make me beautiful? I never thought so, even after all the hours spent brushing my hair. What a negative form of self-deception! Look at all the time we spend squandering life on the trivial, wasting time on wasting time, thinking we're involved with life when we're really missing it.

We rarely pose with Badana's sense of destiny anymore. Instead we snap a zillion photos until we stop noticing most of the details. I prefer writing to preserve and recapture memories of certain moments, turning points, that demand to be recorded. I look back and there's my story.

If only I could leap further, jump higher, travel farther through time and look upon new sights or the same sights differently. I would float down a stream to the river, ride the glory of a falling star back to earth. I would float through the endlessly rich world of memory, remembering intentions, secrets, desires, and energies. I pull sudden laughter from my serenity. Although my coppery hair has whitened, and I avert my eyes away from the mirror, there's innocence left. I still live two lives, day life and dreams. Someplace in those blurred boundaries, they quietly merge like modern art -- until the memory of them pops out into the air, the luxury of reclusive hours.

<hr>

Three Moments at the Picture Window, April 1954

I never have any place to be alone. In North Bergen, the best I could come up with was to stare out the window looking down on Hudson Boulevard. In Bloomfield, there wasn't a private place or a window offering much to view. Now back in Edgewater, I gaze through our picture window towards the river. Most nights I can barely find the moon struggling through the cloudy night sky. However, tonight our windows are cranked wide open to follow the moon as it forms a piercing bright arc on the softly rippling water of the Hudson. I follow the lights of a large barge slowly moving downstream from the George Washington Bridge.

Across River Road, the Buena Vista Tavern seems especially quiet, in spite of the full moon. The neon bar sign forlornly beckons, tempts and woos the drivers on River Road. The scent of lilacs from the patio alongside the tavern drifts in with the breeze. I've walked over to smell the soft musky fragrance of those flowers at the river's edge. I study that lilac tree, feeling it growing upwards in spite of gravity. I'm intrigued with the mystery of one branch undulating in the evening breeze. Its leaves still drip from this afternoon's rain, a brief spring sun shower. Why is one branch more reactive and vibrant than the others? I twist my head to see if other trees or bushes are affected by wind. No... We study nature as if it is different from us, but we are nature too -- with a propensity for evil and love.

The Buena Vista isn't a neighborhood tavern like the one in North Bergen. On crowded nights, there have been knife fights. Mostly riled up guys at Italian weddings in the back room We hear yelling and watch for the Edgewater police to arrive. The next day, the neighbors' gossip tells all. Just like the movies.

Edgewater isn't densely populated. Instead of neighbors walking over, most of the drinkers drive and park their cars in spaces between the bar and River Road. One car calls to me, a teeny, lime green Nash Metropolitan convertible, just my size. I wish it could be mine. Last Sunday, when Dad joined me at the window, I pointed, "Dad, look how neat that car is!"

"Someday, when you're old enough, I'll buy you a car just like that. I know the man that owns it and he might just sell it to me."

Wow! Now I imagine it becoming mine. With my diffident family life, this is a moment to hang on to.

No one's home, so I dance in our parlor with the picture window as my audience. I bought a green hi-fi Victrola with money I earned at Easter break typing minutes of meetings and wills for Uncle Ted. I pile on my stack of Perry Como and Frank Sinatra's 78s, take off my shoes and start moving outside my mind. Stretch, warm up, loosen up head to foot, then let go, moving whatever, wherever, aware of the rhythms settling into my body. Dance stirs up hope, power, aliveness. No one to care if I start on my right or left foot. I move from outside my body to inside my soul. A sure-footed movement to new places down deep, those places that I hide away. Everything comes loose, mingles with the rest of my mind.

Mom walks by with her arms full of laundry and catches me dancing. Dad follows her, whistling to himself. Mom yells, "Be careful, Di-ann, you might hit the window and cut yourself. Worse yet, men in the Buena Vista might see you dancing at the window." There's that word 'careful' again and I'm not allowed to dance anymore, at least when she's around.

Mom drops her clean clothes on the cluttered table, red-faced and on the verge of tears. "Di-ann, did you see my laundry basket? Mrs. Pietsche's yelling at me because my sheets are still in the machine."

Mom often forgets to take the laundry out of the washer. I don't know why. You'd think she'd be afraid of losing our clothes. Dad arrives home and refers to Mrs. Pietsche, our fat neighbor from the next unit, as a 'tough broad'. Next thing you know, Mr. Pietsche comes into view, walking up the sidewalk to our picture window where dad and I are standing. Uh oh, he sees us.

"Keep your wife away from my wife," he yells at dad. "I don't want your wife using the machines when we're home."

Dad's hands clutch the window sill. "Calm down," he tells Mr. Pietsche. "Keep your pants on. It's just laundry. It'll get done eventually."

"So you say," he screams back, waving his fist and stiffening his big belly. "You may have all the time in the world, but I don't."

As the yelling continues, I watch Dad clench his hands to his chest. 'This is insane,' I think. 'I need this to stop so Dad doesn't get sick again.'

"Go eat some hemlock." I shout and pull down the window shade, hitting drowsy flies on the windowsill. I didn't realize speaking out would be so easy. The fight's over; the shade stays down. Dad smiles.

…And I still dance in the dark, alone, leaping in the air, touching the quiet, becoming the dance.

When I boogie, my feet feel the floor and my arms feel the air. I touch the world around me with my body. It's when I forget or am too busy to dance, or I feel I can't sway any more, that I pay the fiddler. I'm driven to twirl and pursue the playful and adventuresome feelings gained from the world around me. Dance brings hope, my steps take me in new directions. Other people may dance too, sometimes with me, but there are people who may see my dancing as my weakness. So I leave them, even though it means finding a new partner. For the really high price comes when I try to pirouette to someone else's music.

I write these memories of dancing at our picture window in the timid first light, as the day's early glow suffuses the sky and the first hungry birds through the bedroom window of my home. They're only moments, but they guide our life. Hope returns in the morning. Daybreak and our creator smiles—before my hours of being boxed in by uncertainties and the day's demands. Everyone's hemmed in to some degree. Pop by religious and cultural beliefs from the Old Country. Dad became the boy Pop wanted to carry on the business, until the business failed during the depression. We all have someone who influences us, burns inside us like a pilot light, and we spend our lives fulfilling that legacy. Writing accelerates my transformation into a clearer perspective of my dance with life. Yet, I'd still rather twiddle my bum than my thumbs. I long to spend my day soaring like a bright balloon, going wherever the wind takes me, until the skies darken and my window reflects only me writing in my room.

I wish my father could see me, see what I look like, what I have become. I want to say: "Look at me dad; your little skinny girl grown into a woman. I know you'll be glad I finally got the car you would have bought for me."

Diana Ruth Krohn

Mom and Me, spring 1954

People call me uninhibited, but I just never learned Emily Post's social rules. Since starting tenth grade, I've had minimal experience with kids outside of school. Dad's uninhibited too. He's a high school grad, but the only son who didn't go on to college. Mom only finished eighth grade. She takes pride in her beautiful penmanship, but never feels secure with reading or discussing world events. We're not like the rest of my father's family. My cousins' dads are healthy. They don't move, except to larger houses. We don't own a house and our apartments are never larger than one bedroom.

In our small apartment, Mom accumulates as many knickknacks as she has freckles. They sit on tables, windowsills and dressers, silently witnessing our family's activities. Lately, Mom's generous giveaway moods are becoming more indiscriminate and chaotic. Family heirlooms disappear. Aaron and I tried to recover a painting of three mountains painted by mom's cousin, but we failed. Dad finally gave us five dollars to buy the painting back from the Geralds.

Mrs. McMahon, a volunteer at the local Salvation Army, claims Mom is their prize contributor. "Where's my corduroy shirt, blue sweater, belt…" are cries of frustration heard around our apartment after Mom's just donated one of her bundles. She mixes up what we need and don't need. She looks at us and says, "Poor children are starving," and I just can't be mad at her.

When we travel to her sisters in the Bronx, Mom stops at a bakery to bring a cake or freshly baked rolls. We visit more often now, crossing the George Washington Bridge to New York City, the center of the universe. All races, rich and poor, exploiters and oppressed, walk the same sidewalks speaking many languages. Color everywhere, even though the sky is nondescript as the concrete buildings, as we make our way to the Grand Concourse.

Sometimes we stop for lunch at Horn & Hardart's Automat. I like choosing foods from those glass-walled food slots. I slip in nickels in the slot next to the food I like. There are over 400 foods, but I turn the chrome knob to the same choices every time. The glass door of the compartments open and I place my apple pie and chocolate milk on the tray. However, the rest of these Bronx visits are torturous boredom unless my cousin Barbara happens to be home getting ready for a date. She wakes up late and sits in the light from the parlor window, her face covered with Ponds cold cream, polishing her nails and pinning up her hair. I watch with envy, planning to be just like her someday.

Mom suffers from hay fever, corns and hemorrhoids. She wears old lady's shoes with open toes and thick straps.

I don't envy Mom or feel protected by her. I won't dress like her; it's bad enough to inherit her freckles. While attempting to do good, Mom often does the opposite. Sitting on my new phonograph records, bleaching the red dress Barbara gave me, cutting people out of photos—her mishaps constantly frustrate us. Aaron and I follow in her footsteps, trying to help by putting away the vacuum cleaner left lying on the parlor rug and those over-scoured pots left on the kitchen chairs.

Mom rarely cooks. When she does, despite how good it turns out, Mom takes only a taste. She's one of those people who thinks, "I've already had my life. We laugh and say, "Oh, well, that's our Mom." But our laughter is merely a smokescreen. It isn't fun. The prevailing wind in our house becomes tension, tempered with outbursts of anger and sarcasm, like breathing in the smell of harsh soap. We play hide and seek with words. Even though I see through it, I can't blow the smoke away.

I tried to rescue and reshape my parents so I could feel safe. I didn't want to lose them. I read their moods. I clung, yelled, explained, prayed for second chances, but parents don't fix easily. Yet, a child's initial source of power is over their parents. Now I realize there was pain my parents tried to hide. Neither one of them was pain-free. I didn't know the details of their struggles or why they were like this. Without this backstory, how can we see our parents objectively. We only see them through our eyes.

◦◦◦◦◦◦◦◦◦◦◦◦◦◦◦◦◦◦

Practice, spring 1954

Now is the time for all good men to come to the aid of their country.

We type this sentence all the time, over and over, to warm up our fingers. Mr. Garman says, "It uses all the letters in the alphabet." It doesn't. The real pangram is *The quick brown fox jumps over the lazy dog*. Did you know that *stewardesses* is the longest word typed with the left hand and *lollipop* with the right? *Typewriter* is the longest word using letters from one keyboard row. My long fingers help me type really fast. We practice on worn out Underwoods, but next year we're getting new IBM Selectrics.

```
asdfg asdf; lkjh lkj;h a lad has a glad
dad; dad had half a shad salad
dad has a gag; a lass has a sash; a lad
has a lash as a fad
```

'Gag' is a palindrome. I search for palindromes among the combinations we type, like 'racecar, kayak and level.' It keeps me awake. We drill until my fingers are sore and my back hurts. We type letters, lists and accounting spread sheets with numbers in columns.

The most fun is our typing game. We slip a blank sheet of typing paper underneath the cylinder and push the bail back in place. We check our margins and tabs. I look up at Mr. Garmen, trying not to giggle at his strings of hair trying to hide his balding head. I sit in correct posture, fingers hovering over my home keys, until he yells, "Ready, Set, Go!"

```
bevel bevel mended mended sincerely
sincerely helpful helpful incidentally
incidentally worked worked
```

The noise is thunderous even without boys in our class. Thirty-six sets of fingernails click on their keyboard letters and shift keys. Hundreds of silver letters hit the platens. There's smacking noises as we slam the carriage return with our left hand at the end of each line. Our fingers are drumming, definitely not all to the same tune.

```
No one is so old as to think he cannot
live one more year.
A   man   may   know   the   world   without
leaving his own home.
```

After a few minutes of testing, the clatter softens. The rule is: When you make a mistake, you have to stop. You're not allowed to look at the paper you're typing on – only at the copy book.

As we are, so we do; and as we do, so
is it done to us.
Either write things worth reading, or
do things worth writing.

When we first started playing this game, some girls didn't know they had made a mistake. But when you bring your finished copy up to be checked, the teacher always finds typos and says things to embarrass you. After a few weeks, as we gain more expertise or to avoid embarrassment, we start to feel when we make a mistake and we automatically stop typing.

December 5, 1952, December 5, 1952,
December 5, 1952
9 ½ bushels @ $67; #27 @ $1.35; (58 -
43); 4% of 102

The room grows quieter and quieter. Only a few of us still type in the hollowness, defying the odds. The clicks seem far away. They echo. I slow down a bit. I don't want to lose. I hate losing. But if I slow down too much, the girls will call me "Cheater, cheater." Finally it's only Cora and me. I keep typing, trying not to hear the expanding silence.

Mr. Kenneth T. Cooper, about whom you
inquire, was a student in my class of
journalism at the State University.

Suddenly, I'm the only one typing. My ankle itches. I bite my lip, but I keep typing while the teacher counts the typos on Cora's paper. She has two. Only then do I stop. The keyboard noise is finished already, but it still resounds in my ears. I know I'm blushing as Mr. Garman checks my paper -- no errors -- and I win! Now I can become a member of the Order of Artistic Typists!

Newscasts and songs from the radio helped me practice my Gregg shorthand and improve my typing speed. Too Young, Cry, Be My Love, Vaya Con Dios, Oh! My Papa... I'm lucky to have almost eighty years of song lyrics in my brain. Words woven into music add color, definition and a spirit that doesn't die.

We can make so many words out of so few letters. Yet, so many are misused, exaggerated, ambiguous. The realization that abstract words don't hold their shape over time comes very slow before it bangs you in the head. Words put out roots, arousing people, painting out memories. Yet we still ache for meaning from these letters. There's spirit in everything. We just have to find it. Inevitably, words weave a tapestry from seemingly isolated events, until the patterns reveal truths that each of us must eventually face.

⋄⋄⋄⋄⋄⋄⋄⋄⋄⋄⋄⋄⋄⋄⋄⋄⋄⋄

More Practice, Spring 1954

I carefully cut into each rib of a grapefruit and place a maraschino cherry on top. I'm learning to cook in Home Ec. My yummiest success is Southern Fried Chicken made in our electric frying pan Dad bought because he loves these foods I cook. I bake raisin spice loaf cakes and oatmeal cookies from my free Sun Maid Raisin cookbook. My secret recipe for tuna noodle casserole has peas. My hamburgers taste like Aunt Miriam's. I kept trying spices and crumbs until the taste matched my memory. I cook boiled potatoes with sour cream like Grandma Krohn. I've learned to iron and Dad appreciates when I iron his shirts without wrinkles or brown burn spots. It's not as easy as preparing supper.

When I'm not practicing my cooking or ironing Dad's shirts, I think about clothes. I wistfully skim outfits in the latest Sears catalog, planning what I'll buy when I start working. The latest model cars and sports statistics interest me more than the progress of the police action in Korea and who's running for president. Except I'm hoping for Adlai Stevenson. I remember when he once said, "A hypocrite is the kind of politician who would cut down a redwood tree, then mount the stump and make a speech for conservation."

I know we test hydrogen bombs 'for practice.' Yet even important scientific accomplishments contain the seeds of terrible things. I remember the frequent times I fell learning to ride my cousin Daron's two-wheeler on Aunt Jean's gravel driveway on Washington Street. Practice makes perfect isn't always a true axiom. I'm still not great at riding a bike and so much of what we're politically cooking makes me afraid.

I learned so much in that holding pen called 'vocational high school.' I still use some of those recipes, knit, mend my own clothes, but hardly iron. I'm so glad I didn't major in Home Ec as so many girls of my generation did. We didn't realize there were other choices waiting for us. We all have roles: the secure and the restless, the intellectuals and the practical-minded, the charismatic leaders and their uncertain followers, the sophisticates and the naifs, the winners and the losers, the fun-seekers and the complainers. I've learned to observe people from this perspective, searching for signs and symptoms that identify them.

◁◁◁◁◁◁◁◁◁◁◁◁◁◁◁◁◁

Returning to North Bergen, spring 1954

Mom weakened at last. She's letting me visit Maureen. It's been almost three years. I wonder if we're still friends or just former friends facing an awkward reunion. I step down from the bus this Saturday afternoon, into a past that's familiar, but smaller, hotter and shabbier. Maureen's already arrived, standing at the corner, grinning and waving. I stare at her, comparing her today self to my memory of her. She's shockingly short. I'm at least a head taller. She stopped growing and I didn't. This should not be, I think. But the logic eludes me.

This isn't the North Bergen I remember, but more like a dream in which I see only bits and pieces on an old face. As we walk down 90th Street immersed in catching up chatter, I have trouble fitting into my new view. Things are too distant and too close at the same time. A feeling passes over me, like a shadow crossing in front of the sun. The street feels clearly diminished, paled into impotence. The brown and gray houses still squat towards the narrow street. The buildings fade in the distance, as if seen from a departing train. Everything looks clean, no clutter, trash or rotting houses. It's as if all the polishing held the houses and the possessions of these immigrant families together. Glossy furniture, sheltered with doilies and photos of the dead covered with icons. Edgewater doesn't have that same luster.

We started in front of our former apartment building. The boxlike trimmed hedges have been replaced by concrete sidewalks. But the short strip of brown dusty dirt still divides the concrete sidewalk from the street, the place where boys played with toy cars, emitting vrooms, rumbling, crashing sounds. Just past this dirt strip, our hopscotch is faded. None of our peach pits ever grew.

As Maureen talks about our neighbors (no one else moved away like we did), I glance up at the roof with its clutter of clothes pinned to the lines and blowing in the breeze. I wonder if there's still piles of flattened tin cans by the coal bin in the basement. I wonder if our apartment now has kitchen smells.

As we continue walking, I glance at Mario's house next door. We never had seen anyone from Mario's family. Even Mario never went out; something secretive was wrong with him. "His father is dead," Maureen says matter-of-factly. "He was killed by a gang." I stare at his house which seems even more quiet, blank, shut down. I imagine the police investigation and how his wife must miss him.

We stop in to visit the Sinagras. Everyone's in the kitchen. Rosemarie has a job. Carmella has become boyish with a pony tail. All the girls have pony tails. No more barbershops for me either. My hair is finally long enough to copy the hairdos of movie stars. Mrs. Sinagra admires my new skirt, the one I made in sewing class. Old Grandma Sinagra stirs her tomatoey pasta sauce (with garlic, of course) as I hug everyone goodbye.

Maureen and I head down Hudson Boulevard towards Horace Mann School. The traffic noise has gotten worse. We run into Barbara and Deanna at the soda fountain. As we greet one another, the sounds of everyone's voices seem far away and something, it seems, has happened to their faces. Barbara is definitely chubby and older looking, but Deanna is the real shock. Her face seems scrunched, like she's wrinkling too soon. Her shiny page boy has changed from 'smooth as glass' to bleached, shortened and permed. Why did she do that? I don't know what to say to her.

I'm happy to be with Maureen, but I don't want to see anymore. It's too hard to keep smiling at everyone. My memories are fading, becoming an illusion. The fragments are breaking up, emptying out from disappointment, as I walk in the present. I prefer to keep my memory. North Bergen has become as ill-fitting as the hand-me-down clothes I used to wear before I started sewing my own clothes. I tell Maureen, "I need to return home."

We head back to the bus stop through the lot, although I feel no desire to wander the paths. The horrors don't stop. Our sledding hill's been truncated, flattened like a super tool cut it off with a knife, to become a Sunoco gas station.

"Our hill. Who cut it down?"

"Oh, that happened right after you left. The gas station was in use before the first snow."

It's sad when the world goes this way. I don't fit here

anymore. Yet the trees still have their glassy green umbrella of beauty in the late afternoon's shadow and sunshine. They can't run away when they're unhappy. They stay put until the end.

The past is a small world, made smaller and darkened by our great distance from it. Was there more truth in the beginning than now? I inevitably felt the need to return to my childhood street -- slung low, weighed down by the lineup of buildings, poorly lit by street lamps -- still searching for something. Not all memory fragments become mundane. Certain people and events manage to meet or exceed my sense of expectation and retain their significance over time. They take up space in my brain and read like ghost writing, like the pages in our reused workbooks where some pages erased better than others.

I can leave places without returning, except for Arizona, but leaving people is hard. Although I never got used to her being short, Maureen and I are still close friends. She married Tom and raised five children. After forty years, our relationship quietly dwindled in the mid-eighties from distance, moves and name changes, like so many do. Then we found each other on Facebook. On a recent visit, we combined memories and played catch-up for three days. She still has her Raggedy Anne and Andy dolls. I'm sure by now the kids we played with have left 90th Street. I hope the vitality from those days playing and growing up together has stayed with them as it did with us.

Many times, going back to our childhood home fixes what's missing or changes our life. It demands the challenge of painting memories clearly, openly -- with words. They carry too much power to be used carelessly. I use them to break the delusions, realizing that perspectives change, accepting that memories may never come close to reality. I thought truth was like the right answer to a math problem, the solution to the situation. So limiting! True knowledge is a form of unknowing, observing things in a different light, not always comfortable, recognizing the possibility of a different outcome — like scrutinizing life with shmutz on my eyeglasses and cleaning them to discover my truth.

I never returned to North Bergen again. Timelessness is an illusion. It seemed like the silver, polished so long ago by the Sinagras, had also lost its luster. But the street and its people always remain a part of my life, like the words of an old favorite tune. How do you remember and interpret the past? As it happens and in hindsight, in shreds and patches. In retrospect, our struggles may even strike us as beautiful.

⚬⚬⚬⚬⚬⚬⚬⚬⚬⚬⚬⚬⚬⚬⚬

Evening City Views, summer 1954

I walk at a leisurely pace along the top of the Palisades, the setting sun lengthening my shadow. This is a place I call my own. I'm sure lots of people have been here before, and there will be others in the future who will, in turn, enjoy its beauty. I call it my own because I wonder if anyone will ever feel about it exactly as I do. Looking down the riverbanks of the slow-moving Hudson, I spot my apartment building in the narrow town where we live.

Summer nights are never quite dark. But in the gradually deepening dusk, across the river lights begin to glow from the tall buildings defining the world-famous skyline. The Empire State, Chrysler and RCA buildings stand tall over the evenly spaced street lights of Riverside Drive. Headlights from moving cars dance across roads and down side streets, lighting houses, stately churches and tree-lined paths in parks that we might otherwise miss. My everyday view becomes magical.

As the moon takes over the work of the sun, it glows silver through the clouds to the inky river flowing under the George Washington Bridge past the downtown piers, rippling on its way to different worlds. Moonlight reveals what darkness hides. The river bubbles like champagne, so beautiful it needs no embellishing. More city lights appear, uniquely alive, gay and giddy as a fairy tale. Neon advertisements flicker on and off, to a tune of their own, punctuated by red and green traffic lights. Ocean liners sit at their docks, their shapes revealed in sparkling strands of white, awaiting their morning departure.

The lives of New York's people also lie open to my imagination. They work, play and sleep unaware of the significant part they play in my river world. The lights, so important and necessary to their well-being, become thousands of jewels strung into a glistening crown of diamonds, bringing a glow of eternal youth to the city. The rising moon above pulls me up into its midst. Where do I begin and where do I end?

That afternoon, the sun seemed to set so fast. If it traveled through the sky as fast as it set, we'd have so many more days and nights. I never find the moon boring. I dance inside when the dim dusk defers to the moon's rise. That evening, above the crown of the Manhattan skyline, it sat on the horizon like brilliant lunar booty, announcing a new season of warmth. As the sky darkened, I claimed the blue moon at the top of the buildings as mine.

I've always felt the closeness of the moon, although I can't explain the theories about the forces between the moon and the earth — on agriculture, religion, eclipses, crime, craziness and babies born. Remember the widow in 'Angelina's Line' who howled at the moon. We refer to moon faces, mooning as a prank, legends about the man in the moon, shooting at the moon. It's said that a new moon brings rain within five days and that the reddish colors in the ring around the moon indicate impending rain. I stare at the moon, sometimes thru telescopes, observing its very predictable shadows. Why does it shine so strangely bright? Why the reactive interpretation of the Greeks—that the moon held the feminine quality of the sun, wisdom and intuition? We no longer interpret the moon based on fear, yet its certainly more than mere romanticism. The pale eloquent moon is not even half of the sun, sort of like me at this moment.

my coppery brown tresses
whitened into weak messes
this is the night...tonight
the light so strangely bright
thru my silhouetted elm
my child eyes at the helm
things are told...are told
and I grow cold...so cold.

To simplify things, I close my eyes. It sure slows down the process.

∞∞∞∞∞∞∞∞∞∞∞∞∞∞∞

The Student Prince, fall 1954

Art, especially music, can free memories imprisoned in us. That's what I realize when Dorothy and I see "The Student Prince" at our Fort Lee movie theatre. I'm smitten with the story of the Prince, incognito among his fellow students at the university, trying to live an ordinary life. He falls in love with a waitress at the beer garden. But normal isn't his fate either. When his father becomes ill, the Prince must return home and take on his inherited responsibilities.

Sigmund Romberg's music awakens our emotions. For the first time, as we begin walking, Dorothy tells me stories about growing up in Germany. Hearing her experiences during the war helps me stop worrying about the dilemma of having a German friend. Before this, when her father tells Juden jokes to her brother, Carlheinz, it made me uncomfortable and cautious when I visited their house.

We skip and dance our long way home like young girls, counting our steps: "Ein, zwei, drei, vier, lift your stein and drink your beer." We sing: "Drink, drink, drink to eyes that are bright as stars when they shining on me."

Not at all like boys from Edgewater talk. Mario Lanza's voice! Edmund Purdom's good looks! What a movie! I carry home the set of 78's I bought in the lobby. I'm sure Dad will love this music too.

...and I'm right. As I sit in the living room, unwrapping my records, I watch Dad shave — the razor skimming his lathered face, the hot water steaming the mirror. But as soon as the songs begin, he joins me in the parlor. As he sits in his chair, I play record after record, telling him the story line. When I play "Golden Days", his eyes tear. So do mine.

"Golden days in the sunshine never having youth..." Wish I'd know Dad at fifteen. I wonder if he liked school and had scads of friends. He sure had a large family.

"...Golden days full of gaiety and full of truth..." Wish I'd know Dad when he was in the Army. How do we conceive enough information to get closer to gaiety or truth in this complex, chaotic world?

"...In our hearts we remember them all else above..." I remember stories from his eight years as president of the Elks and I know he's a Mason because I've seen his books hidden on the top shelf of the closet.

"...Golden days full of gaiety and full of youth..." Dad even knew Frank Sinatra when Frank was a young crooner in Hoboken's taverns.

"...How we laughed with the joy that only love can bring..." I watch Dad's softening face. I see him differently now. I grasp there's been more in his life than I ever saw or realized, shelves of memory.

"...Looking back through memory's haze..." I wish I'd known Dad when he lived the Life of Riley, marrying Dolly, owning the awning store and fathering Bob and Wally.

"…We will know life has nothing sweeter than its springtime…" I recognize our stories are a moving train. We climb down the steps when we get to our station, but the train still continues into the late night.

Now, from the couch where I lie on threadbare sheets trying to sleep, I hear Dad cry out to his mother and first wife. It's the first time he's called out, "Mom, help me. Dolly, help me." in his pain, as if the songs broke through his veneer of stoic humor. He begs for help from these two women he loved. As if he can now communicate with the next world in the bleakness of the winter dawn.

Few relationships transcend the barrier of death. My father's cries to Grandma Krohn and Dolly revealed the power of love and the importance of never-ending connections. Love never dies; it exists quietly someplace inside you. Years later, I sensed my father on my ten-day backpack along the Silver Divide. I didn't understand why, but I felt his presence, alone on the boulders along the waterfall. Into the gurgling water, I whispered the names of those gone from me: Dad, Mom, Bobby, Wally, Buddy, Dorothy, Michael, my friends Kathy, Lois and Ann, cousins I never knew well enough, all my aunts, uncles and grandparents, my little baby boy that miscarried...

Facing My Truths, November 1954

Winter forces us to turn inward. Dad is now in the hospital more days than he works. Each time he comes home, he's different in a way I can't pinpoint. It's like he's learned new things and I haven't. As if time is strangely passing more quickly for him than for those around him.

People keep telling me Dad is dying – Aunt Miriam, Dr. Kolodin, even Dad. But why should I listen when he's there, on the steps, telling jokes to Mr. McMahon and Mr.

Geiler? I stand in the parlor, feel the floor with my feet, then my back, until even my head grows clear with surges of strength from the floor. I look out our picture window, watch Dad and Mr. McMahon laugh at what's, even now, my favorite punch line, "That's when the lightning hit the outhouse!"

Dad is still young. Dying is something that happens to old people. Except soldiers die. People die in accidents, fights and concentration camps. Dave died of his disease that made him so skinny. Life seems shorter when we are vulnerable to early death. I thought as I grew older my head would be filled with all I need to know, but there are still so many blank spaces I'm still seeking to fill, like the dark spots and abstract shadings seen when our eyes are closed. When I open them, what has been in front of them all along is revealed.

I wish I had known my father in his dapper golden days before the frustration of failures and desperation over his loss of Dolly. The doctor said, "Take her to Florida." But he didn't. I wish I had known him before he was worn down from worrying, smoking too much and drinking his two beers.

I only know him now, when he's sick. Even now, he's still fun and funny. I watch through the window as he coughs and holds his chest with clenched fists. At that moment, a truth connects. Someday I will look out the window and his deep cheerful voice will be gone. I'll never get that sewing machine or car. I don't remember my father ever touching me, even to hold my hand. But I know he loves me and is proud of me by the way he looks at me sometimes. He says he wants to see me turn sixteen and walk me down the aisle at my wedding.

Ordinary things. He's dying without doing anything but ordinary things. Working, eating, watching TV, his joke repertoire, a short stint in the Army, a trip to Cleveland, hardly seeing his sons or his family. Ordinary people die and all around them, people go on doing their ordinary things.

My mind rarely rests. It's full of inside thinking, paths of endless association. What does impending death do to dad? To all of us? His doctors are amazed by his ability to survive with his deformed, enlarged heart. I think about his pain, his twenty hospital visits, his courage, his humor. I become uneasy in my own skin. Maybe we only understand how to appreciate life when it's being taken away from us.

As his body shrivels, I picture his heart growing larger inside. Many nights I sit on the stoop with him, seeking any breeze the evening might offer. The men drink their pitchers of beer, laughing at his 'Can you top this?' He has so many good ones, probably even better when he doesn't clean them up for my sake. Yet he's never made fun of Aaron or me. This cycle of school, picking up my dad, his nightly pain. The courage expressed in his humor and 'Dear Folks' letters has only been broken during the year of my mother's nervous breakdown. His letters are photographs in writing.

I meet him at the bus and I hear his raspy breathing as I help him walk up the hill. I bring him an umbrella when it rains. He no longer goes to the Buena Vista for his two beers. Even so, nothing stops his pain and his body from deteriorating. So quickly, it seems. We do not talk. We watch TV, the serials and sitcoms, comedy shows and ball games together. But it's getting harder for me to sit; I'm outgrowing the ritual. The humor doesn't make me laugh and the sit-coms deaden my thinking. I find myself twiddling my thumbs. I don't want to waste my time like this, so I read books until the words come alive and help me forget my world.

I was fifteen, ready for a world without TV. In those days, the home I wanted was created by Louisa May Alcott. The March family. I had three brothers, but always wanted a sister. Maureen had a sister, but my favorite character, Jo, had three. They lived in a house with bedrooms. Jo's mother coped well with her family, the neighbors and community. She loved her girls. My mother never said she loved me and didn't hug or touch me. She had to live in mental institutions when she became afraid. Mr. March, like my father, was hardly there. But everyone anxiously awaited his letters. Jo's neighbor Laurie, the tall boy next door, added to my fantasy. Funny how you never forget your childhood wishes — how much they affect your life.

I still find books fascinating, retaining them in my mind like films. Their colors, aliveness and mystery remain ready to be replayed, reworked and enjoyed. Yet some books disappear like life experiences that don't load into memory. Maybe the fictional characters seem improvised or coincidence becomes the vehicle to tie the story together. It's difficult to write words and actions that earn the advantages of hindsight. I search the secret places in my head where my words are stored, waiting for me to find them.

◊◊◊◊◊◊◊◊◊◊◊◊◊◊◊◊

The Hospital, December 1954

Christmas break. Mom, Aaron and I stayed overnight at Aunt Jean's so Uncle Dan could take us to visit dad. His twenty-first hospitalization.

He lies zipped up in an oxygen tent. I want to ask him about the pressure of the air inside the tent. He cannot talk to me. His impatience at his helplessness is communicated by the way he looks at me from his dimmed eyes. Everything seems white through the clear plastic oxygen tent. Tubes cover part of his face. His hair is covered by a hooded sheet. Jewish men are buried in white, but this shroud is not deliberate or religious. Is God even here? I only feel my father receding.

Realizations are unfolding so fast. Now I know. We grow small and quiet as the life goes out of us. Shriveled, losing color, wearing tubes and bags of fluid. I glance at my father sheathed in plastic tenting. He's slipping away, beyond where he can will himself back. With curiosity, I study his eyes, the only part of his now small body not enclosed by hooded covering. He knows I'm here, but he isn't crying out for help anymore. We don't talk or communicate. We just see each other.

We leave the hospital so Aaron and I can return to school. Uncle Dan drops us off at Bloomfield Station. Mom waits on a bench, Aaron asleep on her lap, at the empty dark station. Alone on the yellow line by the track, I hear the distant warning whistle of the approaching train. The sound reminds me of the way my father's distant voice grew stronger and more familiar --faint, then steadily louder as I grew. There's music in the steady, secure 'ca-chunk ca-chunk' that kept us together. As the train screeches to its stop in the station with such furious intensity, that voice also begins to fade. Suddenly, no more high-pitched horns blow. No more train sounds. Only my memory of Dad and the path of track the train rolled on.

So often, we don't face a situation and achieve the proper goodbye. We tell ourselves that we will return. The words remain imprinted on our brain, left unsaid, leaving scars. On that train home in the heavy morning air, a slow, nagging sorrow began in my stomach and rose to my chest. Everything seemed beyond hope. I couldn't breathe and when it finally entered my throat, I held it there. It lives there now.

The End, January, 1955

Questioning haunts my sleep. My body seems compelled to speak its truth at night when it meets the shadow. This is the third night I've had the same unnerving vision. Nocturnal thoughts become so repetitive. I lie in bed listening to the rain that accompanied my dream. 'Again, I'm in second period history class at Dwight Morrow High.

The principal comes to the door to tell me that my dad died.'

Why history class? I don't know, since the class blurs as I wake up hurting in the predawn quiet. Funny how you feel the right moment to get out of bed…

…January 4, 1955. In second period, I notice Mr. Kindig outside the door of my history class, whispering to my teacher. I know what this means. I don't want this to be happening. From far away, I hear her voice, "Diana, the principal needs to see you."

It's one of those moments when my mind takes a long time to catch up with my ears. Fear keeps me pinioned to my chair. I don't want to live my dream. I want it to be anything else. I slowly leave the room, at whose direction I'm unaware. Aunt Jean stands in the hallway. It feels like I'm walking into a cold pocket of air filled with silence. I don't understand death, even after over four years of illness. Is this quiet hovering, the menacing stillness around me, a refuge? I don't fight it. It just is. I'm not in my dream anymore. My Dad is gone. I don't know what comes next. I have no faith, no understanding. I feel too numb to grieve, too alone. Where is Mom?

At home, I keep thinking Dad's still here, telling a joke to whoever is his audience, or watching TV, or moaning in bed. His things have become useless ornaments. I feel remote and directionless. The calm inside me feels eerie like a pump or a generator that allows me to focus on what's next, to stay afloat. A way of saying '*later*', there will be time to deal with the rest later.

Time passes too quickly. I'm confused in the blur of people at the crowded funeral. I don't see Aunt Molly or Estelle, or even Aaron. Only two people say anything to me. Mimi, my cousin Arthur's wife, tries to console me, "You'll always remember the good things."

Mimi's never talked to me before, but she seems caring. I don't know what to say. By the time I get words unlaced, it's too late. Grandma Seaman, Dolly's mother whom I've never met before, tells me "I'm 87 and I've still got my own teeth."

Her face is fanned out with wrinkles and threads of white hair. I stare at her chicken neck and the shelf of her bosom because I've never seen anyone this old. I wonder which of her wrinkles are etched by time, by laughter and by sorrow.

Death is too awful, empty and unfair. I think, 'My father's hair never got white. He will not see me turn sixteen this month.' Now I understand what dying means. I used to think that spring returns every year. Now I know that it does not. It's not only knowing that his cold body is in the coffin that frightens me. In that crowded funeral room, I sense my own death. One day my life will be over. Then I have another terrifying thought. Mom will die too. Everybody at this funeral will die and then Dad will truly be dead, like he never lived. I don't believe you go to heaven in a hydraulic truck anymore.

The finality sinks in as I try to recall the last time I was home with dad. Were we watching TV or was I listening to his fitful sleeping, his cries of pain? Were his tears the same tears that come with laughing deeply? Maybe he wasn't home that last day. Did he get sicker at work? Why wasn't I there to help him?

Oh yes, the oxygen tent. Dad just lay in that tent until he died. Even with over four years warning, there was no goodbye, no advice on how to live my life, no words of wisdom on how to deal with mom. We've never been a whole family, but now we are permanently more imperfect. Who will love me now? I need to cry, but the room is teeming with people.

We are driving in a long line of cars, slowly, to the cemetery, Oheb Sholom, in Hillside. The light rain, little more than a mist coming from a distant time zone, moistens the dancing arms of trees as the dewdrops scatter into the silence. Inside the stalwart iron gates, the cemetery has streets, like a city for the dead, where visitors stand in the past. A lone bird floats between the earth and sky. Fog chills the moss-covered granite gravestones, inundated with thirsty patches of grass. I feel hidden in that fog. People keep arriving to pay homage to dad.

I watch the military ceremony, focusing on the handsome soldiers, so solemn in their uniforms. After the resonance fades from their fired weapons, they hand the folded flag to mom because Dad was a soldier in The Great War. The soldiers march off, replaced by Masons bent over dad's coffin, performing their secret ceremony. Tears wash my face of hope. We leave Dad there. His coffin will be buried, covered with grass, fused with the earth. At least beautiful, sheltering trees live near his burial place.

As we walk away, I feel the space growing between us, an uncrossable distance. Yet death seems bright, like now, the way my eyes see when I'm not tired. Maybe death brings strength, like my body feels when it is almost winter. Maybe people who once lived are like roving sea life, floating in and out of our minds.

Back home, I realize that the previous deaths I experienced evoked worry about others dying. But Dad's death gave me a vision of seeing my own. Now I understand 'the past.' Dad's parlor chair is just a chair, an inanimate object, empty, unless his soul is occupying it. Dad is now in the past. He doesn't exist anymore except in my mind. In my dreams, he returns, sitting in his worn chair, to watch me sleep. Our house has fallen silent, yet there's so much noise in my head. I stare out the window for a long time trying to remember if Dad ever hugged me. I'd like to remember it, but I don't. The Hudson sends out chills, clearing my head.

I ask 'why…why?' My only answer is vibrant silence and the tension of immeasurable space that implies distance and closeness -- the space between me and someone who died. In that interval, I acknowledge Dad's not dead as long as I remember him. When I die, he'll die again. I cannot take my leave of him without, someday, writing about him. Whoever reads my story will remember him and keep him alive.

Restless birds insistent calls
disturb my wet winter night,
memories of my father's agony
cry in the dark,
extend beyond their space.

"I am here,

   alone,

      I need solace."

Our past with its overlapping layers piled behind us, transforms into an agreeable illusion with an afterlife like rocks that live on in the soil. I write to answer my daughters' questions and understand what I have lived, the mythology that began my sense of identity. Interpretation writes over the experience. Judged by what has come afterwards, those unexpected moments and confusing events now seem inevitable.

Freed from my father's illness—from cooking, caring and concern for his pain—freedom from attachment. Nothing mattered. I became directionless, shapeless and restless. Nothing to hop onto and ride until, thanks to Uncle Buddy, I moved into the blank pages of Arizona, mine to fill. I learned very quickly why he chose to live in such an intriguing place. Arizona conjured up impressions of cowboys, Indians, snakes and scorpions, but certainly not Jewish pioneers. After two years, I welcomed my mother and younger brother back into my life when they moved nearby. My brother became directionless too. He's out there somewhere, doing his thing, occasionally staying in touch.

My mother died in 1992, as the gates of heaven were closing during the end of Yom Kippur. I brought her back to be with my father. Her funeral was simple, attended only by a caretaker, my cousin David and me. Lots of trees and grass, small and secluded. I walked around the gravesites: Ted, Ida, Art, Mimi and Irving, my father. His had the copper Masonic plaque and cited his WWI service. I said the prayers myself, watched her coffin being lowered. I felt the power of the ground as it osmosizes the bones of my parents lying side by side, their differences forgotten. Death opened the lens of truth; I envisioned an expansive view of God. I may choose to be buried with my parents. At least we can be together in the ground — the way we never were in life.

After all these stories for my children and grandchildren, celebrating searchlights, the chicken store and dumbwaiters, my interpretations lost their rose-colored recall. I'd always considered my childhood as a happy, relatively easy time, much more good than bad. As I travelled backwards, they turned into 3-D recall, more coming into view than I expected or asked for. Small epiphanies, subtle and life-changing, leaving a profound internal and unexpected shift. Life has a way of confounding our higher expectations. The past can become resentments under construction. Mine sure turned out different than I planned.

Sometimes I still feel like that little girl at the train station. The train windows speed up into a blur. The hands I hold on to change, the scenarios change, and I'm still trying to gain the perspective that only comes with time and the retelling of the story. More whys than answers. I don't have the keys to complete this chronicle definitively. Beneath every history lies another history. I don't grasp the whole story. Yet now my truth gained more depth. Joseph Campbell wrote, "There is no truth; there is only experience." Although still unsure whether truth emanates from our ego, soul or life experience, understanding my childhood helps me to understand my world, and to respect and be open to other people's truths and perhaps a glister beyond. With so many moves, no one shares all my memories, so I write to keep the years from vanishing.

My childhood taught me that courage may result from the visions in my daydreams, or purpose from my walk past the iron lung, or from inexplicable and unexpected places and events. Time for me to live in the present, although I still carry the light of my family members and friends who have passed. Especially my father, my brothers Bobby and Wally, Grandma Krohn and Uncle Buddy.

Nobody I know has convinced me there's another world, the one we fear to cross into, even if only our souls survive the pilgrimage. Nobody I know can convince me that there is consciousness buried in the dark earth, even though from that stillness, flowers emerge every spring. Perhaps if I knew the answers, I wouldn't have been motivated to write these stories. They've become my childhood memoir, a place where my years of unsaid words fell onto the paper, like slow glimmering movement of motes of dust caught in occasional soothing rays of sunlight. I remember a lot, but who can remember it all? Nobody I know can tell me...

APPENDIX

You Can't Dismiss Ancestry

Zelig and Sarah Eisenberg
circa 1890

You Can't Dismiss Ancestry

My song began with innocence,
a winter day's awakening.
Brilliant first reds unfold
the symbolic tale--a new life.
Connected to my predecessors
by their skeletal instinctive song,
offering distant comfort, shielding me
from their tragedies.

How can we isolate where our lives begin? The only revealed stories from Europe came from my paternal grandmother. I grew up in a generation of assimilation. People did not want to remember. They kept a code of silence, perhaps to forget, perhaps to protect their children. I stare across time and the unreachable silence of old bones -- my genes declaring themselves, a puzzling sensation.

Some of my ancestors play more prominently in my life than others, emerging as surviving influences because of their strong spirit. So I add their charged stories to the lore. I am descended from a long line of dispossessed people. My sparse genealogy of my parents' relatives begins in the Pale, the land of the most tormented peoples in our turbulent history. Jewish men were conscripted into the Army for a minimum of twenty-five years. Why would Jews ever settle there? Probably because they had no country and the Russian mandate to allow settlement gave them a chance for a better life. They lived, among millions of enduring peasants, in a region with freezing winters and hot summers. Their era was commemorated in the penetrating rhythmic music of Tchaikovsky, and in the dark, tragic prose of Dostoevsky. All this and more carried in their blood and spirit.

Truth is more than facts, but on these pages, facts serve to anchor my stories. It has been said that we never really know our parents and their families. In my case, this is exasperatingly true because I waited too long. Now there are so few storytellers, so few stories. My attempts at genealogy truncate in the frustration of insufficient information, merely sparse notes from my father and his sister Miriam.

My great grandparents, Zelig (Selig) and Sarah Eisenberg lived in a small village, Kovna Gobernya, near

Minsk, Russia, on the Polish border. They came to the U.S. in the late 1800's (1890 or thereabouts). Zelig and Sarah had thirteen children, six boys and seven girls. Five of the boys died early in life. It is believed that they were killed in the pogroms. Florence, while still a child in Russia, just disappeared. Zelig and Sarah traveled everywhere, on foot, in their search when people would say they had seen someone with Florence's description. The rumor was that she had been picked up by gypsies or by Catholics bent on conversion of Jewish children.

The family left The Pale, still searching, following tips that led them to London. Florence was never found. The family left for America, arriving at Ellis Island with their remaining son and six daughters. Alter died from tuberculosis within a few months after disembarking. Dora, my grandmother, was immediately married to Aaron Jacob Krohn, my grandfather and the younger brother of Sarah.

There is a story that this may have been prearranged. Because of her age and non-existent birth records, Dora had to have someone responsible for her, or she would be sent back to Russia. Her four sisters lived with their parents on Barclay Street in Newark, New Jersey: Bessie, Tillie, Sophie and Ida (Edith). The sixth sister, Nellie, eventually moved to New York.

Zelig was a *shochet* and Hebrew teacher with a synagogue in his living room. They were very religious. In addition to teaching, Zelig conducted services every morning and evening. He was the fifth in the lineage of rabbis. He brought his family Torah from Europe, a treasure from the four previous generations of rabbis in his family.

Zelig and Sarah were a devoted couple who lived for each other -- a real love affair. In later years, Zelig lost his sight and Sarah would take him by hand to a local shul twice daily for services. She pre-deceased him and he was a lost soul. He kept calling for Sarah. My grandmother Dora said it was heartbreaking. Two of her sisters, Bessie and Edith, lived in the same three-story house with him and they took care of him until he died in the early 1930s.

Aaron Jacob Krohn
My Paternal Grandfather
(1870-1932)

My grandfather, Aaron Jacob Yaffe, (Sarah Yaffe's nephew) was born in the same area around Minsk in 1870. His parents changed their name to Krum, attempting to avoid military service for their boys. Aaron came to the United States in 1890, a timely desertion. He arrived with six brothers and sisters in their teens and early twenties: Fanny, Chiah, Isaac, Hannah, Sarah and Barney. The officials at Ellis Island could not understand the word Krum and Aaron could not spell it, so the clerks wrote down Krohn as their last name.

I visited Ellis Island, the giant hall that had served as the amazing gateway to their new start. I imagined their misty arrival scene: people lining up for interviews, providing information for forms when they didn't speak the language, harassed officials interviewing new arrivals who seem old, even when they're not. I saw photographs of the humiliating, frightening medical exams that could result in quarantine and rejection. Many languages are spoken as interpreters are bustling about. Only battered coats, shawls and kerchiefs protect the immigrants. What nervous, impassioned moments these were for my seven young ancestors!

I know very little about Pop's family. The many siblings dispersed, seeking opportunities. One brother went to South Africa. Barney moved to Newark and Isaac settled in Bloomfield. Eventually, Isaac owned the tailor shop on Bloomfield Avenue, next to Aaron's awning store. Fanny, Hannah and Hyah lived in New York City.

I was told that Aaron had younger brothers and sisters who remained in Europe. We don't have information on them. They died in the raids, wars or, eventually, the Holocaust. His parents also remained in Europe. They were tenant farmers, taking their produce into town each week by horse and buggy trying to eke out a meager living. On one of their trips, they were caught in a violent thunderstorm and while crossing a wooden bridge, the bridge collapsed and they drowned. How prophetic of the impending deluge; those who couldn't elude the storm died in it.

Pop, the grandfather I never met, struggled for many years as a commercial traveler, a peddler. He had a horse and wagon and sold housewares, pots, pans, dishes and tableware, in New Jersey and Pennsylvania. Around 1912 Aaron moved his family to Bloomfield and became a naturalized citizen. Luck went his way and as his boys started to grow, Pop established a shade business. He solicited business on foot until he opened a shop where he made window shades to order and, much later on, added awnings to make a modest living. This is where my Dad, Irving, became helpful. Aaron never made a great deal of money, but it did not deter most of his children from getting an education.

Although Pop and his brother Isaac were one store apart on Bloomfield Avenue, their assimilation into American life differed. Pop was the only sibling in America who continued a strong bonding with Judaism. His brothers and sisters intermarried, rapidly assimilated and moved into the mainstream. Pop clung to his Jewish values and it somewhat divided the family. It was intimated that Pop grew distant towards those in the family who did not remain religious. Yet most of his sons were named after famous historical figures. Maybe it was his and Dora's attempt at blending and showing patriotism to their new country. Maybe, too, after all the pogroms and anti-Semitic acts committed against his family and friends, it was a way to help ensure survival and a good start for his children in America.

Why, when they were safely in America, didn't Aaron become Yaffe again? He certainly wouldn't go back to Krum with its legacy of mistreatment. They left that terror behind or kept it guarded and private, 'shtum'. You didn't want people to know your business because those who knew who might use that information against you. Few Jewish immigrants reclaimed their names. Many Americanized them, clipped off a syllable or two, or changed their pronunciation. Only after Hebrew became a spoken language again in the country of Israel did Hebrew names regain their popularity. Part of their restoration, mostly first names, was also to commemorate their previous generations.

Today, I study the photograph of you, Grandpa, on the beach with your sons, thin yet strong, no timidity or coyness. Why did no one tell me stories about you? All I have is an impression, a limited certainty. You have the chocolaty brown eyes of my Dad. Except by the time I knew my Dad, his eyes were more blurred, perhaps by events he had to forget. Only when he was being funny, or I said something funny, did the shiny sharpness come back.

l to r: Pop, Ted's son Arthur, Herman, Ted, Irving's son Bob, Irving

How could you know what you were coming to, Aaron Jacob Krohn? Little did you know what you were setting in motion. As a young man, with some of your siblings, you ventured beyond The Pale to America and your children survived. You came from 'no hope' to 'new hope' and from 'Yaffe,' to the now extensive 'Krohn' family.

Dora Eisenberg Krohn
My Paternal Grandmother
(1873-1944)

A year after Aaron came to America, he married Dora Dorothy Eisenberg. She was Aaron's niece, the daughter of Aaron's sister, Sarah Yaffe. Neither Aaron or Dora had any formal education. Aaron may have had a little in Russia. They were very poor, living a hand-to-mouth existence.

circa 1888

Dora was born in Russia. She remembered many stories from the Pale where she grew up. Her stories, told to her eldest daughter Esther, but never recorded, were vivid descriptions of the pogroms that forced as many as were able to migrate. She described bands of Jew haters storming the ghetto, stone throwing, breaking windows and doors, torturing and killing the young men, raping the women.

1943

Dora was very close to her parents. My Aunt Miriam, wrote that Dora was self-taught, but interested in music and books read to her. Her children idolized her. Dora was determined to give her children an education and encouraged them in that direction. All graduated high school. Those that went on to college worked during the day and attended school in the evening. Miriam said she was a wonderful cook, a precious mother and a terrific woman interested in seeing her children educated.

Aaron and Dora's Eight Children

Family, like water, has no end -- only density when contained. But the strength achieved from this density dissipates as families disperse. I found no anecdotes about Aaron and Dora's marriage; I never heard any. They were married in New York City when she was 18 or 19 years old. My perceptions are derived from observing their family. It was large; their life's accomplishment. All their children, except Herman and Florence, who both died before I was born, are mentioned in my childhood memoir. Their names reflect Dora's patriotism and Aaron's Judaism. Certainly, their success in raising children is proven by their children who stayed together and represented them well.

Abraham Lincoln Krohn (1893-1958): My Uncle Buddy left home in his late teens after graduating high school. Pop wanted him to come into the business with him, which he turned down. His primary interest in life was

237

to serve his fellow man. Buddy moved to Boston, became a social worker, met and married Evelyn Bernstein whose father was superintendent of an orphanage in Pleasantville, New York. Buddy worked there and another orphanage in Erie (Fairview), Pennsylvania. He was a scholar and his dream was to follow in his grandfather's footsteps and become a sixth-generation rabbi. In his early 30's, he was discovered and mentored by Rabbi Steven Wise who supervised and financed his study at the Steven Wise Seminary in New York. He attended evening classes and worked during the day. He was proud of his association with Steven Wise and his rabbinate reflected his esteemed teacher.

Even before Buddy was a full-fledged rabbi, he occupied the pulpit in Plainfield for a while, taking the place of the rabbi who died. He was ordained in 1930 and his first pulpit was Temple Albert in Albuquerque, New Mexico. His wife did not choose to leave New York, so they were divorced. Abe met and married Eve Ginsburg in Albuquerque. Although Buddy moved away from his family, he made regular visits home and maintained extensive correspondence with his siblings.

When Buddy's grandfather, Zelig, died, the family Torah was passed on to him. When he moved to Phoenix, Arizona in 1937, he brought his grandfather's Torah. In addition to being the rabbi and, eventually, rabbi emeritus of Beth Israel, he helped start the orthodox synagogue, Beth Hebrew and loaned their congregation of Holocaust survivors our family Torah. When Beth Hebrew closed after twenty-five years in the 1990's, the Torah was returned to Beth Israel, approximately 100 years after it was brought to America. I represented the Krohn family during the service when it was returned. My grandson Oren read from this Torah on his bar mitzvah in February 2004. Now Beth Hebrew is being restored as a historic community treasure.

Why did Uncle Buddy settle in Phoenix? The story I

read on a computer in an Israeli museum was that, while in Albuquerque, he became very involved in the social issues of the depression and post-depression: the plight of the farm workers and Mexican immigrants, poverty and many other social issues. Some of his congregation did not share his concerns and wanted their rabbi to rein in. There was a decisive board meeting to determine whether their rabbi's contract would be renewed. After a long meeting, the board voted to retain him, but Buddy decided to quit.

He became one of the best-known rabbis in the Southwest, the visionary senior rabbi of Temple Beth Israel in Phoenix, Arizona from 1938-1953. He died in 1958, his last few years serving as rabbi emeritus and remaining active in the community. Although he and Eve never had children, he was the 'adopted' father of the hundreds of children in his congregation who idolized him. So did the adults in his congregation who emerged as early influential leaders and developers of the city.

Buddy was extremely active and served on community boards that shaped the growth of Phoenix. He taught sociology and literature at Arizona State University. He supported diverse social causes and had many friends in the clergy. When I lived with him in 1957, he was always helping people, even strangers, in need. I remember stopping by the YMCA with him so he could pay the bill for a visitor who otherwise would be homeless.

His honors, too numerous to mention here, include an honorary doctorate from Arizona State University.

Information is available on the Internet, in the Jewish museums in Israel, in the Phoenix Museum of History, the Arizona Jewish Historical Museum and Temple Beth Israel Judaica Museum, in addition to the historical records of charitable and community institutions he helped found. A low-income government housing project is named for him. One of his super achievements, at least for me personally, was to bring me to Arizona, albeit to help care for him. Even though I only spent time with him for a little over a year when I was a freshman in college, he is the uncle that most influenced my life decisions. Thank you Uncle Buddy!

Herman Ira Krohn (1895-1928): Uncle Herman died eleven years before I was born. As a child, he had rheumatic fever and was ill for seven months after a strep infection. Herman was a quiet man who graduated from New Jersey Law School and opened his office in Newark. He taught his mother to write her name Dora D. (for Dorothy) Krohn. He practiced law for seven or eight years and served as a magistrate in his last two years. Even prior to those last two years, he acted as magistrate many times and would stop at his parent's home in Bloomfield after court sessions and relate his experiences as a judge. He had a close relationship with his younger sister, Miriam, who relates that when he started to court Elsie Davidson, he would take Miriam with him to Plainfield and she would spend the day with Elsie's younger sister.

Miriam wrote: "I can remember the Overland car he bought. I also remember him washing my mouth out with soap. I wanted him to buy me a banana from a wagon and because he wouldn't, I called him a nasty name and he punished me. But among the nice things we did together, were the trips to his office in Newark on Saturday mornings where he would work for a couple of hours and then treat me to lunch (a chocolate milkshake and a sandwich). I thought I was in heaven."

Herman and Elsie had one daughter, Patricia. I only met Elsie and Patricia once at my father's funeral in 1955.

Theodore Roosevelt Krohn (1897-1969): Uncle Ted was the patriarch of the family during my childhood. He was born Theodore Roosevelt Krohn in 1897. Ted was a graduate of The Wharton School of Commerce which he attended in the evening, working all day to pay for his tuition. He became a double profession man in Newark. After establishing his accounting practice as a CPA, he returned to school at the New Jersey Law School to become an attorney. Ted married Ida Cantorwitz and they had three children: Arthur, David and Judith. He was the 'angel' of the family, a very caring individual, always ready to lend a helping hand to any of us in need. He loaned me $1000 to continue my second year at Arizona State. He was very hurt when I paid him back, but I thought my commitment should be kept.

Irving (Israel) Edward Krohn (1900-1955): There's only one line in Miriam's history about him: "He graduated high school and went into Aaron's business." Irving enlisted in the Army at Fort Slocum, New Jersey on July 11, 1918. He was stationed in Jacksonville, Florida at Camp Joseph Johnston as a Private, Quartermaster Corp. Discharged at the end of World War I in January 1919. Irving returned to his parent's house at 38 Berkeley Place, Bloomfield. At that time, he entered his father's business on a full-time basis. It would be easy to question his choice, but from the hard work of both my grandfather and my dad, the rest of the children received help with their advanced education.

Irving married Lenora (Dolly) Seaman on November 25, 1922. He was the only sibling to marry out of the religion. Robert Irving Krohn was born in 1924. They moved to 11 Bay Avenue, Bloomfield. Wallace Leonard Krohn was born in 1926. When Pop died in 1932, Irving inherited the awning and shade family business in the midst of the depression. He was dynamic in an era of dynamic men and supportive women. A born comedian, he was president of the Elks Lodge in Bloomfield for eight years and a member of the Masonic Order since 1927. He knew everyone in those days, including Frank Sinatra and other crooners and comedians. He was always referred to as attractive, and the 'black sheep.'

Dolly passed away in 1936 in East Orange Hospital. Bob was thirteen; Wally nine. They had always been kept spic and span, well-dressed. Irving was full of despair and guilt since Dolly's doctor had advised moving her to Florida or Arizona to ease her condition. I remember my Aunt Miriam stating years later that Dolly was a fanatical German housekeeper and that she shouldn't have been washing her windows in the middle of winter. A year and a half after Dolly's death, Irving married Eva Steinberg and had two additional children: Diana and Aaron.

Esther Teresa (Krohn) Alpern (1905-1997): was named after Zelig's mother. She became a pianist who influenced my love for classical music. She attended Normal School, took evening courses at Rutgers and graduated from Upsala in East Orange. Esther became a schoolteacher, but more important, she was the musician in the family. She played the piano while her family sang the old songs from the family songbook. She taught piano for over fifty years and played the organ in a local church. Esther married Lawrence Alpern and they adopted one daughter, Dorothy, arranged privately by Uncle Buddy.

Florence Leah Krohn (1907-1916): Florence was named for Dora's sister who had been kidnapped in the Pale. Although convulsions were listed as the cause of death, Miriam said it was peritonitis blood poisoning.

Miriam Ella (Krohn) Goldblatt (1910-2001): Aunt Miriam's goal was to be a nurse. She took all the courses in high school leading up to a nursing career, but Uncle Herman died the night after she graduated high school and her mother pleaded with her not to enter the hospital. Her brother Ted asked her to come to the office and help him settle Herman's matters. Aunt Miriam worked in Ted's office as a legal and accounting secretary for forty-four years. Miriam married Joseph Goldblatt and they had two children, Florence and David.

Daniel Webster Krohn (1913-1980): Uncle Dan attended the University of New Mexico through the efforts of his brother Abe. Then he continued at Rutgers where he graduated as a CPA. Dan married Jean Zwerling and they had two children, Daron and Marvin. He worked for the government as a bank auditor and in his spare time helped out in Uncle Ted's office. I lived with Uncle Dan and Aunt Jean for one year in my early teens, absorbing their family life.

Irving's 50th Birthday
l to r: Dan, Esther, Irving, Ted, Miriam

The children of Aaron and Dora continued the family through the twentieth century, the century of war. My aunts, uncles and many cousins are all left behind, fused with the earth in another time and place, and I am someone else now. They missed a lot of my life, but are part of me.

The Steinbergs, Abraham and Badana
My Maternal Grandparents

My mother's birth name was Rebecca. She was born in Bialystok, on the Russia-Poland border, in 1911. Her father, Abraham Steinberg, was a tailor in the thriving textile industry developed in that region after the Napoleonic Wars. Sixty-three thousand people, over half the population, in Bialystok were Jewish. Jews owned many mills and most of the spinning, weaving and knitting companies. The Jewish labor movement, the Bund, was strongly supported. But during the Russian Revolution of 1905-1906, reprisals against the union members began. 1906 became a year of violent pogroms.

It was around this time that Abraham married Badana Weinstein. She liked to be called Dana. Threatened by growing anti-Semitic actions, they migrated to the United States in 1911 with their two daughters, Esther at age three and Rebecca at six months. Abraham's sister, Libby Baboff, also emigrated to New York. Nothing is known about the rest of Abraham's relations in Europe. They did not leave.

Dana Weinstein came from a family with three sons and five daughters. Only three came to America: Dana

(Steinberg) and Mary (Leader), known as Merke, in New York and Esther (Berner) in Miami. Two of the sons and one of the sisters, Frida Weinstein Giladi went to Palestine in that same timeframe. Frida was one of the founders of Kibbutz Ayalat Hashahar. I believe three of Frida's five children and her grandchildren may still live there. Dana's brother Leib settled in Melbourne, Australia. His son is a well-known musician. I only met Tanta Esther once when she visited in New York. I don't know the name of the two sons in Israel or the other daughter. Unfortunately, so far, I have no information on her name or where she went. Unlike the Krohns, the Steinbergs and Weinsteins were isolated by distance.

Abraham worked as a tailor. A third daughter, Rachel, was born in 1914. Their story continues with struggle, trials and tribulations until 1918 when tragedy struck and Dana died during the influenza epidemic. Between 1914-1918, the family moved constantly; Esther attended nine different schools. I don't know if my mother became afraid then, or whether she had always been fearful. Uprooted people lose their orientation. My mother's anxiety and angst still leave me with many unanswered questions. I too have experienced loss and being uprooted, the sense of not belonging, but I can't penetrate her mind. So frustrating, when hindsight cannot bring clarity.

In 1920, Abraham decided to hold together his family by marrying Anna Roman, a widow with two daughters, Jean and Frieda. In 1921, another child, Bernard, was born into the family of five daughters. However, Abe and Anna's marriage did not go well. Best to keep it short and say there was prosperity in a small way and trouble in a big way due to the misunderstandings and fights between the two families under one roof.

Many stories are told of Anna Roman's favoritism for her two daughters, Jean and Frieda. They received attention, clothes and education. None of Abraham's daughters were allowed to continue school after grammar school. By this time, they had Americanized their names. Esther became Estelle; Rebecca became Eva because she hated being called Becky; Rachel became Molly.

Estelle was an attractive, wavy-haired blond who, at 18 years of age, had been approached to appear for a screen test after modeling in a hair styling show. The family talked her out of it. Estelle could also have been a piano player in any lounge. She played all the popular songs, adding her jazzy arrangements. Estelle married Arthur Blosvern in 1932. She met him walking in Grand Concourse Park in the Bronx, one of the most popular meeting places in those days. In fact, it's the same place where her daughter met her husband twenty-three years later. Estelle and Arthur had two children, Barbara and David.

Eva was also very striking with thick, dark hair, deep brown eyes and a great figure. She started working in 1924 as a salesgirl directly after she graduated grammar school at thirteen. All three of Abraham's daughters worked and brought their paychecks home to Anna. That was the expected thing to do. However, one day the youngest daughter, Molly, found a shoebox in Anna's closet. In it was a bankbook revealing that Anna had been depositing their earnings into an account naming Anna's two daughters as beneficiaries. I also got the impression that Anna discouraged suitors for Abraham's daughters, probably because of the potential loss of income.

By this time, Estelle was married to Arthur Blosvern. Anna had made a nice wedding for Estelle, cooking all the food. But when they found the bankbook, Eva and Molly started to pull away, although they stayed close to their father. Maybe it's easier to leave when you're young. Eva married Irving Krohn when she was twenty-six. They had two children, Diana and Aaron.

Molly, the youngest sister, married Irving Solomon in 1939. Molly was the most accepting of her stepmother and maintained a somewhat normal relationship with her. She was the most even-keeled of the sisters. I liked her, even though she never fed us. She was short and always said cheerful things. Molly and Irving had three children: Beverly, Howard and Sharon.

There was a great amount of illness in the family. Bernie was not a healthy child and, as the only son, he became spoiled and uncontrollable. Anna contracted tuberculosis and spent her summers in the country. Abraham smoked and suffered from a delicate stomach that eventually led to colon cancer. When he was dying in the hospital in 1946, Anna did not leave her place in the country to be with him. In the end, it was up to his girls to care for him, and they did, with love. The daughters of Abraham and Badana lived long lives into the 1990's; Estelle even made it to the millennium.

All my Steinberg and Krohn cousins are scattered. We grew up in a time when families were increasingly separated by distance and were not dependent upon each other for survival. What a change from the close knit familial relationships in the ghettos of my great grandparents!

Both lean and rich years
cause trees to gnarl,
spot, droop and bend,
yet continue to grow

MY STREET

Irving and Eva, My Parents

*I am a continuation
of all the above,
for unless
I am part of everything,
I am nothing.*

Irving met Eva Steinberg when she was visiting her stepsister's family in Bloomfield. Across Bloomfield Avenue, near the awning and tailor shops, there was a luncheonette run by Harry Span and his wife Sid. They introduced my mother and father. The family may also have been involved, since they were concerned over Irving's growing despair over Dolly's death and the task of raising two sons.

Irving married Eva on July 18, 1937 after a six-week courtship. Abraham, Estelle and Molly were concerned that this was too quick. Their marriage was performed by Uncle Buddy, as were most of the Krohn weddings. That fall, Irving's oldest son, Bob, started Bloomfield High School.

My parent's marriage might have been considered tragic, but they were not prominent people, so I'll just say sad. Eva never replaced Dolly in my father's heart. Somewhere between 1937 and 1939, both Bob and Wally moved out. As a teenager, I assumed this was due to my mother who could be difficult. She was always afraid and I thought the teenage boys might have been too much for her. Wally went to live with his maternal grandmother, Grandma Seaman.

248

I was born on January 31, 1939 at Montclair Community Hospital. I was named Diana Ruth for my maternal grandmother, Badana. My father was disappointed I wasn't born on January 30th, Franklin Delano Roosevelt's birthday. President Roosevelt was his hero. He was a staunch Democrat and was hoping I'd 'come out' on time!

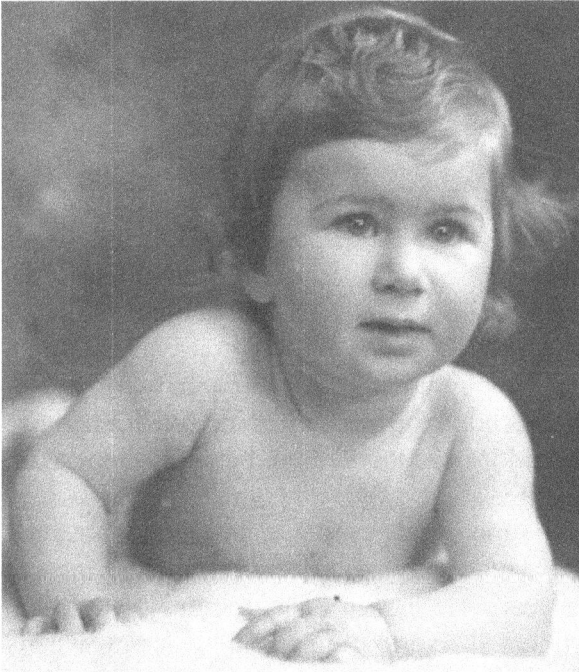

In 1941, my father lost his business, AJ Krohn & Sons, Awnings and Shades. He wrote that it was due to competition and his illness (unknown), but many years later his family told me that Jean Ackerson's husband Billie was hired into the business to give him a job. Jean was my mother's stepsister. Billie was an upholsterer, but he was dishonest, a promoter whose approach put my Dad's business at risk. His actions resulted in my father losing the business. Their bad feelings never got cleared up. My father rarely associated with my mother's relatives after that time.

We moved to Miami for my father's health, but the job he moved for didn't develop. Then I got rickets, afterward referred to as "a tropical infection", which curtailed our plans. Rickets is a condition caused by a vitamin D deficiency that can lead to softening of the bones and deformity. My brother Bobby had rickets too. Maybe it's part of our gene pool, another reason why you can't dismiss ancestors. My mother once told me that we stopped at three doctors' offices on the hurried trip from Miami to Jacksonville. Our only other stop was in Washington D.C. to take pictures. We returned to the known world, my grandparent's home on Berkley Place. Wish I hadn't gotten sick... Would it have worked out better in Florida, or is my guilt unmerited?

Dad supervised shade installations on U.S. Government housing projects, traveling over nine states for over four years. He earned enough money to move us into our apartment in North Bergen, New Jersey when I was two and a half years old. We were the only ones in my father's family to live in an apartment instead of a house. North Bergen could have been Chicago or the South Side of Boston, or Queens or Philadelphia -- any immigrant melting pot. We stayed there when he then became employed as a timekeeper with the Aluminum Company of America (Alcoa).

Both my older brothers were veterans of World War II. Wally served in the Navy and was injured aboard ship during the Battle of Leyte Gulf. Bobby was a navigator in the Army Air Corps, flying missions over Germany. When his plane was shot down, he spent over a year in a

German prison camp. Arriving home, he found his wartime marriage had fallen apart.

When I was in seventh grade, I watched my father hunting and pecking on his Underwood to help me write my first autobiography. Dad typing sounds into the air; me watching. Learning what I never had put together — his biography as well as mine. My father could make our life look so good on paper. That's when I learned that he had another wife before Mom.

Over sixty years later, at a reunion at my Connecticut home, Bob's widow Dorothy, Wally and I were reminiscing. I mentioned my plan to someday write stories about the family. Wally asked me, "Do you know why I was sent to live with my grandmother?" I was shocked, bewildered! Did this mean it wasn't his choice? Beliefs smashed. Then Dorothy told Bob's version, "He came home from high school to find his bags packed out on the front porch. He moved into a boarding house and worked to support himself until he completed his senior year of high school." According to Dorothy, he never knew why. Beliefs smashed again. All things I took for granted as givens began to dissipate like mist...

Could my mother be responsible for kicking out the boys? Did she think it would help my father? Was my birth causing a problem? Who was my father? Was he a failure? Everything began to feel gray like the soiled city air when people live too close together. He had been the tragic hero, but now I didn't know what to believe. I wish I had known my father before his setbacks. I only recall a one-sided puzzle.

I ponder good vs iffy vs bad people. Am I iffy too? Maybe we're only iffy if we count our past. Maybe we become more iffy as we age—from dealing with life's challenges and our recurring mistakes. The feeling of abandonment when my father died has never totally left me. Uprooted, trying to adjust—so many times—so distant from my street. Dust sets in, covering over memories, maybe even creating some distortions of its own. Our past morphs into an agreeable illusion.

We often live ahead of our own understanding. I write to understand what I have lived. Now those unexpected moments and confusing events seem inevitable. I don't have the keys to complete this historic chronicle definitively. I don't grasp the whole story. But if the theory is true that no one changes, then I understand enough. All I can write is what I know, what I wish I knew, and how I feel about it.

I'm beginning to wonder if
questions are dangerous
fragments left behind,
middle-of-the night questions.

They stick in my head
stubbornly seeking answers,
even when I don't want them —
like dawn slicing the night sky
with its pale knife of doubt.

www.ingramcontent.com/pod-product-compliance
Lightning Source LLC
Chambersburg PA
CBHW070917030426
42336CB00014BA/2447